SIMON STEPHENS: A WORKING DIARY

SIMON STEPHENS: A WORKING DIARY

SIMON STEPHENS

methuen | drama
LONDON • NEW YORK • OXFORD • NEW DELHI • SYDNEY

METHUEN DRAMA
Bloomsbury Publishing Plc
50 Bedford Square, London, WC1B 3DP, UK

BLOOMSBURY, METHUEN DRAMA and the Methuen Drama logo
are trademarks of Bloomsbury Publishing Plc

First published in Great Britain 2016
Reprinted 2016, 2018

A catalogue record for this book is available from the British Library.

ISBN: PB: 978-1-4742-5141-9
ePDF: 978-1-4742-5145-7
epub: 978-1-4742-5143-3

A catalog record for this book is available from the Library of Congress

Series: Theatre Makers

Typeset by RefineCatch Limited, Bungay, Suffolk
Printed and bound in Great Britain

To find out more about our authors and books visit www.bloomsbury.com
and sign up for our newsletters.

Written for Oscar, Stanley and Scarlett.

And dedicated to Polly and Mel.

INTRODUCTION

Anna Brewer, the Senior Commissioning Editor at Methuen Drama, asked me to write a book about writing for theatre. I strongly didn't want to.

Not because I don't like books about theatre. I do. And I love books about writing. They nourish me. The possibility of an insight into the decisions that writers make intoxicates me.

But the notion of writing my own book about theatre made me anxious. It seemed to carry with it the idea that I had a clear position on what I thought theatre should be or what I thought writers should do. I have no clarity on this whatsoever. The older I get the harder it is for me to finish a sentence without wanting to immediately return and contradict myself.

This is perhaps a useful characteristic for a dramatist. Drama deals in such contradictions. It is a poor characteristic, though, for an essayist and doesn't lend itself to prose.

I came up with the idea for a diary because I thought it might contain these contradictions. Ideas I have one day are contradicted by ideas I have days later or weeks later or months later. It is in the spaces between these contradictions that any thoughts I have about theatre exist.

I knew that 2014 was going to be an unusual year for me.

At the start of the year I knew that I had three new plays scheduled for production: *Blindsided* at the Royal Exchange in Manchester, *Carmen Disruption* at the Deutsches Schauspielhaus in Hamburg and *Birdland* at the Royal Court in London. I knew that my version of Anton Chekhov's *The Cherry Orchard* would be premiered at the Young Vic in London and that the Young Vic would also take their production of my version of Henrik Ibsen's *A Doll's House* to the Brooklyn Academy of Music in New York. The National Theatre's production of my adaptation of Mark Haddon's novel *The Curious Incident of the Dog in the Night-Time* was also due to open on Broadway in the autumn.

I wanted to capture something of the essence of this year.

It was a year in which I knew I would be working with directors I adore. Sarah Frankcom, Sebastian Nübling, Carrie Cracknell, Marianne Elliott and Katie Mitchell and writing for Ivo van Hove. I enjoy reading play scripts but for me plays only really exist in theatres and the relationships I have with directors define my work. I am indebted to these people, who I consider my friends as much as I consider them my collaborators.

I am indebted too to the actors that I have worked with. I love actors. I love them for their bravery and vitality and the actors I worked with in 2014 were quite stunning. To have other humans give of themselves with such openness and talent in their attempt to make something that I imagined in my head exist in real life never fails to move me. I am indebted to the artistic and production teams that worked on these shows and to the front-of-house staff and the management of these beautiful theatres. I am indebted to the audiences who came and again and again watched these plays with a spirit of openness.

I know that all of these people would write different versions of the events I have described here. I hope these differences and my version upset or offend none of them.

When I told the broadcaster Philip Dodd that I was writing a diary of my year he encouraged me to be fearless and frank and to honestly reveal the truth about a life of a playwright. There was, he inferred, a compelling juiciness to some of the great theatre diaries as their writers have shocked and scandalized people with public revelations of private experiences. That is not my intention in this book. This isn't because I am shy or unduly polite but because I work with a genuine sense of gratitude for my collaborators. That sense is what I hope this book articulates.

The book is dedicated to the most significant of these collaborators, my agent Mel Kenyon. Quite simply I could have achieved none of the things that I have achieved in the working life described in this book without her.

This book would not have been possible without the faith of Anna Brewer who commissioned me to write it for Methuen Drama and painstakingly read it, offered wise suggestions for edits and corrected the appalling typing and terrible grammar and punctuation of my first draft.

It is an incomplete book. The incompleteness comes sometimes from forgetfulness. I had forgotten key details of the events of every working day by the time I settled down to write my thoughts. I hope my omissions don't upset significant people.

It is also incomplete by intent. This is a book about my working life, not my private life or my social life. I don't write about important friends or about my extended family unless they touch directly on my working day. I don't write about my holidays or my time off work. I don't write about the TV I watched, or the music I listened to or the meals I ate or places I visited or the books I read or about Manchester United's miserable year under David Moyes and the joyful possibilities of the club's future under Louis van Gaal, even though this was possibly the thing that most occupied my thinking throughout the whole of the year.

I don't write about my family. Of all the omissions this last one is perhaps most significant. There is nobody more important to me than my wife Polly and my children Oscar, Stanley and Scarlett.

There is an aphorism attributed to T. S. Elliott but actually coined by his peer Cyril Connolly. It claims, 'The pram in the hallway is the enemy of creativity.' In my experience this is pernicious nonsense. Nobody inspires me to write more than my wife and my children. They get me up in the morning. They dictate my working day. I work to pay for them to eat and to pay for them to live safely. They dominate my wondering. They define my fears. They clarify my ambitions. They fuel my imagination.

Playwrights write about human beings. There is no better way to understand human beings than to make a few and live with them and watch them grow up and change. To have made a family with the woman I have loved more than I have loved anybody else and who I think understands me more profoundly than anybody else does has been the most significant achievement of my life.

This book, like everything, has been written for them and is also dedicated to her.

SIMON STEPHENS: A WORKING DIARY

6th January 2014

The first day back at work after the Christmas break. I spent four hours at Moorfields Hospital having my eye injected. I noticed about a year ago that the vision in my left eye was blurred and watery. I had it checked out at Moorfields. They told me it was because my retina was haemorrhaging into my eyeball. I go there every six weeks to have injections into my eyeball that slow or stop this haemorrhaging. It's wretched.

It passed.

I left the hospital and caught a bus to take me to Euston Station and from there caught a train up to Manchester. Back to the Royal Exchange Theatre for rehearsals of *Blindsided,* my fourth play in the theatre's main 800 seat theatre-in-the-round space.

Half of my plays have been defined by that journey between Manchester and London. The M6 – M1 corridor. The West Coast line from Euston to Piccadilly via Stockport. The remarkable flatness of the South giving way to a ripple of physical geography shy of Macclesfield.

The walk from Piccadilly Station down towards Market Street is always defined by an air of menace. Some streets have a psycho-geography that overwhelms town planning. No matter how much they try to clean up that stretch, regardless of the energy of the Northern Quarter or how exclusive those hotels become, there is always a sense of addiction and threat.

As a teenager I'd get off the train from Stockport at Piccadilly to go shopping for records in Manchester and see posters for plays at the Royal Exchange and the promise of the theatre would intoxicate me.

I always caught the bus back home, the 197 to Heaton Moor, from outside the theatre. I remember seeing adverts for Adam Ant in Joe Orton plays at the end of the 80s.

It is a building that graced the edges of my youth. And now I am working here, again.

Rehearsals are looking good and the cast that I saw seems happy and charged.

Sarah Frankcom, the play's director, is remarkable.

This is the third time I've worked with her. She is defined by the precision and the rigour of the questions that she asks the cast. She is fascinated by how she can solidify the interior world of the actors as they imagine the characters they perform. She will more happily ask questions than give notes. She seems to work from the idea, a simple and clear and very Anglo-Saxon idea, that if the actors know the inner world of their characters then their knowledge will be communicated to the audience. The audience will then be able to believe the characters more and so recognize themselves in them and engage with their stories.

None of this is radical. Some of it might seem innate. But it's not. Its very culturally specific and very historically specific and just because it is a central and defining paradigm for anybody who has worked in the UK directing new plays in the past thirty years doesn't mean it is necessarily so. It's not the case, for example, in German or French theatres.

But I think it remains fundamental to me. Despite a decade of flirting around the edges of those considerations that came out of what was described in Germany as 'post-dramatic' theatre, ideas that suggested 'character' to be an idea or a construct that is fundamentally conservative and sentimental, the idea of character remains something I cherish.

I write plays with characters in. I write plays with stories. We tell stories to one another to help us make sense of where we are and who we are in the universe.

I arrived to watch rehearsals of the sex scene at the start of Scene Two of *Blindsided*. Cathy Heyer gives her new boyfriend, John Connolly, a blowjob and then takes her panties off, puts them in his pocket and then fucks him. I enjoyed watching Katie West and Andy Sheridan negotiate the edges of their embarrassment to find something that was as dramatically truthful as it was recognizably human.

Sex on stage is difficult because audiences always know it's not really happening. Its palpable lack of mimetic actuality means they disengage from the idea it might be happening as a kind of metaphor. The trick is to embrace the metaphorical nature of the thing. When the lie is embraced it reveals so much more truthfulness. The scene works best and is most erotically charged when the two actors don't even touch each other.

I never like to follow a script in rehearsal. I don't ever have one to hand any more. It's been three years since I wrote *Blindsided* anyway and the idea that I should know more about who these characters are or what they're doing or what they want than these actors do is ludicrous. I try my hardest to watch what I see and try my hardest to allow that to inform my thoughts. This strikes me as much more rewarding than trying to offer them the truth of any specious authorial vision.

The role of the writer in theatre is to offer provocations to a company of actors as they try to make a night out in the theatre, not to describe how the world is or ought to be. Who fucking knows THAT anymore?

I realized watching the actors that the key to the scene is not the sex but the control. The power play. And the moments when they refuse or allow themselves to be vulnerable.

7th January

There was a moment at the end of Scene Four when Rebecca Callard, the actress playing Siobhan, Cathy Heyer's best friend, stroked her arm against Andrew Sheridan, the actor playing John Connolly. She followed the stage directions to the letter and it felt clumsy and uncertain and awkward. Sarah asked me what I'd envisaged. The truth was that that moment was drawn from two teenage memories of stroking arms. Once I stroked my arm against the arm of a girl I'd fancied for months in a bar and although we said nothing it felt like an electric shock and I still remember it, decades later. Another time a teenage friend confided in me that she found stroking the underside of her arm more erotic than masturbation. That kind of blew my teenage mind.

But neither of these memories was helpful so I told Sarah I couldn't remember. Which was a lie but also partly true. I couldn't remember if I even had envisaged anything on stage so much as tried to evoke the synthesis of two experiences that I'd had in my youth.

More importantly though, my refusal to answer freed the actors to find something for themselves without worrying too much about the stage directions. And they did. They found something much more charged and balletic and truthful than my stage directions would ever suggest.

Sebastian Nübling, the German director who has directed more of my plays than anybody else, told the British actors in my play *Three Kingdoms* that the first thing he ever did when he got a script was cross out all the stage directions. I sometimes think this is what all directors should do. It might make rehearsal rooms more creative places.

Sometimes stage directions for me are an attempt to write myself into an emotional place. They are written as a type of exploration. The most exciting thing to do is to have them as a prompt to find the relevant psychological energy and then leave them behind. This might be better than just trying to copy them or act them out.

We worked a lot on the scene changes. Imogen Knight had been employed as the movement director and she was invaluable. It's indicative of Sarah's confidence that her rehearsal room is so democratic. She is dependent on Imogen's input and mine and others to work together to find a satisfying solution to the problems suggested by the play, rather than working from the position that she knows everything and is in control of everything.

We realized that the worst thing to do would be to make the scene changes hurried and pragmatic. In this production the moments between the scenes can allow the actors to build a sense of dread.

This is a play built on Euripides' *Medea* and that sense of something inexorable happening that the characters can't control or avoid or change feels very true to that classical Greek spirit.

Some plays have a life because the characters have no idea what is going to happen next. Sometimes it's better if there is a sense of something inexorable and awful and impossible to control.

The older I get the more I think that what all playwrights should really do is read and re-read Euripides and Aeschylus and Sophocles. Everything else is kind of colouring in. I mean I know that's also bullshit but there's something in it and it would be easier anyhow.

David Simon said that was all he did when he wrote *The Wire*.

The writer John Gray talked about this in his 2012 essay on *The Wire* in *Prospect Magazine*. Just as in Greek Drama the characters are powerless under the whims of malevolent Gods so in *The Wire* the characters are powerless under the whims of a malevolent economic structure. They have no individual character. The economic forces of neo-liberal free market capitalism are too controlling.

Maybe the characters in *Blindsided* have a similar lack of control.

And, anyway, audiences enjoy watching scene changes. This is sometimes because they add a new layer to the play that is somehow in its original metabolism but also invented and found in the room. So the scene changes are more indicative of the rehearsal process than some of the scenes.

As long as theatre makers don't try to pretend that scene changes are not really happening, as long as we embrace the innate musicality of the scene change – they can be the most deeply theatrical element of a night in the theatre. It's in the scene changes that we enjoy that the whole thing is made up. It's one thing you can't do on film or in a novel or in any other narrative or dramatic form – change the scene. We may as well embrace that theatricality.

It feels like such a joy to be rehearsing on that stage in the round. The theatre in the round celebrates the audience in its architecture. We are aware of one another. It was fun today finding moments in which the actors could enjoy the presence of the audience too.

The more I write the more fascinated I am by acknowledging the presence of the audience and inviting them into the transaction. Not out of a cod understanding of Brechtian alienation because my understanding of Brechtian alienation is indeed cod and half-baked, but because we are all in the room together sharing the process of imagining a story.

There is a scene at the heart of the play in which a baby is murdered on stage.

Sarah is exploring the idea of having an absence where the baby might be. Not miming the baby as such but not using a doll or a sound effect. I saw it for the first time today. It was chilling because it placed the baby necessarily in the imagination of the audience and so we are forced to imagine ourselves more in the position of the characters.

8th January

Leaving rehearsals and heading back home for a week. The afternoon light faded as we sped from Stoke south down to London without stopping.

I found the rehearsal of Scene Eight stupidly moving this morning. It might have been because I'd not eaten anything. It might have been because I drunk too much in the Grey Horse last night or it might have been because of the openness and imagination with which Katie West and Andrew Sheridan played the scene. I watched it with tears pouring down my face and felt like a bit of an idiot when Sarah asked me if I had any thoughts.

I didn't. I just told them it was stupidly well acted and a ridiculous way to start a Wednesday.

There is something though in watching actors inhabit a character like that with a remarkable sense of care and attention to detail and imagination that is extraordinarily moving. It's like they make your dreams manifest and that is necessarily remarkable.

We ran Scenes One to Eight afterwards and it didn't work quite so well, which, at this stage, is exactly as it should be.

I've got about ten notebooks filled with notes on rehearsals and they all say fundamentally the same thing.

Ask the questions as though you don't know the answer and genuinely want to. Questions aren't rhetorical in my plays, normally.

The last word on each line is often the most important one.

And play the action, not the feeling or the atmosphere. That started happening this morning after a while but at first the actors were mediating their playing by flagging up how weird the play is. The weirdness of the play is for the director to release and the audience to discover, not the actors to play. They have to inhabit the normality of the thing because this allows the audience to recognize themselves in this weird and bewildering world.

At least in a play like *Blindsided* this is true.

So they have to be specific and clear about what their characters are doing with each line and not mediate it through feeling or mood.

And they need to listen as hard as they can. As though the words they're hearing have never been spoken to them before.

Listening is the hardest thing for an actor to do. Just bloody well listen. It's hard if you're rehearsing in the wrong order, as we were this morning, because it means you bring the end of the play into the beginning and that always means you bring the mood in. It's hard anyway to not worry about your own lines or the energy of your own delivery or the fact that you've heard these words spoken twenty times already. But if you can do it it's startling.

And in the production, in this play, imagining a concrete world can help specify behaviour. Especially when a set is abstract this can be really useful. For actors to really imagine what their world looks like.

As I write this I'm aware that it contradicts a lot of what we've been exploring with the Secret Theatre Company, the permanent ensemble of ten actors Artistic Director Sean Holmes established at the Lyric Hammersmith for a year. I've worked closely with him as an Associate. In our work with the ensemble we've celebrated the actuality of actors being in the same rooms as audiences and as each other. We've encouraged them to not play their character but commit to their moment.

But maybe that's fine. Each play is a different gesture and each production of each play demands a different process. The only thing that's really important is a consistency of approach.

Not imagining that some rules are innate but finding the right and appropriate rules of each production of each play and committing to those with consistency.

Building that on what the action of the play in the specific conditions of the theatre is, not cranking it into everything or defaulting to it each time.

Maybe that's the joy of working with a range of directors. I get to see that fluidity.

Julie Hesmondhalgh, who is playing Cathy's mother, asked me how to act her surprise that John Connolly's flat is richer than she thought. I didn't really know what to say to her and felt like a bit of an idiot.

But maybe it's about imagining that world in detail and playing the action not the feeling. Maybe. I told her she'd find it out.

It's good to have questions. Questions are the best thing about making theatre. Not answers. Problems and questions are the metal of our work. When we answer them we may as well stop making theatre. All we can do is ask them and then find different ones and ask those and insist upon the question. It's all we've got.

I leave encouraged, completely encouraged that they will find these things.

9th January

I was back in the office for the first time this year.

My office is built out of the converted staff toilets of an art deco furrier factory on the New North Road that leads from Old Street to Highbury & Islington roundabout in London. It is the only art deco building remaining in a sprawling wasteland of social housing on the borders between Hackney and Islington.

My windows look out onto a huge block of flats. Sometimes I watch the people come and go. Mostly it's quite boring because they're just leaving and arriving, which is exactly what you would expect it to be.

An undercover policeman did once use this room to carry out surveillance on a flat that belonged to a drug dealer across the car park from this building. I've never seen anything so illicit as that. Sometimes people shout up from the car park but that's about as transgressive as it gets.

I spent the morning answering emails. The only thing I wrote was a dedication to Berit Gullberg, my Scandinavian agent who is seventy today.

I wrote about the problem of never really knowing whether what we're making in theatre is any good or not. Writers don't know it. Directors don't know it. Actors never know it. All of us are defined by the response of others but have no way of really anticipating what that response might be. And so we end up completely dependent on collaborators we can trust.

Often I hear people complain about their agents. I think I must be lucky. Berit, like my German agent Nils Tabert and Mel Kenyon who represents me throughout the rest of the world and found Berit and Nils for me, is a friend and an ally. I've known Mel for seventeen years. My relationship with her is almost as long as my relationship with my wife.

I had lunch with the actress Liz White who I've known for years and who was in the production of *Port* at the National Theatre last year.

I asked her about whether she ever reflected on her own work. She said she never did. She couldn't even watch herself on film. It's odd this part of the actor's life. They have an absolute need to remain intuitive. I think that every other profession I know cherishes reflection and the improvement reflective practice can bring. No actor I know has found a way of properly reflecting on when their work was good or bad and why this was ever the case.

Marianne Elliott, who directed *Port* and who, as Associate at the National, is one of my closest friends and longest collaborators, asked me to think about writing a response to Marlowe's *Dr Faustus*. I've spent a lot of this week reading that play and thinking about that.

I love the idea of writing a play with supernatural forces in it. I love the moments when Faustus is killed and comes back to life. I love the glee that could be found in having somebody so transgressive. Having him go anywhere in the world. Having him conjure up Alexander the Great or Helen of Troy. Or sprouting antlers on the head of an enemy.

I love the presence of eternity in the play. The speech at the end of the play in which Faustus asks if he could only be in hell for two hundred thousand years and then be saved.

It put me in mind of the conversations I had last week with my fifteen-year-old son, Oscar, and my friend and his mentor Jon Sedmak about the size of the universe. The expansion of everything, the distance between things, the size of the whole beast of the universe leaves me in awe. It makes me want to fall over. The scale of the thing. And the finality of death. The impossibility of continuing after death. It's in contemplation of these things that I feel a sense of awe that both terrifies me and makes me want to write.

I love the idea of a transaction in which that eternity is flaunted or toyed with. Imagine wanting something so much that you would risk far more than you could ever conceive in order to get it.

The stakes on that would be remarkable.

Faustus waits twenty-four years and then we see the last hour before his death.

Imagine if this brought you the capacity to make the world different to how we knew it to be. To come back from the dead. To get any girl you want even if you're bringing her back from the dead. To rid your enemies of everything.

And then the clock ticked and time passed and soon everything was coming to an end and everything was going to disappear. Imagine that. That is kind of extraordinary.

I like the idea of writing with a chorus. I like the idea of the chorus being a band. I like the fantasy that this band would be playing songs written by Nick Cave.

I like the idea of having a character that could break the paradigms of the world.

And then leave him alone and isolated and understanding the eternity of death and the size of the universe.

I like the idea of writing a play about how God is no longer a superstitious idea and nobody believes in the devil anymore. How do you dramatize contemporary ideas of what the devil is when nobody believes in the devil anymore.

I think the play is hamstrung by its satire. Its satire dates it. So the references to the Catholic Church don't really resonate at the moment.

The specific politics of Germany. I guess the point is to find a contemporary institution that is just as powerful now and to make the fallibility of that seem palpable. I also think Marlowe takes an easy line on Catholicism which is a bit boring. We have to love the voices we oppose to make a play any good, more than we love the voices we support.

10th January

I judged the Susan Smith Blackburn Prize for women's playwriting this lunchtime. This is an annual prize given to a woman who the judges have decided has written the most outstanding play from all of their entries. There are two separate meetings of judges. One set of three judges meet in New York and one set meet in London.

They don't seem to have any set of criteria against which we should measure our taste. They don't really have a mission statement. They're working from quite an old-fashioned notion of trusting the judges' instincts as to whether something is good or not. These instincts are perceived, erroneously, to be neutral.

What we really end up judging is how well the writers write in terms of being a bit like us.

But they buy lunch and reading ten plays by women writers in a fortnight was bracing and largely inspiring.

I met with director Phyllida Lloyd and actress Lia Williams in a restaurant in west London which wasn't as nice as its veneer suggested and together we agreed that the best play on our shortlist of ten was Lucy Kirkwood's *Chimerica*. It was everyone's first choice in London. It was the first choice of all of the judges in New York.

It's a play that takes the remarkable leap of imagining what the celebrated protestor at Tiananmen Square in 1989 had in the plastic bags that he held as he stood in front of the tanks there and builds, from this, a remarkable and moving love story about characters who regret the missed opportunities their lives are defined by.

It's an extraordinary play of range and ambition. It is politically searching while remaining humane. It is funny and touching and angry and bold and theatrically compelling and smart and sexy and kind of just great.

I read it after missing it in the theatre all last year. I've no idea why I didn't go and see it. I think I assumed it would reek of cultural imperialism as a British writer passed judgement on both the US and China, and that was a fucking stupid assumption because Lucy was too smart to do either of those things.

It is a terrific play and deserved to win the award.

I walked from the restaurant to Wardour Street with Lia Williams.

We talked about how actors reflect on their own work. I asked her if, as Liz suggested, it was entirely intuitive. She said it was largely intuition but she was also dependent on interpreting the responses of her audiences and the other actors she worked with.

I like the idea that an actor's measure of his or her own performance can never be solid or concrete. But rather that it is the sum of the interpretations of the reactions of other people to their own actions. It strikes me that this is a bit like life. We can never really know what kind of person we are. We can only make conclusions based on the accumulation of different interpretations of other people's behaviour towards us in an attempt to infer what kind of person we might possibly be.

Our identity is slippery and inchoate. It is not fixed. There is, in the end, no such thing as character.

Went to see *American Psycho* in the evening. It was directed by Rupert Goold at the Almeida Theatre, where he is the new Artistic Director, and starred Matt Smith as Patrick Bateman.

Matt is a subtle and nuanced actor who can communicate a lifetime of feeling very simply and with real effect.

This was kind of beautiful to watch but I'm not sure how happily it sat with a satire on the emptiness and soullessness of capitalism.

It was like the production was suggesting that everybody else was going insane and the only way to really feel anything anymore was to cut somebody's legs off and write on your walls with the blood from their stumps.

I enjoyed the rather soulful a-cappella versions of Phil Collins's execrable *In The Air Tonight* though.

13th January

Read *Long Day's Journey Into Night*.

This is a fucking incredible play. It is one of the most raw, most felt, saddest, bleakest, most angry plays that I know.

There is an off-stage character – a dead baby called Eugene killed by his elder, toddler brother.

It is a play about addiction and disappointment.

It is a play about illness and real despair.

The key to this play is in the stage directions. The stage directions, despite being unfashionably lengthy and prescriptive, are actually expressive rather than helpful.

The key to staging the play would be, rather than following the prescription to the letter, which is what Anthony Paige and Lez Brotherstone did last year, to excavate the metaphor from the atmosphere that O'Neill describes. It's hard and sad and frightened and brutal.

Had lunch with Christopher Hampton. Christopher is one of the most significant post-war English playwrights to have continued to write successfully into his sixties. I asked him how the hell I'm going to keep on writing throughout my next two decades.

This is something I think about often. I like writing. I like making my living as a writer. I would very much like to carry on writing throughout my life and I worry that all my ideas will dry up and I'll have to go back to being a schoolteacher in Dagenham again. I quite like Dagenham but I like playwriting more and so I've started talking to older playwrights to get their counsel. I spoke to one of my playwriting heroines, Caryl Churchill, about this last year and today to Christopher.

He told me that he realized that the key is to diversify. Caryl suggested to collaborate. Both seemed to encourage me to not try to endlessly scratch plays from the inside of my head but rather to nurture craft as much as a post-Romantic notion of genius.

Hampton started writing musicals and operas and screenplays. He's had sixteen movies made and written fifteen stage plays as well as opera and musicals. He's written about thirty unproduced screenplays.

He writes by hand in a notebook and has somebody type out his plays for him.

He says he has the capacity to remember four or five lines of dialogue at a time and then transcribes them. He can do that as quickly as he can type or write.

He writes his films and his plays in exactly the same way.

I like thinking about the relationship between the gesture – the physical gesture of writing something down and the intellectual gesture of crystallizing thought into language.

I like Christopher Hampton's plays enormously. His third play, *Philistines* written when he was about twenty-four ran for three years in the West End.

I'm interested in the bizarre way that only in the UK and the US would there be this strange relationship between commercial and artistic work.

Sometimes I think this is a brutal limitation to the work of a theatre maker in the UK. We need to constantly peddle our work in the market place. It means we can't ever make anything really daring or push our form or challenge the relationship between forms and content because we can't alienate our audiences too much. It matters to us if the audience are laughing or not.

We become a bit addicted to whether or not our lines are going to get laughs because laughter is the most tangible and legible measure of how happy our audience is.

In other countries, particularly in Germany I guess, there is less concern with this and so perhaps the work is less compromised. Sebastian Nübling is perplexed by why we are so dependent on the laughter of others.

But on the other hand there is something brisk and bracing about having to step out into the market place and sell our wares.

We can't indulge ourselves

We can't allow indulgence.

We have to prove it.

Met Marianne Elliott at the National. She gave me a raft of good notes on *Waterfall*, the film I'm writing for her. We talked about whether we should try to make a play inspired by *Dr Faustus* or by *Long Day's Journey* and she didn't really have a favourite. I am working on a few ideas for the National Theatre at the moment. I've been writing a version of Brecht and Weill's *Threepenny Opera* for a year or so. I would love Marianne to direct a production of my play *Heisenberg* that the Manhattan Theatre Club in New York have commissioned and will open in Spring 2015. As with these plays we will wait until Rufus Norris, the incoming Artistic Director of the National, has had time to consider the question of *Faust* or *Long Day's Journey* before rushing to a decision.

Probably by the end of the month.

My play *Carmen Disruption* started rehearsals in Hamburg today, as Sebastian Nübling started a week's work with Rinat Shaham, the mezzo-Soprano for whom the play was written and on whose life story some of the play is based. He rang me last night to tell me he was happy with my new pass at The Singer's section.

On the Shore of the Wide World opened well at the Griffin in Sydney over the weekend and received astonishingly warm reviews.

Sarah Frankcom texted me from Manchester to tell me they ran *Blindsided* today and she really loved watching the play in one whole. She seemed surprised by how much she'd enjoyed it. Maybe she always secretly thought it was a bit shit until now.

Walked over Waterloo Bridge in a hailstorm with a strong westerly wind blowing into the east estuary of the river and got quite stupidly wet.

14th January

Grabbing mouthfuls of air between rehearsals I did re-writes on *Birdland* today. *Birdland* is my new play for the Royal Court. Carrie Cracknell, who directed *A Doll's House*, will direct it in the Spring. She directed a reading of it last year.

I tried to make Paul, the play's rock star protagonist, more inquisitive. I think he should be more informed by a spirit of inquiry and less by hatred, and the suicide of Marnie, the girlfriend of his band mate with whom Paul has a one night stand, should tip his spirit into despair.

I tried to reign back on misogyny in that first draft.

It's alarming to me that when I was writing so unconsciously I should produce a character whose apparent hatred of women was so inchoate and uncontrolled.

I met the playwright Charlotte Macleod at the Tate Modern this morning. We had a coffee, talked about writing and gazed out at that remarkable view of London.

The city seemed pregnant to me. It seemed ready to blow. It made me think of New York ten years ago. That was a city that rendered itself uninhabitable. The same is happening here.

I wandered briefly through a new standing exhibition, which I think was called 'Facing History'.

It was beautifully curated. Ninteenth-century masterpieces of early modernism were hung opposite contemporary work. The pieces threw each other into relief.

Whenever I see art of that standard it galvanizes me. I seem fixated at the moment with the extent to which new theatre sits in a fault line between art and entertainment. It is a particularity to this country. And one, weirdly and against my expectations, I find myself enjoying this week.

The need to get up and get to the market can be inspiring. The need to get out of bed. The need to remember we are in a conversation, not engaged in an art of expression, can clarify our thinking and make us better.

And yet there was something about the Richter canvases or Hrair Sarkissian's series of photographs *Execution Squares*, a series of photographs of places in three Syrian cities where people were executed, that chills me and inspires me to feel uncompromised by a need to sell.

I guess what is essential is that it remains a conversation.

We live through an experience. We use our craft to transform it into something metaphorical. This process helps us understand the experience and also helps others understand that they are not alone.

The point is to practise the craft until we are deft with it. This involves hours and hours and hours and hours.

And to be alert to experiences. Sometimes that is the hard bit. Keeping our fucking eyes open.

It was a beautiful day of cold sunshine in London and that is my favourite type of weather in this city.

15th January

I did no writing today.

Pottered around London and met folk.

Walked from Euston Square to Bedford Square for a meeting with Anna Brewer at the Bloomsbury Offices. They have a new reception which is done up like an old-fashioned reception with a table rather than a receptionist desk and a woman sat behind the table with lots of books around her.

It was a brilliant simulacrum of something old fashioned.

Anna, who is my editor at Methuen Drama, gave me a handful of books by brilliant young writers. And there are brilliant young writers around. I love Alistair McDowall and Brad Birch and Tim Price and Rachel Delahey.

The concertina of a decade's investment in new writing ending with a significant contraction of funding has created an odd bottleneck. There are more playwrights than there have ever been. Probably statistically that's kind of true.

And the amount of stages that can do their work is decreasing. The best way for writers to learn remains by having their work produced. I hope they persist. I hope they don't become bitter. I wish them tenacity.

Sometimes the notion that it is possible to have a first play produced at the Royal Court, say, or the Bush can mean that it becomes an imperative and so the notion of a play in a fringe theatre can be dispiriting. The best of them will avoid losing spirit and just keep writing.

I had lunch with Hofesh Shechter, a choreographer, and Ramin Gray, a director, and we talked about *Seventeen*. *Seventeen* is a project that we have been working on together for a year or so. Ramin, who is the Artistic Director of Actors Touring Company and who has directed three of my plays, brought the three of us together to make something. Hofesh is currently perceived as one of the world's leading choreographers. We made some decisions about our project in development.

We will definitely use dancers that dance to a standard that Hofesh is happy with. This is largely on the grounds that I rather enjoy non-actors speaking my text but he gets very impatient with non-dancers. Sometimes I think non-actors can have an honesty that mediocre actors can't ever have again.

We will make a show about sex. We will make a show from the position of three heterosexual men projecting their fantasies onto beautiful women.

It will be like the bits of *Three Kingdoms* that feminist critics hated but ten times the case. It will be more unapologetic.

Hofesh made the point that sex was the one psychological area about which we three remain most vulnerable. So we should explore it. We should look at those things we are most afraid of, or if not afraid, shy or uncertain about.

And then to the Lyric for a run through the first three acts of the new Secret Theatre show *Glitterland*. Written by Hayley Squires it is a re-imagining of Webster's *The White Devil*. It's kind of extraordinary. It relocates the drama in a contemporary political world that evokes Kennedy's US. At its best it feels like *The Godfather*. It has that level of fear and betrayal.

The Secret Theatre Company is starting to show signs of the brilliance of lengthy collaboration. The level of trust and play and friendship they have with one another is remarkable. They play with each other and attack each other.

I wish that we didn't make it all a secret. The decision was made, when we put the company together, that we wouldn't announce the titles or content of any of the shows we produced but just number them as Show 1, 2, 3, 4, etc. It's an idea that never ceases to annoy me.

It wasn't our idea. It came from the theatre's marketing department and has, ironically, made the work impossible to sell.

It just mediates audiences in a way that isn't helpful.

Ellen McDougall has directed it with clarity and simplicity and it is powerful.

The story needs work. We need to hear the story in order to buy into what will be a very long play.

People don't mind plays being long. It's not the length of plays that people find boring. It's the sense that the artists involved in the plays haven't controlled the length of the things. Thirty minute plays can be unwatchable if they feel like they will go on forever.

Six hour plays are compelling if they feel controlled.

This seems to be a recurring thread in my thinking at the moment. Story is an urgent means of manipulating time in theatre. It is fundamentally human. It helps us make sense of our own position in a universe we understand to be eroding.

We understand our behaviour to play out over time.

Our lives have no narrative. But narrative is not mimetic. We don't tell stories because our lives have them. We're not that stupid. We tell stories because they contain metaphors.

The more I work outside an Anglo-Saxon context the more I enjoy the tension that narrative can give to formal provocation or exploration or expressionism.

Went to the Paines Plough birthday party. Paines Plough is a theatre company that is committed to touring new plays. I'm on its board. It's forty years old this year.

David Pownall, the founding Artistic Director, made a speech which drifted in and out of audibility in a massively entertaining way. But forty years ago he had an idea that is still worth fighting for today.

There are still new writers who want to take their plays throughout the country and there are audiences that want to hear these plays. There is something inspiring about that.

16th January

Back to Manchester and back on that train.

I spent the train journey making cuts to my adaptation of Mark Haddon's novel *The Curious Incident of the Dog in the Night-Time* before it plays a month-long residency for London school kids, and in preparation for the probability of having to cut it for its Broadway run.

In December the plasterwork in the ceiling of the Apollo Theatre was dislodged, most probably it seems by a lightning strike in a brutal London winter storm. The plasterwork fell on the audience. I initially heard about it leaving a reading of *Birdland* in the bowels of the National Theatre. The reading was held there because Carrie Cracknell, the play's director was working on another show at the National.

I left the reading to hear from a technician there that the roof of the Apollo had collapsed. I struggled to make sense of the probability that audience members would have died.

Thankfully, though, it wasn't as dramatic as that. Thankfully nobody was seriously hurt and the last remaining patient related to the accident left the hospital by Christmas Eve. But it closed the play for six months.

The current cast will play out their last month performing for free to London schools. I cut about twenty minutes from the play to facilitate that.

It should be no surprise in light of recent thought that I was drawn towards cutting those parts of the play that colour its tone, in an attempt to make the story as clean and as clear as possible. It felt like cutting out adjectives from sentences.

The Curious Incident of the Dog in the Night-Time has changed my life. I never envisaged that it would be possible to earn upwards of fifteen grand a month from working in theatre but for the past four months I have done so.

That will change for a while and then maybe will return.

In the meantime I bought three suits that I have enjoyed wearing. Oscar took the piss out of me. He couldn't understand why I would wear a suit at all when I work the one job that means I don't need to.

The Curious Incident of the Dog in the Night-Time is such a democratic show. It is predicated on a gesture of celebration of theatricality towards the audience. The idea that an audience that had saved money to see the play before Christmas should be so affected upsets me.

We will be back.

I arrived in Manchester to watch a run of *Blindsided*. It is a strange and sad play. I worry that it needs to be more built upon a driven central protagonist. I worry that it is unduly bleak for a Manchester audience. But the acting is sublime.

I worry that at times it is overly written.

But I normally have the experience of watching a run of one of my plays and thinking it is shit. Normally it indicates that the actors are ready for an audience.

Blindsided is a play about murder. It is a play carved out of a sense that the Manchester I was raised in remained haunted by the

ghost of the Moors murderers. It is a synthesis of Emlyn Williams'
biography of the Moors murderers, *Beyond Belief*, and Euripides'
Medea and Terrence Malick's *Badlands*. It is a play about how the
psychosis of love at first sight can lead to despair and violence.

The actors thought they were muddy and unclear. They felt like they'd
fucked the play up.

That didn't seem the case to me. I thought they listened with clarity
and played with grace. I just thought the play, my own play, was
slightly broken-backed.

There were moments, though, when I believed I'd dramatized what it
felt like to kill a child and those moments left me proud.

Went drinking with the actors afterwards and had dinner with them at
the pub Tom's Chop House next to the theatre. I went there for a
stiffening whiskey fifteen years ago before my first ever professional
meeting with the Exchange, which was in fact my first ever
professional meeting with any theatre company. So to go back there
for my fourth play at the Royal Exchange meant a lot.

Andy Sheridan and Katie West and Julie Hesmondhalgh said they
were nervous about me watching. This is partly because the British
rehearsal room is built around the writer and partly because I'm old
now and my plays have been around for half their lifetimes. Certainly
since Katie West was a teenager.

She is a rare and astonishing actor who fills a stage and makes it
sing.

She has no idea how good she will be.

Sarah has directed with psychological precision. This is the greatest
strength of English directors. They work with a sense of really wanting
to stage the way people are in real life. At least in that which they
perceive to be real life.

17th January

I worked on notes with Sarah this morning. I sat down low on the stage with her and did a lot of whispering in her ear.

One of the elements of my working life that I am most proud of is that I have a handful of very close collaborations with directors. One of the earliest and most important is with Sarah.

I first met her when she was Literary Manager at the Exchange. Her work, now that she is Artistic Director, remains defined by the imagination and rigour of her reading. Watching her work with the Movement Director Imogen Knight, though, I noticed that much of Sarah's instinct for movement is brilliant. It's as if she dare not acknowledge that she might be good at it.

She told me this evening that it is only now that she is starting to think of herself as an artist.

The word 'artist' is a poisonous word in English theatre and probably in England as a whole. It is because theatre sits on the spectrum between art and entertainment and we value the lack of pretension implicit in the notion of being an entertainer. It makes us think we are workers, which I like, but sometimes we need to step up and acknowledge that we are making things exist that didn't previously exist and the function of those things is entirely emotional or intellectual.

You can't sit on a play. You can't open a door with it. You can't move around on it or heat your house with it or eat it. A play won't keep you safe. It won't teach you grammar. It makes us nervous that something should have such a limited function. The function of art might be subliminal but it is urgent. Without it we would atrophy and grow arid and piss away.

It is possible to live without art but our life would lack any sense of self-reflection or nuance and we would only live through paradigms of making money.

Sometimes it's important to reclaim the importance of thinking and celebrate it.

Without it we would be in some way less human.

Another of the notes I write again and again in my rehearsal notebook is to encourage the actors to have the nerve to look each other full in the face and to be in the moment.

We did good work on that this morning and ran it this afternoon and the play was revealed. It is revealed when actors play in the moment, moment after moment after moment.

This company's capacity to do that today was shattering. Especially when the actors know of course the horror and fear into which this play will move. To hold the nerve to stay in the moment demands concentration and rigour.

They got close to achieving this today and now they need to tell me fuck off back to London on my train so they can own the play and kick the shit out of it.

I give that note about my plays all the time. Actors need to attack it.

They need to swagger.

Harold Pinter apparently told a director that he always felt it his responsibility to declare his true feelings about a production.

I don't know if I agree with him. When I'm in a rehearsal room I like to think that I'm working *for* a director and so I need to do all I can to facilitate their work and the best work of the actors. Sometimes that can involve being blunt and frank. Sometimes it must involve being encouraging and encouraging them to swagger.

I enjoyed spotting the bits in the play most directly taken from my life. The frankest moment of this is when Cathy Heyer tells Siobhan that

John can't pair his own socks. It's a line that reminds me how dependent on Polly, my brilliant wife, I am.

A kid I taught when I was a schoolteacher in the 90s at Eastbrook School in Dagenham, now working in Manchester, came to see the run. He emailed me last week to tell me he was in town.

It was nice to see him. He's thirty now. He was fifteen when I taught him. He's older than I was then.

Afterwards he described the play as 'lovely'. This was the best compliment he could have paid. That we had excavated love from a play about a woman killing her own baby felt important to me. 'Lovely' is also the word that most recurs in Sarah Kane's plays. Her plays are not plays about violence but plays about love, and the possibility that there is life in the world that is lovely, defines her work. She remains one of my favourite playwrights.

The adjective 'lovely' is one she returns to use. I noticed this on the day I read all of her plays sitting on a train from Euston to Stockport as I tried, and failed, to see Dad before he died.

To have shared her adjective meant a huge amount to me.

Went for a drink with old friends afterwards. I have no sense of the physical geography of Manchester at all.

I love, though, seeing it as a traveller. It is a bruised and beautiful red brick place.

The train is crammed. And overly warm. It's like an EasyJet flight. I can't wait to get home.

20th January

Up at five to get a taxi to Gatwick. We drove south through the centre of the city.

EasyJet flight to Hamburg for the start of *Carmen Disruption* rehearsals.

I re-read this play on the flight between dozes and was relieved to realize that it wasn't shit.

Gaby, the theatre's driver, came in her brand new Mercedes to collect me at the airport. She's collected me every time I've worked here. This is the fourth play I've had in the Deutsches Schauspielhaus. A 1,200-seat nineteenth-century playhouse that looks exactly how theatres are meant to look like. A huge proscenium. An enormous auditorium. It astonishes me that my plays are played here. Partly it astonishes me because I don't consciously write plays that will attract a large audience. Partly because it humbles me.

We drove out to the rehearsal room in the industrial areas in the east of the city. It felt exciting to see Sebastian again.

He chaired the opening of the rehearsals with charm and energy and we talked about why I wrote the play. Sebastian gave me the idea of writing it. He became fascinated with the dislocated life of Rinat as she parachutes into productions of *Carmen* again and again. He shared his fascination with me and it led to the play. She's sung Carmen thirty-nine times now in every continent. We talked about how the play was carved out of the themes and structures of the opera and built around the four principal characters.

It is a play, it strikes me tonight, about love and death. It is important to me that the structure of the play is defined by monologues. Our obsession with technology drives us further and further into isolation from one another. But the human form lingers in theatre. No matter how atomized by technology we become the necessarily human presence of the actor survives. Weirdly, in an increasingly technological world, this, it strikes me, has made theatre a more radical art form than it has been in my working life.

The theatre is a space where strangers sit next to one another to look in the same direction at other humans living in the same space and time as them.

The play read fine. I like hearing my plays in German. I like German. It is an erotic and gentle language. I like hearing my plays in a language I can't understand because it reminds me that our work is not in writing ideas but orchestrating energy.

The set designed by Dominic Huber is a beautiful recreation of the edifice of the theatre. It will move slowly towards the audience throughout the play.

It is a bold and dramatic gesture of a set but it works not through its boldness but because it is rooted in ideas contained within the play. He has taken a simple and core idea and built the set out of that while also creating an acting space for the actors.

This synthesis of imagination and simplicity and grace in creating an acting environment is what defines the German designers as great.

Dinner in an Indian restaurant in the illicit red light district of St Georg. And then back to the Schauspielhaus to figure out how to perfect the character of The Singer. The play is made up of five monologues and a chorus interweaving them. The choices of the other four characters based on the opera principals work fine. The chorus is manageable in its re-write. The voice of the Singer, the character Rinat will play, is harder to pin down. We couldn't figure out why and our conversation in two languages was fractious.

Not in an aggressive way. It was fractious out of frustration more than aggression.

We resolved to return tomorrow and went for a beer. Sebastian asked me what it was about the opera that most lives in the play. I said it was love and death. These are the two characteristics most absent in The Singer, I realized. I must listen out for that tomorrow.

It is wonderful being back in the Maritim Reichshof – the old nineteenth-century hotel connected to the theatre. I've stayed here so many times over the past decade. This was the first hotel I stayed in while working in Germany when coming to Hamburg to meet Sebastian to talk about

Pornography, the first play that I wrote for him to direct. It is a central setting in *Three Kingdoms* with its strange repetitive echoing corridors and absence of humanity. And its whisky bar. And its breakfast hall. And its swimming pool.

We've sat, Sebastian and me, in that bar drinking many times.

He asked me to write a trilogy of plays for him for the Ruhrtriennale. I think I would like to try. Perhaps a reimagining of the Oresteia. Many of my recent plays have been reimaginings of classic plays. *Blindsided* of *Medea*. *Birdland* of *Baal*. *Carmen Disruption* of *Carmen*. I think it is a rich source of material and actually a classical way for playwrights to work. It seems a rich heritage. Rather than imagining source material afresh, we assimilate from others and reimagine it and always have done. The vanity of thinking we can think of our own stories is modern.

They are selling the Reichshof to Chinese property developers. They are resolved to keep it as a hotel. I struggle to imagine it as anything other than a hotel. But they turned the Chelsea Hotel in New York into apartments so the same may happen here.

21st January

Second day of the rehearsals for *Carmen Disruption*.

We read the play again testing the new beginning. The work we were doing was trying to accommodate a different time frame for The Singer, the role that Rinat Shaham will play. Whereas the other four stories in the play take place over a day in the city her story plays out over one moment of decision.

We had to focus on getting her logic to work in a different sphere than theirs. Her world is less realistic. It's less natural and more psychological.

We worked on rigorously honing the logic of her psychological deterioration. I think, by the end of the day, we found a model that worked.

This is the first play I've ever written a chorus for. A body of voices articulate the inner spirit of the city, refracting and reflecting the lives of the principals against a broader social structure, one defined by the erosion and dislocation of intimacy in a world defined by technology.

Sebastian had Rinat read her lines in German. It gave her work a beautiful and strange quality. English is her second language so she can't intuitively find the rhythms with the effortlessness of a born speaker. But she is comfortable enough in English for it not to become an interesting interruption to her fluidity.

By having Rinat speak in German, a language she is self-conscious in, attention is drawn to how difficult her character finds it to articulate her sense of her world.

It reminds me of the qualities that the dancer-actors bring to spoken text with our work on *Seventeen* and the observation that the worst thing is to have mediocre actors. Far better to have language taut and strained through an interruptive thought.

We listened to the music that I'd laced through the play. Sonic Youth and Roy Orbison and Kraftwerk.

It made me wonder if the main reason I write plays is to have my favourite music played very loud in a theatre. I remain a kind of irritating DJ. Sonic Youth emptied the rehearsal room in the way it used to empty dance floors when I played their records when I was an actual DJ in indie-clubs in York as a student. Guaranteed floor emptiers.

The decisions about how to order this play are based more on tone than on narrative. It becomes about marshalling and orchestrating energies rather than telling a story. Hearing the play in a second language tunes my ear to the energy of words rather than their meaning.

The questions we face as dramatists are the same as artists have faced for hundreds of years. How do we best dramatize what it is to actually be alive? In a lot of my plays I've tried to do that by capturing behaviour and language that is as close as I can possibly get it to be to behaviour and language that we might recognize in our own lives. This play is different. The language is more heightened and poetic. The form more splintered. The world less real.

But I'm not sure that we experience life in the way that I've often written about it in plays that might be perceived as being realistic.

Sometimes as we dissolve into our addictions to YouTube and Twitter and porno and emails, where we lose all sense of what room we're in or who we're talking to, I wonder if we also reach a time where we need to reach for new forms of plays.

We experience life in a way that is as musical as it is driven by narrative. Our memory is as impressionistic as it is cogent. I've tried to find a more musical, more impressionistic, more atomized way of dramatizing that experience with this play than I have in other plays.

I've probably failed. We all fail. The point isn't to succeed. None of us succeed. The point is to try.

Hearing Roy Orbison reminded me of Dad and reminded me of John Peel. There is a beautiful simplicity to the lyrics of 'It's Over'. I was listening to the song as I landed in Cologne two years ago to prepare for the writing. And then saw painted in graffiti on the walls of the city the words 'It's Over'.

It felt like a sign. I felt like some kind of middle-aged English situationist.

A lot of the play was written talking into my phone as I wandered round London. I used to write like this into a Dictaphone. It always made me feel a bit weird and feel a bit like a spy. This was twenty years ago in the days before mobile phones. Now everybody potters round cities locked up in a private stream of words, phones shoved against their ears.

I think the stream of thought that came out of those walks defines some of the language in the play.

Got an email from Mel Kenyon via Scott Rudin's office asking me if I wanted to work on the next Martin Scorsese film. This was about the stupidest and most ridiculous email I ever got. I nearly fell over.

The amount of emails I've had from Mel over the past fifteen years that have sent my career spiralling into unexpected directions is considerable.

Polly told me it was a dream come true. It isn't. I would never have dared dream this would happen to me. It's a fantasy come true. Like playing for United or some fucked-up nonsense like that.

It won't happen of course. Peggy Ramsay always said that in film work the point is to take the money and never expect anything to be made.

We'll see.

22nd January

Up. Breakfast in the Reichshof. A glorious old food hall huge and echoing over a significant buffet and the location of the scene in *Three Kingdoms* where Stefan Dressner stuffs his pockets with croissants.

Went in with Sebastian to the rehearsal room but parked myself in the room next door doing the re-writes that came out of the first couple of days' rehearsal. I wrote a new story line for The Singer – establishing the idea of her boyfriend more clearly, suggesting the possibility that he was a fantasy. The best way to dramatize loneliness, rather than describe it, is through an attempt to contact.

I wrote some more of the chorus. Which was good fun. I'm enjoying the idea of a chorus.

And Sebastian entertained me by calling me into his room with Samuel Weiss and asking me questions about Samuel's character background. They wanted to figure out where he came from and what kind of family he came from and how he knew the friend whose money he has come to borrow. He joked that he was working like an English director.

I enjoyed my few days working with him immensely.

The range of directors I've worked with fascinates me. Directors are in a curious position in relation to their work. Because they never get to see their peers work they all assume that their practice is innate. They think that what they do is 'what a director does' because they don't know anything other. But every director I know has a different approach to his or her job and to what makes good theatre.

Sebastian is defined by his restlessness. Sometimes it's almost like he has attention deficit disorder. The word he uses more than many others is 'boring' to describe work that's frustrating him. This week he would kind of squat on his chair as much as sit on it. Poised. Sprung. Ready to go.

It's infectious and defines his work. We've had fun this week. The company seems relaxed and are brilliantly cast to their roles, and they read with real insight and care.

This afternoon we met the actors who will play The Chorus for the first time. I was in the rehearsal room when they came in. Thirty-five people of all backgrounds and shapes and sizes and ages trailed into the room. Each of them carrying their own chair. It felt like a chain of people that was never going to stop. It was extraordinary seeing them gathered in the room.

Theatre is the most human art form. There was something bracing about the idea that so many actual humans were going to be in one of my plays. Who are these people? Where have they come from? Why are they doing this? To get experience working with Sebastian? To work at the Deutsches Schauspielhaus? From a love of the theatre? Because they want to get out of the house? I don't even know if I'll get to answer any of these questions although I'd really like to.

Sebastian did some work with them, exploring different ways of moving people around in space. It was thrilling just watching all those people.

I bet he's cut them when I get back. Maybe not.

Taxi from the rehearsal room to the airport. Bought the kids forgiveness for my absence in the shape of toys. And a Moleskine notebook for Oscar.

Had a sandwich and a beer. Got on the plane. Came home.

26th January

The first three days of previews for *Blindsided*.

Up early to get the kids to school and see them, even only for half an hour. And then back to Euston and up to Manchester.

Staying with my mum and her partner Steve. Which was kind of great and meant I had cups of tea in bed in the morning. This felt like a total luxury.

I like previews. They terrify me.

I like them because they allow me to test the play. I see things for the first time when I'm watching them in front of an audience, and when the cast have worked as well and with as much detail and nuance as this lot, then I see things about the play that I'd never seen before.

Over the course of the first couple of previews it became clear to me that the work I needed to do was in making sure Julie Hesmondhalgh's reading of Susan Heyer came as much from a position of love and vulnerability as it did from anger. Or that her anger was a secondary emotion that sat on a fear that she was unable to articulate. Anger is always a secondary emotion. People are angry when there is something more primal that they can't control. For Susan Heyer she can't control the fear she feels of being abandoned by her daughter and her granddaughter, especially after the early death of her husband.

Julie, a brilliant and generous actor, has been playing Susan with a ferocity. We worked over the previews in grounding her more in tenderness. And over the course of the previews that love and tenderness became clearer and clearer, and so the story became clearer and clearer and the audience became more and more engaged. It was a cumulative build-up of response to the play, which is just great.

The artistic team have done extraordinary work. Lee Curran's lighting design in Anna Fleischle's beautiful set is sculptural and creates a tender and expressive world for the play to exist in. Pete Rice's soundscape is Lynchian in its boldness.

The acting, I think, is off the scale. All five of them. Rebecca Callard's tension between moral generosity and sexual desire. Jack Deam's detail and care and compassion as he explored Jacob. Julie Hesmondhalgh finds herself in the odd position of being just about the most popular actor in England at the moment because of the generosity and openness of her performance as Hayley Cropper in *Coronation Street*. Cropper, a transgendered sufferer of pancreatic cancer took her own life on Monday night's episode. I've never felt a theatre so full of love for an actor. Because she has worked in soaps rather than in Hollywood or TV drama for such a long time, the audience's relationship with her is not one of awe but of love. They feel like they know her. And she holds them in the palm of her hand. Last night, especially, she was just magical.

Andy Sheridan has played in three of my plays now. He is a detailed and intelligent actor and a bold and fascinating writer. He relishes the language of the thing. He plays action and intention with real clarity and accuracy.

I think Katie West's performance as a young Cathy Heyer is as good as any performance I've seen in any of my plays. She stands toe to toe with Lesley Sharp, Danny Mays and Andrew Scott. I hear her say some of my lines in my head as I'm sitting on the train back to London and it brings tears to my eyes. I know I'm a sentimental fuck but it really does. When she tells John Connolly that she 'trusted' him, when she tells Susan Heyer that she's the only one allowed to call Ruth 'Ruthy'. It blisters me.

An article in the Observer this morning talks about how much harder it is for working class kids to make it as writers or actors or directors or

39

musicians or artists. It's getting so expensive now. It's prohibitive. It's an accurate and unnerving article.

The cast of *Blindsided* inspire me even more so in this strangled context.

Loved working with Sarah through our notes. Her capacity to listen and to ground psychological detail is rare and she's made some of her best work here.

I worry about the audience. I worry that these are good people paying a lot of money to see Hayley Cropper and they get a very different experience. I felt like going round the auditorium and individually apologizing to all of them before the shows. But they've been attentive and appreciative. I always underestimate Manchester audiences. They are, in fact, more open and alert than I ever credit them with being. They're less 'cool' than London audiences. In both senses of the word. They are less concerned with being hip and so probably aren't as savvy as some regular London theatregoers. They are also less afraid of reacting before checking what other people are doing.

Less afraid of saying when they find something shit as well as less afraid of laughing out loud.

Some great laughter last night and a gratifying amount of audible sniffing in the sad bits.

They come from all over Manchester now. All over the northwest. The audience is less dominated by the Cheshire set. It's a democratic and open audience.

The relationship between the work and the audience is something Sarah is rightly proud of. It's a relationship that raises important questions about what theatre is for. I feel in my metabolism an instinct to entertain and to get laughs. There is an extent to which theatre in the UK remains an entertainment and I kind of respect that. But it can also be a limitation. My uncle came last night and was warm and generous but said as he went back for the second half 'Right! Entertain me!' and that need remains legible in all British theatre audiences.

Is that a bad thing? Maybe it isn't.

I often wonder why people can't go to the theatre in the way they would go to a modern art gallery. The edifice of the music hall looms large. And in the Royal Exchange, the edifice of a financial exchange.

I value this as much as it unsettles me, I think.

I always acknowledged how much I owed my mum. She was a teacher and fed me with an enthusiasm for books and reading. My dad was a salesman though. I always think I underestimate how important that salesman genetic code is in my sense of self and in my work.

On the one hand every scene is a kind of transaction. Every scene is kind of a deal. On the other hand I sometimes value the energy that a market can give an artist. We've got to get up and get out to the market and keep on fucking going even when it's pissing down and nobody's buying.

It struck me yesterday afternoon waiting for the matinee how tiny and negligible my anxieties are compared to the anxieties and concerns of most other writers in the history of world literature most of the time. The stuff I write won't leave me in prison. My family won't be endangered. I can write openly and not in code about whatever I want to write about. I wont be lynched or pilloried or arrested or vilified.

The only thing I need to worry about is the market. This is, physically at least, safe. How it pollutes or affects the work is for other people to judge.

27th January

Back to Manchester for the last preview of *Blindsided*. Worked some notes and some cuts. I love cutting plays in preview. Previews reveal the awful clumsiness and inclination to over-write in my playwriting and I love the opportunity to shave them back.

The best moments in theatre are moments that don't actually need any words.

Felt a weird sadness when the notes session finished. A nostalgia. It felt like a moment of releasing the cast. Their work has been rigorous and they'll carry on just fine without me. I felt like what I imagine it feels like for a parent saying goodbye to their kids as they start university. Pride in what they could do. Sadness that they don't really need me any more.

One of the wisest observations that I've read on the nature of creativity was written by the clinical psychiatrist Oliver Sacks in his study of autistic patients, *An Anthropologist On Mars*. In one chapter Sacks wrote about a patient who was suffering from a crippling nostalgia. Living in Florida in the eighties he suffered acute nostalgia for his hometown in fifties Napoli. It was so acute that it affected his vision. When he left his flat he saw that hometown so leaving his apartment in eighties Florida became dangerous. But he was a skilled oil painter. He could paint oil paintings of his hometown and in eighties Florida there was a vibrant market for oil paintings of fifties Napoli. So he exhibited and made money as a painter.

Sacks suggested that creativity and nostalgia come from the same place in our sense of self. They come from places of interruption. We don't feel nostalgic about every experience we've ever had. Only those experiences which in some way were interrupted or incomplete. And we create art and feel nostalgia out of the drive to complete those interruptions or repair those breakages.

That sense of nostalgia and its relationship to creativity felt acute as I left the rehearsal room and the actors. It felt like an interruption that would inspire nostalgia and also creativity.

This cast work with tireless determination to make images I made up in my head become corporeal. How could they not break my heart?

The preview was reassuringly shit. There's always one nervous, tentative, unhappy preview where everybody moves a step back. These are the most useful ones. It's in the shit previews that you measure how robust the work is that has gone into rehearsals and tonight it felt robust.

All the actors slurred or stumbled lines or dried altogether. Notes felt as though they were being played rather than inhabited. Blocking was overly conscious. But still the audience were largely held and the play had an imapct. So when the actors are back on it, it could be special.

Lots of coughing. Audiences feel like they can cough in a scene when they don't think they'll be interrupting something because nothing is actually happening.

Play the actions.
Ask the questions.

I wrote a piece on the train for the Volkstheater in Vienna. They asked me to respond to the question what should people ('Volks') do in theatres. I was happy with what I wrote.

In an increasingly frenetic world people should sit still in the theatre.
In an increasingly disconnected world people should sit next to strangers in the theatre.
In an increasingly technological world people should turn their fucking phones off in the theatre.
In an increasingly opinionated world people should listen in a theatre.
In an increasingly godless world people should show a bit of faith in each other at the theatre.
In an increasingly cynical world people should open their hearts in a theatre.
In an increasingly ignorant world people should bloody well think in the theatre.
In an increasingly humourless world people should laugh in the theatre.

Sonja Anders, Chief Dramaturg from the Deutsches Theater in Berlin came. They will do the play next year. She enjoyed Sarah's production but she was struck by how exposed all the actors are in the theatre in the round.

In this theatre character MUST be inhabited completely.

29th January

Fucked. Having drank about three bottles of wine last night.

Back home after the opening of *Blindsided*.

Saw old school friends at the Royal Exchange in the morning and then met Polly Thomas who will curate the Hunger for Trade show in the summer. I chose four playwrights to write short plays in response to the food trade in Manchester. Miriam Battye, Kellie Smith, Brad Birch and Alistair McDowall. Four fine young writers who fill me with optimism about the vibrancy in the craft of playwriting. They've written their short plays. I'm working with them on refining or developing them.

The meeting was fraught as the Literary Manager left on maternity leave rather suddenly and we are all under-prepared for the consequences of her departure.

I like working with young writers. They make me better. I'm a vampire. I suck their ideas. This time I'm nervous I'll let them down.

And then the final day of rehearsal.

The cast was slightly nervous after a shaky preview on Monday. Sarah pointed out that what happened was that, as actors, the five of them started becoming isolated. They were dropping their lines, stumbling their words because they were becoming conscious of themselves. The answer to this problem is always to find yourself located in the other actor.

Worked some good notes.

Then finished working on the play. It is always sad to stop rehearsals. We'll never rehearse those scenes again. We'll never invent or explore characters again. I feel proud of the work on this play and won't read the reviews.

The sense of yearning I get sometimes makes me want to cry. It makes me fall in love with the cast. That they should have committed so much to make my fantasy realized. And then that I should leave them. I won't feel like this in two days but at the time it is very acute.

The play is a dark play. It asks an audience to forgive a woman who they watch kill her baby. It is sparsely staged and acted with commitment. I am not sure if the absence of a single protagonist damages the back of the play. But I'm largely, for now, satisfied.

My wife, Polly, hated it. Not for bad writing or inept direction but because the gesture of asking forgiveness for a child killer felt vile to her. It was odd to have her so angry.

Split the audience as well. You can feel it when people are lying to you. I think the darkness of the ideas or the starkness of the production will alienate some. But many others feel genuinely moved and enthused. The cast was happy. Sarah too. Although she didn't watch it. I couldn't bear not watching a press night.

Went out late. Drank too much. Train this morning. Avoiding reviews. It's difficult. Quentin Letts, I gather, described it as a 'sweary little play'. He's a small-minded Tory with no imagination. I'm always thrilled when he leaves my plays upset. Like most people I know in theatre I wish him nothing more than misery.

Lunchtime meeting to talk with Kevin Cummins about the possibility of a Smiths movie. The speculative nature and unsubstantiated urgency about the film industry always confuses me.

30th January

My daughter Scarlett's seventh birthday and a day at the new Rambert studios working with Hofesh Shechter and Ramin Gray on our show, still tentatively called *Seventeen*.

We were auditioning today.

Twenty dancers came from all over Europe to work with Hof. He ran them through a series of exercises and taught them a dance. We chose twelve of them to work with in the afternoon and tomorrow.

It was heart breaking watching eight people leave.

We posted names on the door of the people we wanted to stay.

The rest were left blinking and thanking us for our time.

The whole project is built on a fascination of how we communicate thoughts in our head through bodies of dancers to heads in the audience.

To go from head to body to head.

How possible is that form of communication?

Actors deal better with the abstract. They respond positively to feelings or impulses. Less well to actions.

I always find in dance audiences that I am compelled to invent stories and create connections where there are no stories and there are no connections. This is the pull of narrative.

Ramin fluctuates between enjoying the dramatic and rejecting it.

His oscillations are both freeing and frustrating.

As a thinker he constantly diverges.

My impulse, always, is to converge. This is where narrative comes from. An attempt to find connecting points between two stars. An attempt to pull together that which is separate.

We like the gaps.

I'd like to find a form that excavated those gaps more fully.

This afternoon some of the work we were doing reminded me of Bill Viola. It was astonishing. Bill Viola and William Basinski.

Beautiful slow stillness punctuated by sudden explosions of violence.

Talked to Polly about *Blindsided*. She said that Cathy's inability to shake off her love for John was what infuriated her. It showed a lack of agency and a refusal to take responsibility for what she'd done.

I told her I was fascinated by the irrational. Drama struggles to deal with irrational behaviour. We reject it. It causes cognitive dissonance when characters appear to do things that make no sense. And yet sometimes sense feels arbitrary and random to me at least. How to dramatize that?

31st January

Negative reaction to *Blindsided* continues to come in.

Marianne Elliott wrote me an email to tell me how much she disliked the play. Her email raised interesting points.

How necessary is ethnic-specific casting? I've seen many Christians cast as Muslims and Sikhs and atheists. Albeit brown people or black people. But Marianne is worried that we cast a non-Jewish actor as a Jewish character.

More she finds herself unable to empathize with the characters. She says that I wrote the play only to shock audiences. She qualifies this with a great deal of love and affection.

I value her honesty enormously. And it makes me interrogate myself. But I think there is a difference between the effect of the play, which may come about as a result of my ineptitude, and its intentions.

An accusation of cynicism wounds me more than an accusation of being a bit shit.

All I know is that I care for Cathy deeply. And some other people claim to as well. I really love her. I only ever write characters I love. My intention with this play was to dramatize the humanity of a woman who killed her baby. Now I may have failed to. But there's a difference between failing to achieve something and trying to achieve something different.

I was, I think, wounded by an accusation of cynicism from a friend and a long-term colleague.

I'll get over it.

But the question of whether people should write characters that audiences care about is interesting. It is a Judaic-Christian narrative paradigm that continues to resonate in post-religious capitalism. The myth of the brave individuals struggling in the face of impossible odds. It's a myth I've based a lot of plays upon.

I think I've often failed to capture it.

But Marianne has always had issues with some of my plays. *Motortown, Morning, Three Kingdoms*. I don't begrudge her that and I value her telling me. But just because they might not dramatize the myth of the heroic outsider that a lot of my work does, doesn't mean these plays are cynical. I really think I'm not cynical and never have been.

A bit shit, maybe. But I take my responsibilities towards theatre really seriously.

Another day working with Hofesh and Ramin.

The key to this project is only ever to use text to juxtapose with imagery; not to write dialogue; embrace the choric and the absurd. Images that live with me. Eighty-one-year-old Ann Firbank dancing with the young company. Her reading them a bedtime story of erotic desire. Their hair hanging in front of their face. Them playing with their own hair. Their slow movements yesterday collapsing into the track changes. The intimacy dance opposite a male cast dancing entropy.

This afternoon – the attempt to dance a stop – holding a freeze until it became agony. Their attempts to speak interrupted.

I need to revise the text. Create something more poetic, more choric, more nuanced, more structured. That builds to an end.

2nd February

I took my son, Oscar and Tom, his cousin, up by train to see the play.

I did a pre-show Q&A with Sarah Frankcom and Dan Rebellato, the playwright and Professor of Playwriting at Royal Holloway University in London and the boys went for a burger and to bum around the Arndale Centre, which is precisely what teenagers should do in Manchester.

The Q&A was lengthy but good.

My favourite question was whether the play would be different if it was set in East London? Do I write with a particular sensibility when I write characters from Stockport?

I'm not sure.

I suspect though that there is a more acute nostalgia in my plays about Stockport. I think in some way for the characters from Stockport the sky is in some way bigger. Their political contexts are, I've noticed, more local. These are not characters so battered by globalized multi-national neo-liberalism as in some of the London plays. But their sense of history and their sense of space is wider.

The play was in good shape. It is always more enjoyable watching a play after its opening. I notice more things about it.

I have noticed that it is a production defined by what the actors do with their heads. Maybe this finally is Sarah's biggest skill – her capacity to interrogate the psychology of her characters. Watching the play I noticed that the bodies keep a weirdly rigid body shape through much of the play. Chest fully open. Arms hanging loosely by their sides. They connect with what they think.

It gives it an odd, dislocated, hypnotic accumulation.

I still haven't read the reviews. I gather Lyn Gardner in the Guardian liked it a lot as did Ian Shuttleworth in the Financial Times. And that most others haven't enjoyed it a great deal. I tweeted Shuttleworth to apologize for not reading it. I told him, honestly I think, that I was just policing my own needy paranoia.

I am surprised how many people find Anne Fleischle's set unnecessarily stark. I love its starkness. It provides an epic arena for Sarah's psychological nuance.

Read Astrid Lindgren's *The Brothers Lionheart* this weekend. Thomas Alfredson who wants to make it into a film sent it to me. It is a huge fantasy epic adventure about two boys fighting to save an endangered valley in the land of the dead. It is beautiful and poised. An odd choice for me – I've never written anything remotely like it. I've not even seen *The Hobbit* for God's sake. But I found there to be something constantly poignant in the ever-presence of death.

Two boys die. They go to an afterlife. They save the world of the afterlife. They die again.

Is it too Scandi for me? Is it too action packed?

3rd February

Coffee in Islington with the playwright Arinze Kene and director Sean Holmes to talk about Arinze's commission for Secret Theatre. It was good to push him into uncovering the emotional core behind his play.

Is there such a thing as real love in real life? What is love? He suggested that love was the ultimate distraction from the chaos of what it is to be alive.

It struck me this week that all stories are basically investigations of different tactics used to distract us from death.

Love being one of those.

Saw *Happy Days* at the Young Vic. It is an astonishing play. It does strike me that it takes decades to really understand Beckett. Death needs to be a tangible probability. The way he oscillates between astutely observed social analysis and observations of marriage or love or memory or family encased in this tomb of form is astonishing.

When I was younger I never realized how accurate his observations were.

4th February

Casting for *Birdland*. It's always a good thing to hear scenes cast. We looked at Marnie, the suicidal girl whose death triggers the protagonist's despair. I became temporarily worried by the domination of middle class actors in British theatre. The best of them were good because they played the action and asked the questions. It's about holding your nerve to be that truthful.

But if this week has taught me anything it's that appreciation of actors is entirely subjective. I always thought that acting was different to writing or directing. There were some people who were just good at it and better than others. But recent differing opinions on actors I love or have reservations about have taught me this is just not true.

Carrie Cracknell is keen to cast a small tight cast according to talent not accuracy. So actors will play the wrong ages. The wrong genders. So long as they play the action truthfully, ask the questions, listen, those qualities transcend accuracy of character type.

And then over to the Old Town Hall Stratford for the scratch performance of *The Curious Incident of the Dog in the Night-Time*. For two weeks this month the West End cast of *The Curious Incident of the Dog in the Night-Time* will stage a performance in the Old Town

Hall Stratford for free to Newham school kids. No video projection. Simple sound. Just the play.

Fifty kids today came from Eastbrook, the school where I used to teach as part of an audience of two hundred. My former colleague and mentor Glenn Anderson brought them. It was a thrilling afternoon. The actors acted with precision and listened hard. And the kids were held. They were moved and inspired by what they saw.

It was good to see Glenn again.

It reminded me of the first conversations I'd had with Mark Haddon about why and how we would adapt his novel. It was always important to me that we produced a script that could be done in the simplest possible form. The video projection and the lighting were exciting additions but the book was so democratic that it felt important to me we should be able to stage it with amateur actors in a school hall. And this came very close to that experience. Except the cast was a cast of National Theatre standard. And the school hall was the nineteenth-century chamber of the Stratford Town Hall. It was one of the better afternoons working in theatre.

5th February

Did re-writes on my Manhattan Theatre Club commission *Heisenberg* this afternoon. A few weeks after the reading in New York with Sir Ian McKellen and Mary-Louise Parker. That was an afternoon to remember and all. They read to each other with nuance and wit, and at the end he leaned over the table to kiss her thank you.

The re-writes I think clarify the story and make Alex Priest the emotionally atrophied butcher at the heart of the play who is woken up by an American stranger thirty years his younger, a more interesting character.

Too late to seduce Sir Ian who has said he's not keen on doing another play in New York. He said he was too tired. Outside the reading on W 43rd he rubbed his hand through his hair and closed his eyes and seemed simply exhausted.

I honestly have no idea what will happen with the play. Maybe something. Maybe not. But it was nice to return to it and find that it wasn't necessarily shit.

It is carved from the same skull as *Blindsided* in that the characters have an odd, playful eloquence and a psychotic love of speaking. But the gesture of the play is gentler than that. It's tenderer.

Went out with Polly and, our friends, Gary and Danielle Lineker to see John Donnelly's *The Pass* at the Jerwood Theatre Upstairs. As an eminent ex-professional football player and leading sports commentator Gary asked me if it was the Wembley of playwrights. I said it was more the West Ham Academy or the Crewe Alexandra of the nineties. This is where many playwrights' careers start. It made me remember the thrill of having *Herons* up there thirteen years ago now.

I remember that production vividly.

Gary said he found himself slightly distanced by the differences between how the footballers were portrayed in John's play and what footballers are really like in life. Never having been a footballer I couldn't relate to this and I found much of John's play compelling and his world plausible.

It struck me that there is a difference between what we perceive reality to be like in our memories, based largely on what we experience, and how we perceive reality to be like in our imagination. It is more important, I think, for plays to accord to this imaginary reality when attempting to create the effects of realism.

What is realism for? By creating a world on stage that in some way reminds an audience of a world in which they perceive themselves to be living may facilitate self-recognition and so allow audiences into the metaphor of the play.

We exclaim at how accurately the writer has captured exactly what a certain experience is like.

This helps us think about what we are a little bit more. It helps us examine our own humanity a bit. This is, I think, the whole point of theatre. The point of any arts. To create a space in which, for a time, we can think about what it's like to be human.

But when the world replicated on stage gets too close to a world in which we have lived, then we actually end up distanced from the play. Because it wasn't like that in any way. We're then more likely to recognize ourselves in the story of a fourteenth-century Danish Prince or a King in Ancient Greece than we are in a world that attempts to be a bit like what our life is like.

And further than that we have imaginary realisms. Worlds and stories that resonate not with how life is actually lived, but with what we tell ourselves life is like or lives which we don't know MUST be like. So, to me, John Donnelly's description of scoring a goal seemed really plausible. I pointed that out to Gary and he looked at me like I was somebody who had never, in their life, ever scored a goal.

Which is exactly what I am.

I recognize the experience of scoring a goal not from my own life but from my narrative of what life is like.

Wouter van Ransbeek the producer of Toneelgroep Amsterdam, the Dutch theatre company led by Ivo van Hove rang to confirm the intended dates of the monologue I am writing with Mark Eitzel, which will have the working title of the Van Wyck Expressway.

It will open in São Paulo or Amsterdam in March next year.

I need to write it by the end of June.

6th February

I turned forty-three today.

A reading day. I read three plays. Sarah Daniels's provocative study of pornography in patriarchy *Masterpieces* – a play which feels both oddly dated with its explicit political agenda articulated through what a character learns and resonant with its frank discussions of the dehumanizing nature of porn.

She writes like a weird cross between mid-period Brecht and quite broad old-school humorist. I liked the play despite its political techniques seeming dated. Whether or not her line on pornography holds true is interesting. Sarah Kane would have disagreed with her. Kane always thought feminists under-estimate the sophistication with which most men use porn.

Enda Walsh's *Disco Pigs* remains a vibrant, impenetrable punk of a play. The narrative is pretty straightforward. The form pretty simple too. It's in the language that Walsh makes this play significant. It is explosive and dangerous and alert and inventive and steeped in a deep Irish tradition of verbosity as code.

And Alistair McDowall's new play *A Forest A Forest*. A huge Gothic study of a religious sect in which the men imprison, torture and murder the women, and end up marrying their own daughters. It's a nightmarish exploration of Mormonism. It's savage and huge and well written. It's funny at times. At others didactic. But maybe this is how I will reveal my fall from fashion. Maybe what we need to start doing is being more explicit about our political ideology. This appears to be something that the young are doing.

Liz White wrote to tell me that she thought Carrie Cracknell's study of gender politics *Blurred Lines* at the National Theatre Shed was the start of something. Maybe that is exactly what she means.

7th February

Spent the day travelling to and from Newport to apply to replace Oscar's lost passport.

The train was massively delayed by the flooding in the West Country. The place is fucked by wetness. It felt apocalyptic.

The Passport Office was in a car park underneath a bridge over the river. A strange, dislocated Ballardian isolated area of absence.

Newport looked desolate. The more I travel outside of London the more compelling I find the idea that in fact London is almost a different country. The poverty and despair of Newport felt like a city in the real throes of economic despair.

Came back in time to watch the first preview of *Glitterland,* the Secret Theatre Company's fourth show at the Lyric Hammersmith.

Beautifully acted and designed it is suffering from a lack of narrative clarity. Hayley Squires has written a rangy play of political ambition. She just needs to get better at telling the story. She needs to let us into it a bit. Use real nouns. Use place names. Locate the story. Without those things it feels impenetrable and elusive.

And then it becomes just boring.

Despite how poised the acting is or how graceful the design. And it is like a Noir-ish Lynch-ian thing. But for too long the audience simply don't know who is who and what they want and what they're doing and so they don't care and then it becomes poisonously boring.

The more I write this journal the more obsessed I feel myself to be with story.

Theatre is a forum to consider the things that people do to one another.

Story is the marshaling of exactly those things in order over time.

10th February

I did an interview with Radio 4 at home this morning talking about the relationship between my writing and home, and the representation of ideas of home in my play. They came round to our house, which felt appropriate and also freed me to chat openly and to investigate my own ideas.

Death is omnipresent in plays. Maybe we feel most at home in those spaces and times during which we come to reconcile ourselves to our deaths. We want nothing and regret nothing. We live in the present tense. We are aware of our smallness.

A couple of hours on my translation of Anton Chekhov's masterpiece *The Cherry Orchard*. I think my first draft is good. It's taut and funny. I think I use too many adverbs to qualify adjectives: 'really hard', 'so cruel', etc. That's an easy pass to do.

Went back to Stratford to watch another matinee of *The Curious Incident of the Dog in the Night-Time*. This time with Mark Haddon. It's so good to see that play in the round and I feel very proud of my collaboration with Mark. He said he was surprised that I remained engaged. I think that I just enjoy watching the decisions actors make. Mike Noble, the young actor playing Christopher, felt particularly alert and fresh in his work today. Every decision felt lived. Which after a hundred shows is remarkable.

Back to the Lyric Hammersmith for a Readers meeting.

A general mood of unhappiness has gripped The Secret Theatre Company as they rehearse *Show 4* through previews. They are whipping each other up into fury. Encouraged to think of themselves as artists they seem to be forgetting that the calibre of the art is more important than how happy they are and so are resisting cuts and changes.

I gather from all my colleagues in Europe that this is exactly how ensembles always work.

Back into town for dinner with Mel Kenyon and to see Lisa Dwan in Walter Asmus's exquisite production of three Beckett shorts *Not I, Footfalls* and *Rockaby*. It was extraordinary theatre. So detailed. Deeply compassionate. Exactly as Beckett should be performed. It demanded a complete immersion in the world of the plays and rewarded that immersion with an experience that felt profound.

In moments like that theatre becomes more than a church. In moments like that it is transformative. The spectrum of audience engagement is taken to its most desperate edge in some ways. But in other ways Beckett writes with such nuance and warmth in his understanding of popular culture, and women's role within that, that it never feels alienating.

I remember the first time I met Mel. I was having lunch in London with Polly and her dad and was annoyed that I had to leave the lunch before the dessert to go and have this meeting with an agent. I was annoyed because I'd earlier met another agent in an agency in West London who I really liked and was keen to sign with. I sat outside Mel's bustling office for about ten minutes while she finished a phone call and rather took against the place.

It was too busy, too noisy, too frenetic. I decided that I would go in and make the meeting as brief as possible and go and join Polly and her dad again. Instead, I sat with her for about two and a half hours.

We talked about my writing and about theatre. We talked about the north of England and about politics and class. She told me about all the writers she represented. She has the best list of writers in the UK.

She represents the best of an entire generation. She represents us with fierce loyalty, reads us with real clarity, finds us work, and fights our corner. She has been the engine behind Sarah Kane, Robert Holman, David Greig, David Harrower, Lucy Kirkwood and hundreds of others.

I love our nights out together. We get drunk and gossip terribly.

11th February

Started work with Katie Mitchell on *The Cherry Orchard*. Katie will direct the play in the autumn. I'm relieved that she liked my draft. She confirmed that it will be taken to Moscow Arts after its run at the Young Vic.

She had very few notes and a lot of enthusiasm and we sat in the Southbank Centre and enjoyed a rigorous interrogation of the minutiae of some of my decisions.

One of my favourite changes she asked me to make was to replace all references to 'stage' with 'room'. So characters no longer cross or enter the 'stage' but rather cross or enter rooms.

For her the commitment to the completeness of the world presented on stage is absolute. I know no other director as ferociously rigorous as her when it comes to making the onstage world total and ignoring the corrupting impact of any audience.

She and Nübling are often lumped together when my work is being discussed but they really couldn't be further apart in their attitudes towards audience.

Or towards the question of where the character begins and the actor ends.

I love the tussle in my own head between their ideas.

12th February

Met with Rufus Norris, the new Artistic Director of the National Theatre and Ben Power, his Artistic Associate to talk about *Threepenny Opera*.

Rufus is very keen for me to radically reconceive the scenes so that they resonate more completely with a contemporary world. The play in the simplest terms isn't very good.

You get the sense that Brecht either was writing with contempt for the innately bourgeois tropes of drama or he was just not very good at making scenes dramatic. There are constant interruptions. Constant subversions of the narrative. Culminating in a ludicrous deus ex machina. But the music is remarkable.

I am slightly unconvinced that it is possible to reconceive the thing. I worry that a contemporary sweeping play about police corruption and corruption in homeless cultures will not accommodate musicals so easily. Or will not fit into that shape of play.

But Rufus wants to make it his first production. It would be a signature production. It feels like I can't turn it down.

More work with Katie Mitchell.

And then to meet he filmmaker Daria Martin to work with her and choreographer Joseph Alford on the show they will make for Tate Modern. An interrogation of the experiences of mirror-touch synaesthesia. People whose level of empathy is so cripplingly high that they feel that which they see.

I was under-prepared but I had an idea about how the film could be an attempt to get a teenage boy out of his house and that seemed to work.

It felt today like I'd taken on too much work.

It felt today that I was drowning in commitments.

Brutal storms lashed the west coast. The weather felt apocalyptical. The meteorological extremities brought about by climate chaos seem to have kicked in.

That felt unarguable.

It may mean that I'm not able to make it to Manchester to see *Blindsided*.

13th February

An interview with Matt Trueman from the Guardian to talk about the influence of music on my plays. I like Matt. He's one of the sparkier young journalists writing about theatre at the moment.

Everything I know about drama I learnt from music. Everything I learnt about dramatic structure or movement through time or rhythm.

Music is nostalgia to me. Everything I remember is refracted through music. The writers who made me want to write were songwriters. Matt asked me about Sebastian Nübling. I said I recognized in him a sense of rhythm scouring through him like a pulse.

I said that my restlessness to find new music was like my restlessness to write. That instinct to keep searching without ever finding that which I'm looking for.

Had lunch with Ben Power and Marianne Elliott to talk about the Faust play. Myself and Marianne have decided to pursue the idea of reimagining Faust, over responding to *Long Day's Journey Into Night*. I think the key to it is going to be how to properly excavate the eternal. The possibility of consequences resonating for all time.

The idea of the devil being incarnate.

The challenge is to make a character we can relate to making a decision that seems inexorable.

I wonder if Faust should be a woman. Mephistopheles a man.

The trick is for her to doubt his existence. When the devil convinced us that he didn't exist – well that was his greatest trick.

Then back on the train to Manchester. England has been battered by the storms and floods. I was lucky to arrive on time.

And back to watch *Blindsided* for the final time.

It was a good performance.

A clean performance. The story was told with clarity and well acted with pace and incision and determination. It really sung out. The audience listened and were moved by it. In a post-show discussion I was astonished by the degree to which the audience really got the play. They got that it was a play about the psychosis of love. They got that it was a play about the possibility of redemption after even the darkest of crimes.

That this audience who came along to see Hayley Cropper got something so deeply was immensely moving to me.

It made me proud of Manchester.

I asked Ben Power and Marianne if they felt Northern over lunch. They said they did. But struggled to define it. I wonder if it's a suspicion of pretension. I wonder if it's a recognition that it's alright to want to leave.

Went out drinking with the actors.

I can't write about how much debt I feel to the actors who commit to my plays without sounding sentimental and stupid but I do. And then it's over. And you don't see them for a bit.

14th February

Battered after a late night and back down through the drenched Northwest.

Lunch with funders for ATC. They were smart, driven, rich people with a love of theatre.

A woman and her son. They were articulate and searching about the nature of our world and our futures and also committed United fans which made me tremendously happy.

Met James Rose, a young writer whose play I read and loved.

And then Andrew Scott to talk about *Birdland*.

He's anticipating something huge. He's nervous. Anxious. Excited. Keen on the play.

This bewildering baton of play to play to play is passed on.

Up till 02.30 doing emails and finishing work.

Holiday tomorrow.

I can't wait.

Simply can't wait.

24th February

In New York for the opening of *A Doll's House* at the Brooklyn Academy of Music.

The artistic team spent their per diems on upgrading the hotel so I'm staying in the achingly cool Standard Hotel on the Lower East Side. A great night's sleep in a beautiful big bed helped me recover from jet lag quite completely.

And then walked a few blocks this morning for breakfast with Trip Cullman who will direct *Punk Rock* at MCC, the Manhattan Class Company, in the autumn.

We talked for a couple of hours about the particularities of the English language and about how Northern these characters are. I always think the richer people are in the North the less pronounced their accents are. There is a wash of affluence in English accents that makes the posh kids of the North sound like posh kids anywhere throughout England.

Again and again questions about casting and production came back to the same idea. As long as an actor can play the action with a sense of clarity and truth, then issues of race, ethnicity, age even are irrelevant. This is striking in the US – a country still rift by the fallout of slavery. Still a relatively recent catastrophe in this country's young history.

It was odd returning to the world of *Punk Rock*. I wrote the play seven years ago. I'd forgotten a lot of it. The weird things characters say to one another. So much of my writing is necessarily instinctive. I spent a lot of time on that play plotting the narrative and the action, and I wrote it quickly. I think my plays tend to be best when a lengthy period of mulling and planning results in a speedy process of writing. This can mean that my thinking about language choice, for example, on some lines is almost irrational, it's so instinctive. So I forget the lines I've written or why I wrote them and the director and the actors have to excavate the texts. I am not some great authority on what I was trying to say in those moments of writing. I was just trying to write the thing. Just trying to create some kind of energy or heat.

Odd looking back at the killing at the end of the play. The shocking nature of the killing is how sudden and irreparable it is. The deaths don't need to be visceral. Just immediate. Life is ended quickly and with no build-up or apology. There is something horrifying about the randomness and the speed of it.

I think productions of the play that cut the last scene are limited in some way. From a world which is built on history and chaos and clutter of the library we go to the clinical interview room in a secure unit of a psychiatric hospital. In the clinical world there is the possibility of some kind of odd hope.

Walked through the Village up to 7th and 14th to get the 1 to go to Columbia and talk to playwriting students there. A beautiful walk on a cold sunny day through one of the most beautiful parts of the city.

The playwright Anthony Weigh hosted a conversation with me and him and Christian Parker. Christian is my oldest friend in New York. Back from when he was my first advocate in New York, reading *Port* when he was Literary Manager at the Atlantic Theater. He has provoked me into thought and given me stuff to read and responded to my plays and pushed me into being better.

I'm proud that the Atlantic have been the first theatre to stage my plays in this city.

It was a good conversation watched by twelve largely mute playwriting and dramaturgy students.

I talked about the relationship between nostalgia and creativity and the five experiences from which I draw inspiration. The experiences I've lived through – those interruptions Oliver Sacks identifies as being the root of both nostalgia and creativity. The experiences I've observed in others. The experiences I've researched. The experiences I've taken from other plays – plays I've loved and want to re-interrogate and plays I've been frustrated by and plays I've written – wanting the next play to be different to the last. And theatrical experiences. I've always written for actual stages and real theatre architecture – this fuels my love for the back stage area – the place where magic is concocted. The energy I get writing for particular actors.

I talked about how every play has been an attempt to in some way interrogate the same question and that every time I write a play it seems in some way to fail. This failure is exactly what gives me a need to try and write another. Because I never get it right.

I couldn't properly identify what the questions are. I think they are questions about a keening to leave home and a need to return. I think they are about the responsibility to be optimistic in a world with an uncertain future. I think they are about having children and being married, and how nourishing and enriching and difficult those things are.

Anthony made the observation that my plays never really have questing central protagonists. This was a fascinating surprise to me because I always assumed that they did. Maybe this is the area that I keep returning to. I'm trying to clarify a character's attempt to make rational attempts to make sense of their life in the face of the knowledge of their death and yet my characters exist in a world that atomizes their unity so their quest is never properly cogent.

How do we live in a world that scatters order?

How do we drive to achieve things in a world that only encourages us to contradict ourselves and behave without reason?

26th February

I met the film and theatre producer Scott Rudin this morning. I sat in the lobby of his offices on 45th Street surrounded by the posters for all the films that he's made: the Paul Thomas Anderson films and the Coen Brothers films and the Wes Anderson films and I felt more nervous than any time I've spent waiting for a meeting since I waited to meet Mel Kenyon sixteen years ago.

He was avuncular and charming and fun and deeply learned and had read my plays thoroughly. We talked about politics and the future and how writers write and why they write and how I manage to write so much and why I need to write so much. We didn't actually talk about either of the projects that he's asked me to think about but the expansive conversation was, I suspect, finally worth more than that.

And then went over to Brooklyn, to the Harvey for the last preview of A Doll's House.

The Harvey auditorium at the Brooklyn Academy of Music where A Doll's House is playing is quite beautiful. The story goes that it was a space found by Peter Brook. People talk about him climbing through a window in what was a disused opera house and recognizing within it the capacity to create a space in Brooklyn that evoked the battered intimacy of his Bouffes du Nord in Paris. The open brickwork and steel work and revealed mortar were evocative and elegant. Daldry and Rickson must have been thinking about this when they re-opened the Royal Court fifteen years ago,

It is a space that combines the epic and the intimate with the same sense of magic, as do the best theatres.

Under its huge wing space Ian MacNeil's elegant design looked more like an actual doll's house than I'd seen before.

I sat with Carrie Cracknell at the very back of the stalls under the overhanging balcony. The space, frustratingly, was an acoustic dead spot. We really struggled to hear the actors. The struggle was tiring. It made me realize that there is a danger that the play can seem dominated by talk. I had a very odd response. I was bewildered by just how much talking went on in the play. It clarified for me the idea that writing plays is not about scripting language but rather about mapping energies. If the actors aren't attuned to this ferociously difficult architecture, then we lose the energy, are left only with a mass of worlds and drop our concern, losing interest in what they're doing to each other, thinking only about how much they appear to be saying.

Carrie made the brave decision to go and speak to the actors at the interval. She was nervous that the impact would be destabilizing but in fact the opposite was true. They attacked the second half with heightened energy. Rather than losing any of the specificity of thought they made it clearer. We didn't lose any nuance but heard it more. It was a terrific second half performance and a testament to Carrie.

The audience was quieter than on previous evenings but responded with warmth and many stood up.

Carrie has a remarkable determination and courage for somebody so poised. It was good to see David Lan there. He is about to become Artistic Director at the new Freedom Theatre at the base of the World Trade Center. He has the capacity to re-energize New York theatre.

He is a visionary producer and his work at the Young Vic has been constantly stimulating.

27th February

The opening of A Doll's House at BAM.

It was fascinating watching the play last night. There's part of me that wishes I'd had time to come over earlier and work on the script. Those huge spaces eat story. All the moments of nuance and uncertainty feel exposed. The bigger the auditorium in a theatre, the more exposed hesitation is and so much harder is it for subtext to work.

I also wonder of the hermetically sealed nature of the on-stage world. Carrie has a commitment to psychological nuance and a shared onstage perspective. She leads her cast to imagine the same worlds as each other. This sense of deep psychology filled the Young Vic with a real sense of truth. I wonder if it alienates the audience in this huge space. I wanted the actors to let the audience in, to acknowledge the presence of an actual theatre, just a touch more.

But they worked the volume with real energy. And by the end of that ferocious third act they were utterly compelling. Never seen Dominic Rowan, playing Torvald, so raw. When he roared, 'I'm saved' on opening Krogstad's letter, it felt as though it came from a place of real despair.

And Hattie Morahan, as Nora, matched him beat by beat.

That final act of the play from the broken tenderness of Krogstad and Mrs Linde; through the sexual tension between Torvald and Nora; into the comedy of the knitting section and the deep, deep sadness of Dr Rank's farewell; into that bewildering and urgent confrontation between Nora and Torvald is playwriting of the highest order.

My favourite moment in the production is when Torvald leaves Rank and Nora on the sofa alone to get his cigar. They sit in silence. They can't speak. The level of love and sadness and fear of death in them is utterly extraordinary and moves them beyond words.

In the stunning Harvey space that felt like a still, silent ballet.

There's part of me that thinks that my favourite moments in my plays are silent.

We need to move towards a position of earning silence on stage. I should try and write a play with no dialogue.

28th February

Landed at Heathrow to get Brantley's review of A Doll's House in the New York Times.

It is the first review I've read of any piece of theatre all year and a fairly unequivocal rave. Even great reviews corrupt us a little bit. It's easy to take my eye off my own thoughts from the way the production and that version of the play sit in the opera house. I don't mean to be a fuck – it's just that I found my problems more fascinating than the NYT review is gratifying and I can't help thinking that in the end that fascination will bear more fruit. We only learn from problems and flaws.

This is my current returning mantra used talking to young practitioners. A generation of young people has grown up in the UK being tested by the government from the age of six. Most of them don't even remember being tested. They are keen to succeed. They are keen to impress their parents and their teachers by their success, the best of them. But success teaches us nothing. We only learn from those errors we make and flaws in our work and the reflections we make upon these errors and flaws.

Met Ramin Gray and a woman from the University of Kent – Dr Freya Vass-Rhee – at the National Gallery café. Freya Vass-Rhee was the dramaturg for William Forsythe for sixteen years. She talked to us about his divergent and alert way of making work. Forsythe would rehearse for months at a time before sometimes finding the true shape of his shows days before the opening. Her process accorded with Ramin's fixation with holding the nerve of the divergent imagination and sits at odds with my more convergent way of thinking. My instincts in my work involve my bringing disparate ideas together. Ramin's involve shaking his apart. This tension sits in our collaboration in a way that I think is quite useful.

Freya described her thinking as 'tentacular', which is a word I enjoyed.

She distinguished between the use of juxtaposition and the use of counterpoint in the making of theatre. She was excited by the way Forsythe counterpoints elements of sound, language, movement, image rather than simply juxtaposing. His dancers work like a jazz ensemble, listening to the way each other thinks.

She talked about the way Forsythe uses language. As a rhythmic phenomenon rather than a means of communicating ideas literally. I found the conversation thrilling.

It tied in with my thinking about trying to use silence and tension on stage as a means of communicating idea rather than language. It reminded me about my thoughts on the unspeaking scene between Rank and Nora in Act Three of *A Doll's House*.

Walked across Hungerford Bridge to the National Theatre to see Ben Power to talk about the questions we have for the Brecht estate on a possible re-think of *Threepenny Opera*. Can we cut the inter-scene titles? Can we change the back story? Can we swear? Can we change the narrative? Can we change the setting? . . . are amongst some of the smaller questions we have for them. Their response will dictate whether or not we pursue the project.

3rd March

First day of rehearsals of *Birdland*.

It is a strange combination of the exhilarating and the weirdly familiar to be back in the Royal Court. It feels a bit like coming home. But as though home is an impossibly exciting place. Although at the introduction to the staff at the end of the day I recognized maybe two people. We leave work places and they carry on just fine without us.

First day of rehearsals often have the same routine. We gathered – the cast, Carrie Cracknell, Ian MacNeil who is reunited with Carrie after *A Doll's House*, the stage management team and Vicky Featherstone the Court's Artistic Director – nervously in the Site, the old location of the Young Writers Programme, in the morning. We read the play. We saw the model box. We had lunch. We started work in the afternoon.

It is the familiarity that makes it nerve-wracking. Actors dread the exposure and the first-day-of-school horror.

But the play read beautifully. It is a terrific cast. The play is a reimagining of Brecht's *Baal* set in the world of contemporary stadium rock. Like a synthesis of *Baal* and Grant Gee's film about Radiohead's OK COMPUTER tour, *Meeting People is Easy*. Andrew Scott plays the lead role of Paul. He is joined by Nikki Amuka-Bird, Yolanda Kettle, Alex Price, Charlotte Randle and Danny Cerqueira. They read with clarity and nuance and a sense of play.

I was relieved to hear that the funny bits are still funny. I had some thoughts for possible re-writes. But they were little enough to not be daunting. This is all exactly as I would have hoped.

We tried an experiment with cross-gender casting and all agreed it didn't work, and that experiment and agreement was smashing.

The play is not as misogynistic as it was in the first drafts. It seems, instead, slightly humane. I worry about my own unconscious impulses but I'm pleased that with Carrie's help I was able to police them.

In the afternoon Carrie started the slow but important work of establishing the intentions of the scenes. She breaks the play down into sections that normally last about half a page and invites the company together to identify what the actual events of each scene are. What are the events that change the inner world of the scenes irrevocably? How do the characters act in the wake of these events and what do they intend out of their reaction? We identify the sections, then work together to agree on these intentions.

This rigorous detailed work gives us a structure from which to build performance.

It means the actors are all imagining the same world, like they're acting in the same play. They have a shared language. They are working in real detail.

At the end of the morning session, Ian MacNeil and the costume designer, Holly Waddington, talked us through their ideas for the play.

Ian has created a kind of deranged Technicolor cabaret of contamination. A set of surprising stillness is built under the looming shadow of the Court's back wall sunk in a pool of sump oil that rises and rises as the play goes on until it touches everything.

Holly's costumes, inspired by the photographer Alex Prager, touch on the edges of the hyper real. I think there is potential for something quite extraordinary in the tension between this luminous heightening and the psychological truthfulness of the acting technique.

The tensions in this production will sit against the exposed back wall that was so central to all the thinking of Jocelyn Herbert and Andy Phillips. Every production at the Court is made better by tussling with its beautiful legacy. We step onto that stage and it's the same stage as all those ghosts – from Osborne to Bond to Churchill and beyond. Their legacy frees us more than it deadens us.

I'm put in mind of something Wouter van Ransbeek, the producer of Toneelgroep Amsterdam said, when we spoke in London last year. He travels all over the world meeting people. Whenever he's asked where the next burst of creative theatre will come from he now tells people that it will come from London. He says people in London are starting to catch up with the possibility of the astonishing in design and direction. If we can combine that with the sense of truthfulness in acting, rigour in writing and a metabolic instinct to engage an audience, then we have the capacity to create theatre that makes that produced in Germany seem old fashioned.

4th March

Second day of rehearsals on *Birdland*.

Carrie continued to work through the play looking at intentions. It's a rigorous and detailed process based largely on work around the table.

This can unite the company and give them a sense of a shared world.

It can also equip the production later in the rehearsal process because they have a road map written out for them. They are not so dependent on instincts or intuition but have something that is solid and considered.

Some actors fucking love it. Some find it alienating because it seems that they are being separated from their capacity to trust their own instincts.

I'm just not altogether sure how trustworthy actors' instincts are, finally.

I sometimes think that the actor is the last person to judge his or her own performance. I realize this might seem like I'm sceptical about an actor's intelligence. I don't think that is my concern, though. I think rather that, as Max Frisch once said, the actor is the one artist who can never see his or her own work.

This is the hardest thing about a stage actor's working life. They can NEVER see what they do.

I've seen many performances of my plays that have borne out how unstable the actor's perception of their own work is. I've seen performances of my plays when actors have been left buzzing by how successful their work has been only for me to have to bite my lip at my own disappointment. And others when actors have been frustrated by performances that I have felt to be clear and nuanced.

I suspect that this is similar to the impossibility of the writer ever properly assessing his or her own work.

The play seems to return to the same questions as I always do. How can we be optimistic in a world looking so hard into shadows of uncertainty? Once we leave home how can we ever return? How can we love in a world so atomized?

A new question is how do we know when anything is real anymore?

This seems to manifest itself in the play's relationship to its actually BEING a play. The mechanics of being an actor in a room with an audience seems more explicit in this play than in others I've written. But also in Paul's increasing uncertainty that anything he's doing is real. The impossibility of finding stability in an unstable world. Rather than making the need for stability pathetic, I think it renders the attempt to find it dignified.

Sean met me after work to tell me that he thinks, for reasons of scheduling, that Joel should dramaturg *Show 5* for the Secret Theatre Company. In a sense I'm a bit sad about this. In a sense I'm worried it's because I let him down. In a sense I think it's a relief. Either way it makes perfect sense and frees some time up for me.

Then had an interview with a journalist from Tokyo who had just seen *Wastwater* there and was here to talk to me about my work and about my status in Tokyo.

She told me I was known there. This is an idea that I find utterly odd.

She asked me if I thought theatre was important.

I told her that I don't think theatre has ever been more important. In a world dislocated and disengaged by technology, it is the one forum in which we are encouraged to sit next to people we've never met before and look in one direction and share a live experience that exercises our brains and our sense of aesthetic.

It is necessarily a mirror to ourselves. The responsibility of the artist is to decide what that mirror will show and how it will allow light to fall.

5th March

There is a rigour and determination to Carrie Cracknell's work on plotting the intentions of a play that is kind of awesome.

But what she is very good at is listening to when actors are frustrated.

Today with one of the cast she recalibrated her approach. She asked him how he was getting on with the methodology and accepted his frustrations, and of course that simple task of acknowledging the validity of his reservations took the edge off them and he totally changed his approach. He relaxed. He became playful. Creative. Alert.

She shares with Marianne Elliott a suppleness of approach. Rather than having a fixed methodology that is immovable she is able to shift and change it to release the best of her cast.

It was an exciting moment.

Went to see Peter Gill's *Versailles* at the Donmar Warehouse in the evening. It is a cripplingly over-long play, a study of the tensions sitting in Europe at the time of the signing of the Treaty of Versailles. The entire middle section is un-dramatic. It is a section in which characters do nothing but expose the historical context of the play. Their function is only to reveal history. It was deadening.

He is a great writer of silences and of women. To have an entire act of men talking was unbearable.

But God! The best bits, when he allowed the women in, when he allowed the silence in, were devastating.

To be writing with such ambition and achieving something so rare at his age is galvanizing.

I live in terror that I've already written my best plays.

I look at the narrative arc of the best of England's playwrights since the Second World War and most of them have written their best work by the time they're my age.

So Gill in that sense is in some way heroic.

6th March

There was a fascinating conversation with the *Birdland* cast today about whether they will use accents when they are playing multiple characters.

Carrie and myself tried to usher them away from doing so.

What interests me in the relationship between actor and character is not an accurate representation of how they speak or the capacity to imagine what they've lived through before the play but rather the capacity to achieve a specificity of intention.

What matters is not how accurately they can mime the characters but with what detail they can excavate and recreate the things that they *do*, psychologically, to one another.

In this sense accent is utterly irrelevant.

They were nervous about how such an approach would sit at odds with the set but for me this is the force of Carrie's idea.

To completely invest in the things these characters do to one another in a way which is compelling but in a stage which is odd.

When actors don't disguise their work on intention with accent but rather really get into the nub and detail of what they're doing to each other, it creates gaps between the audience's understanding of who the characters are and what they see. But it is in these gaps (which might manifest themselves in questions like – why aren't they speaking like they're from Dundee, where is the food he is enjoying, why are they talking about a bed when there is no bed there?) that the imaginative space is created. It is this space which, finally, allows the audience to recognize themselves. It is in this space that the play might become more than just a play about rock and roll, and become, maybe, about humanity.

Saw Vicky Jones's *The One* at Soho Theatre. Vicky has worked as a director of new plays, normally by men, over the past decade. She's just written her first play. It won the Verity Bargate Award.

It is a savage, funny, sexy, problematic, dark, elegant comedy of manners.

I loved it.

If a man wrote it I wonder if I would have despised it.

I wonder if that matters in any way at all.

7th March

Another excruciating trip to Moorfields. While I was getting anaesthetized a nurse told me off for chatting to the doctor – she said I was only doing it because I was nervous about having my eye injected and she was right. I went back to the Royal Court this afternoon for more *Birdland* rehearsals.

The difference between the intentions that Carrie has been meticulously mapping and the actions that Max Stafford Clarke works around and has written about beautifully was really clarified for me this afternoon.

An intention follows an event.

An event is a thing that happens in a scene. This can be a deliberate change in the direction of a conversation, an entrance or an exit of a character, a physical action, or an event brought about by an outside source.

The intention informs how the characters marshal their response to the event.

The action is the behavioural tactics they use to control that marshalling.

Character A shoots Character B in the head in front of Character C. That is the *event* that charges Character A and C alike with a new intention.

Character A's *intention* might be to persuade Character C to hide the gun on their behalf.

Their *action* might be to threaten them or to entreat them or to frighten them or to charm them.

There can be a thrilling tension between the intention and the action.

Often scenes are at their best when there is a real tension between these things.

In the rehearsals of *Birdland* we are enjoying noticing how often characters have strong intentions and play soft actions. If anything this carries a bigger threat or sense of menace.

This is true of Andrew Scott's character, Paul, especially.

It struck me this afternoon as well that this type of work, especially carried out to this level of thoroughness, would have been absolutely unthinkable in German theatre. Maybe that's not true. Maybe it's not interesting. There is a lazy inclination to generalize about 'German' theatre on behalf of British practitioners and critics and I've just been guilty of it.

But it is the type of work that Nübling would not in any sense be interested in.

I write this sitting in my kitchen on the Saturday morning after finishing the first week of *Birdland* rehearsals and before going to the last week of *Carmen Disruption* rehearsals.

It feels like I'm at a hinge in the middle of my work in England and my work in Germany. This capacity to switch between the two continues to provoke and stimulate me.

I learned this week that I would be commissioned to write a new play, a trilogy of short plays in fact, for the 2017 Ruhrtriennale. This is one of the biggest festivals in German theatre. At the same time I'll write a new play for Marianne Elliott to direct at the Olivier. This conversation between German and English theatre culture and aesthetics continues.

I bumped into Nick Tennant in town. I'd not seen him since he played the lead role of Ignatius Stone in *Three Kingdoms*. I was staggered to hear that his daughter is two and a half. She was born just after *Three Kingdoms* left Tallinn.

The furore surrounding *Three Kingdoms* was fairly pronounced. It's the only play to date that Sebastian has directed in England. It created a schism between mainstream critics who despised it (Michael Coveney saying that any audience member who enjoyed it would be necessarily 'depraved') and a young generation of theatre writers working predominantly online (Andrew Haydon describing it as the best play and production of the year). It is, oddly, a production that is still talked about today. It becomes like a badge of honour for people who either loved or hated it.

In the wake of it kicking up sand, a lot of things changed. A lot of young directors started to explore abstraction or juxtaposition between play and world. Joe Hill Gibbins's *Edward II* in the Olivier leaps to mind or Robert Ickes's *1984* or the work that Ellen McDougall has done. Most obviously in the work that Sean Holmes has led at the Secret Theatre Company. It strikes me that unconsciously it has been a theme I've returned to in these pages.

This is because it looms large in my thinking about theatre. But also because it is a concern of many people I work with.

Sebastian rang me during the week to tell me he was cutting the bulk of the text of the chorus – something no British director would do, I think. And that he was changing the ending. I am completely fine about this. The text was written with the intention that it could be cut and re-shaped and refined and language taken out and re-ordered and added.

There is a daring to this gesture that I find stimulating.

But I also thought, watching Carrie work with such rigour and imagination and care, and watching her company of brilliant actors galvanized by what she was doing and then drained by it, that it is easy to underestimate the great strengths of British theatre. That level of psychological insight and detail is exceptional and not to be dismissed. It will, I am certain, embed itself in their performances.

10th March

This morning was my first morning back in the office for a month. Emptied my inbox of emails and did some work on *Seventeen*, the piece which I am working on for Ramin Gray and Hofesh Shechter for ATC.

I was synthesizing some of the images that I wrote while in New York in 2013 rehearsing *Harper Regan*. Lonely erotic images drawn from the loneliness of being away from my family, with some of the theoretical thinking that has sat under *Seventeen* for the last three years. The piece is a consideration of the human consciousness of the inexorable movement of time.

I think the key for the piece is to juxtapose a sole voice with a more choric presence.

I like the idea that the sole voice being the sole voice of the sexual desire of a woman in her seventies. Keening for one last sexual experience before she dies.

I came up with the new title of *Nuclear War*. This is a fucking great title and I can't believe it's not been used before.

Had a phone call with Scott Rudin and agreed to take the commission to adapt the David Ignatius novel *The Director* for Paul Greengrass. Rudin's reputation is as somebody who can be driven, almost to a ferocious degree, and there's part of me that is daunted by stepping into his arena.

But Greengrass is a great filmmaker and I think the amount I may learn from both men will outbalance any nervousness I feel about working for somebody singular and committed.

And then I had lunch with Wouter van Ransbeek of Toneelgroep Amsterdam. We went to Blacks, a private members club on Dean Street in Soho. He likes Blacks. I've been a member there for eight years now. It was beautifully empty today. For much of the lunchtime we had the entire ground floor to ourselves. There in the heart of Soho we sat in quietness and talked.

We talked about *The Van Wyck Expressway*, the piece I will write for Ivo van Hove. The play is a monologue about a businessman returning to his home in Amsterdam after learning, in New York City, that his teenage brother has died of a sudden heart attack. The play takes place over the week between him hearing the news and flying back to New York after the funeral. It will have music written for it by Mark Eitzel.

He likes the idea of the epistolary form. This gives scope to make something that is jagged and interrupted. There is less need to iron out the form to make something cogent.

There is the possibility of building up to a date as a climax – the date of the funeral. There is more scope to introduce the songs in a way that is tangential and surprising.

We liked the idea of the music being an attempt to complete or to write a song.

We talked about the fear of death in a secular culture. When humans no longer feel their life is a contribution to something bigger than they are, then death is final and cruel.

We talked about people who commit their lives to the building of a building they will never see.

We talked about the human scale of Amsterdam in comparison to the epic scale of New York.

We talked about the need to find a home and the need to return home and the fear of that.

A home is a place where there is no desire and no regret. If somebody lives in isolation, then there is an acute power in regret and desire.

And then money becomes a chaotic force.

We talked about the cultural fear of talking about death. It is the one ultimate truth that all of us face and yet it is acutely taboo in conversation.

We walked to the British Museum and looked at the exhibition of the drawings of Georg Baselitz and his contemporaries. There was energy in all the arts in Germany in the sixties, a decade and a half after the horrors of the Holocaust and of Dresden, and the decimation and splitting of Berlin and the rest of the country. It manifests itself in the great films and rock and roll music of the day and it manifested itself in these drawings.

Baselitz was evicted from university in East Berlin for being politically immature and his work has a grotesquery and comedy that is dirty and muscular. Some of his colour work was breathtaking.

Gerhard Richter's sketches for his bigger work were astonishing. They revealed an imagination of restless force.

I was taken too by the vivid scrawls and paintings of A. R. Penck. Another Dresden-born painter. I'd never heard of him before.

I liked how so many of the works were woodcuts. These artists reclaimed this ancient German artistic tradition in a time of urgent rupture.

I love the idea that in order to make something contemporary they were returning to an ancient form.

11th March

I worked this morning on *Nuclear War*. I like the bombastic gesture of calling a play *Nuclear War* and I like how it is a title that is both completely irrelevant and also refracts the deep metabolism of the piece.

On one hand the piece is nothing whatsoever to do with nuclear war, which makes the title much more playful.

But the play is also a consideration of the consequences of human consciousness and our dread of an uncertain future and the extent to which catastrophe plays out on an atomic level.

I found a structure for the piece based on an old lady's determination to have sex one time before she dies and the failure of this attempt. The form of a day gives the piece a narrative drive. Thematically it's a more playful way into a consideration of sex and death. It allows me to explore the choric nature that Ramin encouraged me to explore as she moves around her city.

I am drawn to the idea that the New York playwright Mark Schultz talked to me about when I asked him what God was. He said that for him in some way God was a city. The force of the collected spirit of millions of strangers. I think this is something I return to in my plays.

Then I got the plane to Hamburg for the final week's rehearsal of *Carmen Disruption*.

On the flight I started reading Russell Shorto's *Amsterdam* in preparation for writing *The Van Wyck Expressway*. I listened back to the first of the interviews I made in Amsterdam a year ago, with Mark Eitzel.

The rehearsal was in poor shape.

Sebastian told me that the actors had been tremendously difficult to work with. He told me later, too, that he found there was a lack of plausibility in the original ending of the play, a naïvety in the gesture of The Singer leaving the Opera that led him to try something different.

It was unsettling to watch my play with an entirely different ending.

But more unsettling to watch underpowered performers. Actors weren't listening to one another. They weren't playing in the same space. They were indulging themselves and taking too long over entrances and exits.

It took three hours. It was stopped several times to deal with problems the actors were having.

There was no sense of cogency to the piece. The characters didn't feel as though they were from the same world. In my mind the world was the world of the subjectivity of The Singer but much of the text that clarified that had been cut.

It was more fascinating than dispiriting.

I mean finally it's a play, not a real catastrophe. Finally it's not a death or a war. It's always, in the end, defined by a kind of frivolity.

I was more sanguine than Sebastian who said he was in a kind of crisis.

The only thing to do in these situations is to work with patience and detail.

To go back to the original basics of our work. To listen to one another. To pick up the cues. To try to enjoy one another.

I momentarily speculated in my head that the flaws in the production were indicative of flaws in the theatre culture. Ensembles of this size are perhaps unsustainable. An auditorium of this size, selling 1,200 tickets a night may finally be unsustainable. The room is so large that if Sebastian wants to give an actor a note in private it takes him thirty seconds to get to them. A room this size may not, finally, lend itself to real creativity.

But there were also moments of beauty and imagination that sparkled. If the actors can play their action and also play with each other, if they can hit their entrances and pick up their cues, then it may be a way of revealing the play.

12th March

We worked on the play. Sebastian seemed more energized and worked on contracting the thing. Exactly those contractions the play needs and also on giving the characters an energy and a sense of awareness of one another on the stage.

He told me over lunch that the intendant of the Burgtheater has been sacked for leaving the theatre thirteen million Euros in debt. It felt like an emblem of the unsustainability of German theatre.

The run this evening was much better. It was shorter. It was sharper. The actors felt as though they were listening to one another and playing with each other. I was buoyed.

When they play those simple actions, the more complex structure of the play and of the production, built on the juxtaposition of images of loneliness and the random arrival of death in the form of the unifying incident of the motorcycle crash that unites all the characters, is revealed.

Sebastian's work is built upon juxtaposing image and text rather than allowing them to work together, and it is by simple pursuit of quite orthodox ideas that this juxtaposition is released.

He told me in the bar afterwards that one of the key flaws was that there is a dramaturgical weakness in the heart of the play. I never happily reconciled the characters to be in the same space at the same time in a way that didn't feel forced in.

It was wounding to hear these thoughts so late in the rehearsal.

But maybe he's right. Maybe if I am to write for theatres of this size again then I need to avoid the subliminal or the sub textual. Maybe Aristotelian action is really what works in these spaces and rather than writing in opposition to that I need to embrace it.

Maybe it goes back to my idea that the real work for playwrights to do is to engage in the Classics. It's in the Greeks that the essence of dramaturgy is found. In Euripides and Sophocles and Aeschylus.

Thinking about the German post-war visual artists returning to the woodcut reminded me of the same thing.

It is nevertheless frustrating that I may have let him down. The response from readers to *Carmen Disruption* has been largely positive. Some people have really fallen in love with the thing. What I don't know is whether or not Sebastian has failed to grapple with the metabolic dramaturgy of the piece and is blaming the piece for his failure. Or he's right and the play doesn't work on a simple

level. I suspect any failures of the piece lie somewhere between
the two.

It was an odd gear change though to leave a rehearsal that I was
inspired by and then to hear this toughness presented in quite a gentle
way from a friend and a collaborator.

It's odd, this year, with its fistful of plays. Maybe none of them will
work. Maybe in some way all of them will alienate audiences, one after
another.

13th March

Dramaturg Sybille Meier and Sebastian were both slightly mortified when
I told them I'd spent a lot of the night worrying about their comments.

They hadn't intended to destabilize my faith in the play.

There are some things though that you only learn about a play when
it's on its feet.

I think the technical limitations of Rinat as an actor exacerbated the
problems. Her work is really good but has taken time. She still finds
listening to actors' dialogue on stage unusual. As an opera singer
she's never needed to listen to another actor with quite that precision.
Normally she will be guided by a conductor and playing against an
orchestra. Nuanced listening is the most demanding element of the
stage actor's craft.

When she sings she effortlessly stills your heart.

Another morning of compressing the piece together.

It seemed to go well.

Sebastian was more alert and more precise and more driven with his
notes.

An afternoon of writing fifty emails, none of which sent in this hotel's shitty wi-fi.

I've stayed in this Reichshof for ten years now off and on. It feels very much like a hotel closing down and there's part of me that isn't all that sad that I won't stay here again but part of me that is so angry with the wi-fi I think the whole place can go fuck itself.

14th March

There is no culture of first previews in German theatre. No preview culture at all. After the opening night, which is both the first time a play has been put on sale to the public and the night the press go and watch and review the play, the artistic team often leave and go to another city.

They don't refine in the wake of audience response.

Instead there is what is known as the public dress rehearsal.

On Friday night 140 people came to see the dress rehearsal of *Carmen Disruption*.

Amongst them was Karin Beier, the theatre's intendant.

It was frustrating because it was nearly brilliant. There were moments that were quite astonishing. The choral work and the singing and some of the images.

But it was too long and flat and the actors were flat and the ending dragged.

I spent two and a half hours sitting with Sebastian and his team afterwards rethinking the ending. I wanted to cut the equivalent of about two pages. Sebastian told me, finally, that it was too late.

This was a position very different to the British system. I quite enjoy press-night cuts. I always think they're like little presents. They mean the actor has something to dwell on other than the living hell of opening night. And I was sure my cuts would have helped.

But again, in this production, the weaknesses of the ensemble system were revealed as clearly as on earlier visits to other productions, I've seen strengths. When an actor lives in no fear of their job – when actually they're not choosing to go for particular jobs but rather are just taking what is given, when they have no need to impress the director but rather the director needs to win them – then they can be aloof, uninterested, disengaged.

They don't understand that cuts might benefit the entirety of an evening and they feel bruised from having lost words to speak. I don't mean it as a personal objection so much as a structural observation.

There are advantages and disadvantages to both structures. All I know is that Sebastian confronted more obstruction in giving notes on a last performance before an opening night than I've seen given to any other director from actors in that position.

I don't blame the individuals. I think it is a structural flaw.

Finally some new ideas were stumbled upon. Some cuts were made.

Let's see.

15th March

The opening night performance was as good as I've seen it, which, finally, is all you can ask for from an opening.

It may be that the company hated one another and that the theatre is just too huge to ever do interesting work, or that this play doesn't fit a huge stage, or that the removal of the chorus ruptures the structure to render the play thinner than it is, but thankfully we pulled it off.

Some cuts were made so the play was tighter.

The ending was entirely reconceived so that there was a compelling sense of escalating tension. The Opera House at the heart of the set started moving towards the audience earlier to build that sense of imminent doom even further.

The cast were really buzzing. They punched the piece, really attacked it. The music was calibrated with more volume and aggression. Rinat really sang and placed all her notes and had a powerful sense of play.

The audience was amazingly attentive. Their applause was loud and long and when Sebastian and I came on for the press night bow that is de rigueur in Germany, there were some vehement boos which were really thrilling.

It reminded me of being in my old band, the Country Teasers, again. I played with them for ten years from the middle of the nineties. Often audiences would respond to us with a mixture of glee and fur. The audience tonight had that same sense of attack.

We had a big old party. I thanked all the actors.

Polly said she loved it. She even enjoyed the set, which was a big test and a relief.

I'm sure it could be better. It could have been tighter. There could have been more scope for more play. There could have been more juxtaposition of imagery and text. Sebastian wrote to me after to tell me he thinks he kind of failed with the play. But finally it was the best telling of the production that they'd told so that is all we can ask for.

I won't read the reviews. Because they'll be in German.

17th March

I spent the bulk of the day cleaning out my inbox after a week away.

But also listening over to some of the tapes Mark Eitzel and I made in Amsterdam. Some of the interviews. And today, particularly, his thoughts.

We want to make a play with a human scale in which somebody returns home after the death of his brother to recover his humanity. It struck me that the mistake would be to make him too vehement or too cynical. He is a human. Not an artist. Not a wild rebel. Just a normal guy.

Somebody who works in money not as an evil fucker but just because that's what he does.

And he lost his little brother.

Mark has sent me some beautiful, beautiful music.

I want to read my books and watch the Ozu and Terence Davies this week.

I want to get on with that.

18th March

I went back to the Lyric Hammersmith to see the Secret Theatre Company again.

They, with playwright Joel Horwood, are making a new devised show. I had lunch with them yesterday to try to refine its central idea. We stumbled our way towards making a show that celebrated the dignity and humanity in continually trying to change those things that are impossible to change. Trying to change the impossible is much more brilliant than giving up on discovering its impossibility.

The show will be built out of a series of improvisations. In between these improvisations there will be a series of scenes from Shakespeare's plays. Sean spent the day looking at how to act Shakespeare's language.

It was fascinating joining them for a while.

The most exciting discovery came when the actors really hit the second half of their lines.

Or when they hit the second syllable in iambic verse.

It lifted the language from the poetic to the massively active.

It created vitality and question.

I thought it was thrilling.

To watch Leo Bill, one of the actors in the company lift, Macbeth. To watch Nadia Albina lift Viola.

Shakespeare is the most democratic of writers.

Because his work is charged and electric and the body of words – that monumental amount of words carved at a time to coincide with the definition of England – takes my breath away.

I was taken by the idea that this language came out of a culture where there was no rehearsal, there was no director.

The actor simply had to respond to text – text that was often even written in performance.

If they could master the idea that leaving air, a small breath of silence at the end of a line, and hit that second half of the line then it could charge the text – if they did it with dry technique then they didn't need rehearsal.

The life comes from the technique.

19th March

A day in schools in the South East Midlands. Bilborough College where an amazing woman called Sharon MacInnes runs a further education drama department of 200 AS and A-level kids with commitment and passion and inspires them.

And then up to Chesterfield to see the Catholic school Mount St Mary's to talk to sixth formers there.

I should spend more time talking to young people. They inspire me.

I talked to them about the importance of failure and reflection upon failure. And tried to encourage them to at least think about writing.

It's easy to be judgemental about the privileges in private schools but Trent College in Derby inspired me to write *Punk Rock* four years ago.

And both places, today, were equally provocative and charged.

Drama teaching is imperative to the future of this country. It exercises our sense of humanity. It makes us better humans. To build education departments around that seems dignified. Sharon MacInnes, in this sense, exemplifies the best of England.

At Mount St Mary's I talked about why there was so much swearing in my plays. This, it seems, renders them tricky for schools, even sixth form colleges, to produce. I talked at length about how great swearing is and all the nuance and visceral force of swearing in English. Their drama teacher agreed with me. I think the head teachers didn't.

20th March

A lengthy schlep up to Belsize Park in London to see rehearsals of *Birdland*.

It's a fascinating gear change from Nübling's rehearsal room with his desperate keenness for his actors to pump up the pace and the attack and the volume.

Having figured through the intentions of each scene Carrie sits back and watches the actors play the scenes. She identifies moments which are useful and worth holding onto.

We rehearsed the scene in which Paul tells Johnny he doesn't like the new songs. Together Andrew and Alex and Nikki found a real nuance and playfulness and psychological detail in the acting.

My job was to just sit and watch. Sometimes that's the wisest thing to do. To not intervene. To let good actors find the scene. It felt refreshing to go back to a freelance structure as the actors were so charged by a keenness to work together and to build collaboration together.

Carrie has a cool poise that supports the actors and allows them to feel creative.

And then down to the Young Vic to meet Ivo van Hove to talk about the monologue I will write for him.

A single man sits at a piano and writes letters to his young teenage brother. The brother he will never see again. Letters written in the week leading up to his funeral. The piano he plays should be his brother's piano.

The epistolary form allows him to find a new energy with each page, with each day. Letters written in the seven days leading up to his funeral. Punctuating these letters is an attempt to sing a song. To find the purity of soul that will lead him towards music.

Inspired by Terence Davies and Ozu and Cocteau. A play about the search for light in the darkness of a young boy's death and the darkness of a world in which value has been replaced by cost.

22nd March

I spent the morning with Joseph Alford from London theatre company theatre O. He was the movement director on *Trial of Ubu* at the Hampstead Theatre and is working with me now for the filmmaker Daria Martin on her new film.

Daria is an art filmmaker who has embarked on a series of films about synaesthesia – the sensory, neurological confusion that results in the attribution of emotion to inanimate objects.

We are making a film about empaths. People whose mirror-touch synaesthesia is so acute that they experience the physical sensation that they watch in other people.

We met to find shape in a film that will be played on loop.

What is fascinating is practising communicating ideas only through moving image not through text.

The text needs to counterpoint or juxtapose rather than explain. This counterpoint allows an interpretative space for the viewer.

I will try and write it by the end of April.

And then back to the office to work more on the Amsterdam play.

Letters from The Faraway Land?
Songs from The Faraway Land?

The company for *The Faraway Land* was the original Dutch company exploring the East Indies. Ivo wants us to find a new title. I wonder if *Letters from The Faraway Land* might grace on Dutch history, death and America.

Maybe.

I watched Ozu's beautiful *Late Spring*. And read Richard Ford's short story *Rock Springs*.

Listening to Schubert's *Winterreise*.

I have a feeling that the play exists somewhere in the space created by the triangle of Ozu, Ford and Schubert. That sadness and specificity. Something huge in something tiny.

The Ozu film was shattering. There was a demotic level of smiling that quite broke my heart.

In the evening I went to the National Theatre's Lyttleton space to see Kate O'Flynn who was in *Port* here last year and Lesley Sharp who played the lead in *Harper Regan*, in Shelagh Delaney's *A Taste of Honey*.

I found it a beautiful play. It was strange to me that while I've never seen this play it felt like a massive influence on me. It must be that writers I have loved from Morrissey to Jim Cartwright owe so much to the play that it has filtered its way down to me.

Lesley and Kate were astonishing. Their riffing together was beautiful. It meant a lot to see actors who have given such voice to my plays working together.

23rd March

A rare Saturday instalment. I tottered down to the National Theatre to talk with Jane Horrocks and the mighty Jim Cartwright about representations of Manchester in the drama that has come after *A Taste of Honey*.

There was so much to say. Many of the mythical tropes attributed to the North apply elsewhere. From Glasgow to Tunbridge Wells people have found humour in despair or found emotional frankness difficult or built family structures around matriarchs and found influence in music. And Manchester now is a major European city. It's comparable with Munich or Lyon or Barcelona as it is with some bizarre mythical town from the sixties. The cobbled streets of Salford are probably extremely desirable residencies for people who work for the BBC. And the working class in the country is no longer defined by their capacity to find wit and compassion and community in straitened times so much as their capacity to work in Amazon factories to pay for Sky Sports subscriptions.

But two things struck me as true. The physical geography of the Northwest, carved out of the valleys where the Gulf Stream hits the Pennines, leaves a place defined by rainfall. The capacity to find optimism in the rainfall, or 'light through the pouring rain', as the photographer Kevin Cummins has it seems to be a product of this physical characteristic. We defy the rain because it rains so heavily. And the proximity of the town to nature through the rivers and the valleys gives the urban spirit of the place a constant undertow of the possibility of nature.

We looked at extracts from Jim's plays and some of mine and from *A Taste of Honey*. The recurring tropes of mothers trying to bond with their daughters as peers, trying to use food in order to do that, was striking. The absence of food in the kitchen. The tussling over attractiveness to men.

All of the scenes were on Hildegard Bechtler's naturalistic set for *A Taste of Honey*. All of them had the vapour of mimetic naturalism to them. All the plays were written kind of as an attempt to make the actors talk as people talk in life.

A woman approached me at the end – an academic – her voice shaking with feeling. She urged me to write a play about the Amazon factories. She urged me to carry out a new exploration of the new working class in the North.

24th March

I spent the morning in the office with Scott Graham and Karl Hyde. Scott is the Artistic Director of leading physical theatre company Frantic Assembly and Karl is a musician, most celebrated for his work in Underworld who has expanded into theatrical work over the past five years, especially working with Danny Boyle. He worked on his films and on *Frankenstein* and then helped curate the music for the Olympic opening ceremony.

We've been plotting for six months or so to make a show in response to fatherhood. We hope to go to our hometowns and interview five men about their experiences of being fathered and becoming fathers. We're experimenting at the moment by interviewing each other.

Trying to get the questions right.

So yesterday morning we talked to Karl for three hours.

It was maybe an hour too long. I think we need to focus our questions around being fathers as much as we are, at the moment, talking about our fathers. I also think we need to speak to a wider range of people from a wider range of backgrounds. But it was a remarkable morning.

Karl spoke with honesty and frankness about his upbringing in the borderlands between England and Wales. How he would sneak off to be on his own. How this informed his perspective on the world as an artist. The way he would see the world from the bottom of a bin. How he would return to this image in adulthood when he was drinking.

The question at the moment is how we might turn this thing into a piece of art. How we might structure the material and shape it. How we might mix text and change it.

How we might create music and physical imagery out of it.

There was a remarkable sadness and love when he spoke.

25th March

An excellent meeting with Marianne Elliott this morning and Camilla Bray of Sixteen Films and the script editor Scott Meek. Scott was brilliant on the *Waterfall* script. He was illuminating and clear and precise and it was like taking a lesson from a master.

I have no idea what will happen with the film but it felt, briefly, that simply for his clarity of thought and detail the whole thing had taught me enough to make it worthwhile.

And this afternoon Marianne and I went up to Air Studios in Belsize Park to meet Nick Cave. We talked to him about our idea for a Faust play. A play of real terror. As somebody really sells their soul to the devil and faces an eternity of agony.

And their consciousness will never end. And they will always suffer. And they will always be aware of it. And they will get so tired they can't breathe. But they won't sleep. And everybody they love will suffer too. And they will see all of it. And those people will blame them. And wherever you turn they will be there. And you will never, ever, ever die. And that will always happen. And that is a consequence of the things that they did.

Nick was charming and avuncular and searching and sceptical. But finally won round. He liked the idea of making people horrified he said. After years of making music for scores that are atmospheric he wanted to make something visceral and direct.

It couldn't have gone better.

We left trying to contain our glee.

It was an astonishing moment to be in the presence of somebody who I have revered all my life.

If it goes well I will move from revering him to respecting him. He'll stop being a hero. He'll become a collaborator.

26th March

I spent the day reading Russell Shorto's *Amsterdam: A History of the World's Most Liberal City*. A lucid, clear-thinking history of Amsterdam. Built on the premise that after the vicissitudes of physical geography and subsequent social dynamics, after the fallout of the Reformation and the development of capitalism, and through the philosophy of Spinoza and the painting of Rembrandt that all that we come to understand about what it is to be Liberal was born in one small, unrealistic city in the space of a hundred years.

I'm reading it to research the new play with Mark Eitzel.

I like the idea that the play becomes a study on the nature of liberalism from the moments that feel like its end.

So our character heads from New York, the place that perhaps marks the end of capitalism and liberalism, back to the city where it started and to see the burial of his younger brother.

He doesn't hate Amsterdam because it is naïve in its idealism. He mourns it because this was where everything that he knows now to be ending started.

So the death of his brother is mapped with a historical metaphor.

27th March

Back to the *Birdland* rehearsals.

There is a real grace in watching Carrie Cracknell work. Her approach is the antithesis of Nübling in a lot of ways. She has no interest in demonstrating her personality or amping up her charisma.

She is meticulous and clear-headed.

She watches rehearsals, makes clear, specific notes, which are informed and intelligent, and feeds them back to the actors with real clarity.

She uses the word 'draft' to talk about a run of a scene. 'That was a very clear draft', she'll say. Empowering the actors with authorial status. I like this enormously.

In theatre we all author our work together. My drafts of my scenes are infinitely less interesting than the drafts we make together because mine don't speak or move about.

I love the theatrical language Carrie has created for the show.

It's a modern cabaret of the decay of the West.

I always, though, watch one run of my plays and realize that the play is actually very, very shit and that is what happened today with *Birdland*. A poor play that is fundamentally a whine on behalf of the male, heterosexual rich white boy. Acted beautifully. Directed with imagination. But basically me wringing my hands with agony.

I know that when I see it tomorrow it will be much better.

Had dinner with Ivo van Hove. He very much likes *Songs from A Faraway Land* as a title.

28th March

A much better day of rehearsals today. Work carried out with rigour and detail.

I spent a lot of time talking to Andrew Scott about making sure that when he has a question he asks it like he wants to know the answer. This felt like it really released something in him.

We practised and practised and ran the play against the end of the day and it was much more alert and alive and much less elf pitying and better. Just better.

Ask the questions like you don't know the answers and really want to. My rehearsal room notes are peppered with this advice. My plays peppered with characters that could seem demotic or destructive until the reader realizes how many questions are being asked.

I think my plays are just kind of inquisitions.

Into something or other.

I don't start plays because I have something to say. I start plays because there is something I don't understand. I create characters whose default grammatical position is the question and build my plays around those questions and those characters and Paul is one of those.

31st March

I spent the morning on the 3rd floor of the Southbank Centre with Katie Mitchell working through the first draft of my version of *The Cherry Orchard*.

We got through Acts Two, Three and Four.

Katie's commitment to the imagined world of plays being a hermetically sealed actuality is a startling contrast to the worlds of Nübling or even Carrie's *Birdland*. With Nübling and Cracknell there is more seepage into the auditorium and the imaginary world is always acknowledged to being present in a theatre.

She also has a ferocious hunger for cogency and consistency in the back-story of the play and the relationship between characters, utterance and characters' world. She distrusts the irrational unless it is only apparently irrational and actually built on a logical, cogent world. She is keen for me to edit out the contradictory and the uncertain.

I like the rigour of her approach enormously. I like working with her hugely. Despite a reputation for austerity she is actually very, very cheeky, has a great, dirty Sid James laugh and a lovely line in gossip and postcard humour.

My main objective is to get her to chuckle. I was desperate to persuade her to cast Vic Reeves as Lopakhin but she was having none of it.

Working through my own draft it strikes me that the real work lies in removing the tripling and the adverbs and adjectives. I think I need to work towards a leaner, tougher text.

Went to the opening of the tech of *Birdland*. The costumes are remarkable. The lighting looks startling. The set quite beautiful. It could overkill the play. I trust that with Carrie at the helm it won't.

And then to Guildhall School of Music and Drama. To meet the actor/director Jo McInnes and a group of first-year students there who

are working on my play *Marine Parade*. Jo directed the
world premiere at the Brighton Festival in 2010. I wonder if, as Jo
is keen, we will restage that play in the autumn. I think there's a
tenderness to the play that I'm still fond of. I think it might bear
more scrutiny.

1ˢᵗ April

I spent the day travelling to and from the Royal Welsh College of Music
and Drama to talk to the students there.

I'd anticipated a room of about twenty people. There were about a
hundred.

I'd anticipated talking for an hour. I talked for two.

I spouted the usual guff about the fundamental nature of drama to the
human animal. Gripped by our own consciousness of what it is to be
conscious we define ourselves and others by the behaviour we
partake in. We are the cumulative sum of the things that we do. I
talked about technique and process and the dignity of failure.

It is so important, I think, to encourage young people to fail. It is only
through failure that any of us ever learn things. Young people
nowadays are raised to revere success. Success teaches us nothing.
We learn from failing and failing and failing again.

As long as we have the intelligence and clarity to reflect upon our
failure.

On the train there and back I implemented Katie's notes on *The Cherry
Orchard.*

Make the story simple.
Cut the adjectives.
Cut the adverbs.
Make the corners sharp.

2nd April

The first dress of *Birdland* at the Court.

I took Oscar and Tobias, the 15-year-old boy who is here staying with us, as an exchange student.

I am so brutally tired that all I will do for these few entries is cut and paste highlights of my emails to Carrie.

ON THE WHOLE I FEEL CONFIDENT THAT IT WILL BE GREAT
IT FELT A BIT TECHNICAL. IT FELT LIKE THE ACTORS WERE
STRUGGLING TO REMEMBER STUFF AND I'M VERY GLAD
THERE IS ANOTHER DRESS.
MUCH OF WHAT I THINK THEY NEED IS PRACTISE.

BUT NEARLY ALL THE ARTISTIC DECISIONS ARE SMART AND
EXCITING.
I LOVE THE SOUNDSCAPE.
I LOVE THE BLOCKING AND THE SHAPES YOU MAKE AND
THE COLOUR

I FOUND THAT DESPITE AN ENERGY THAT MIGHT BE READ
AS BOMBASTIC IT IS ACTUALLY A VERY TENDER
PRODUCTION
ITS A TENDER PRODUCTION DISGUISED AS A BOMBASTIC
ONE AND I LOVE LOVE LOVE THAT ABOUT IT

I AM WRITING THIS BIT IN CAPITALS BECAUSE IT IS THE MOST
IMPORTANT BIT OF THE EMAIL AND THE BITS BELOW SEEM
AUSTERE AND MIGHT MAKE YOU THINK I WAS UNHAPPY

I'M NOT

BUT I DO HAVE THOUGHTS. . . . .

The only urgent headline that I would LOVE to be implemented by the dress, let alone the first preview, is to revert to the original lines about Johnny's mum in the dad scene.

I think the re-write is wrong in every possible way.

I hate it and want to apologize for it.

Please can you ask them to go back to the original lines.

I don't think we lose Marnie at any point at all.

Please.

Others:

1) I think the first scene isn't working. I wonder if the boys are banjaxed by playing everything out. I don't know.
But they're not playing the scene to each other at all.
The reason they're not enunciating is that they're not listening.
The reason they're not listening is that the stakes are too low.
So the play doesn't START until half way through the second scene.
Which after the bombastic intro feels very odd.
I think they need to ask each other the questions like they want to know the answers. Right from: 'How's your head?' That is a proper question and Johnny needs to be concerned about Paul's head.
I think they need to play the actions in the scene more.

2) That need to play the action is acute in the first four scenes.
Their annunciation will come when their actions are landing more clearly.

3) I think in the opening scenes (while the line of chairs is still there) they need to really land and delineate the different worlds much more clearly. They need to try to not carry previous scenes into the new scenes. They need to find new energies with real confidence. They need to reimagine their physical spaces as completely as possible

4) Do they play that type of music in the Café Pushkin?

5) As a general rule any actor playing out needs to include the circle and upper circle.

Otherwise they read as being introverted. If an actor plays to the stalls they seem introverted. They have to play to the circle.

6) I think Andrew needs to avoid playing darkness or regret and just play as much enthusiasm and energy and need for connection as he can. The darkness is in the words. He doesn't need to illustrate that. And when he avoids illustrating that darkness it gets far darker.

7) David needs to carry Marnie into the room with 'Is Johnny alright, better off without her probably eh?'. That should be a huge event. Blasphemy needs to be a bigger outrage for Louis. A heartbreaker. He needs to play the actions of the last David scene much more precisely. He needs to relish nailing Paul.

8) I thought the dance before Veuve Clicquot either got really low energy or it went on too long.

9) I'm really not sure about the oil rising for the dad scene.
I don't like the actors wading in the water on the whole, if I'm really honest.
But if they are going to do it, it should be just for the cops and the David scene – not the dad scene. I reckon.
At its best that scene is beautifully acted but I was distracted all the way through it by the wading in the water.

I hope that gives an insight into my thinking.

Too fucked to add to it.

3rd April

First preview of *Birdland*. I sat transfixed in terror jumping and shaking and twitching with fear. I anticipated every word. I had to fight to not mouth them out. I had to fight not to grab the Assistant Director's arm and squeeze it.

It passed. People loved it. People stood up.

I hate previews because I don't really know when people cheer
and love something if they're just lying or not. I suspect they're just
lying.

It feels like a start. Like a moment to kick on from.

They can pick up the cues. They can fill the space.

They can attack it now.

4ᵗʰ April

Second preview of *Birdland*. Andrew fucked the life out of the third
scene that had been tampered with by a re-blocking. He pulled
himself back. Gathered himself and then gave a really strong clean,
clear show.

Afterwards he was slightly distraught.

The girls were too.

Second previews are always like this. The actors hate them and think
they're awful when actually they are normally cleaner and stronger than
those first previews, which are normally a cocktail bomb of adrenaline.

The crowds gathering outside stage door to meet Andrew are huge.
He is mobbed. Normally by teenage girls. I worry it's going to freak him
out. To spend two hours playing the disorientation of celebrity and
then come out and face that must be very strange.

Slightly more confident that the play is not awful.

Although Ola Animashawun, an Artistic Associate at the Royal Court,
and my former boss when I used to work at the Young Writers
Programme at the theatre, worries that the drive runs out of the play.

Carrie has the last four scenes waded through water and I don't quite think that works.

10th April

A ten-day break for the entirety of the opening of *Birdland*.

I'm not sure if that break is reflective of how important the production is to me or how tired I am after opening four shows in four months.

Probably a bit of both.

The final two previews play out with grace and largely success. With Cracknell at the helm calmly pushing the actors and the artistic team in the right direction.

Looking back now they've blurred into a mesh of paranoia and fear.

I am trying to think of what I've learned.

I think I watched the press night genuinely and generally gripped by a sense of how over-written the thing was.

I must remember this.

There were whole riffs of call and response that could be edited succinctly into simply a line or an utterance.

I wanted to stop and do a re-write.

But wasn't able to.

The most powerful moments were moments unspoken or that existed in the gaps between the lines.

I think on the whole the synthesis of the bombast of Carrie and Ian's vision for the production and the detail and clarity of the actors' work was a successful one.

I think all of the cast rose for the opening night and were greeted with real warmth and affection. Andrew was startling but the whole cast were in fact.

And the piece felt like an ensemble piece.

I was genuinely a twist of anxiety.

There were truckloads of kind people there who came and were lovely.

I don't know why press night makes me nervous. I've successfully avoided reading a single theatre review all year. I honestly don't care what any critic writes. I feel soiled when I enjoy their approval and contaminated when they offload their bile on me.

More though I'm sad that I don't REALLY respect them. Not really. They are necessarily reactive. I don't think I learn from any of them. So better, I think, to not read them at all. The best of them are benign but never astonishingly insightful. Maybe Andrew Haydon is. Lyn Gardner. Maybe some other bloggers.

So why be so fucking nervous?

Maybe it's because it marks the end of our work on a play.

The work has finished now.

So all the mistakes that we made can't be unmade.

And the nature of being a writer watching a play in performance is one of such acute powerlessness that it just leaves me wrecked.

Wrecked.

I think the reviews have been mixed, including an apparently savage demolition in the Telegraph from Charlie Spencer who claims to have NEVER enjoyed any of my plays despite having given me four stars for *Port*, *Country Music*, *Harper Regan*, *Herons* and *Punk Rock*. So fuck

108

him and the horse he came in on, the cunt. I say that because he claims I'm an affable chap and maybe use my writing to exorcise my demons. If I'm ruder to him maybe I'll write better.

See. I don't care what they say, clearly.

Michael Billington, from the Guardian, and the Independent's Paul Taylor and Michael Coveney, of WhatsOnStage, enjoyed themselves. As did Time Out.

So.

A range. Split right down the middle.

Also, I think, my third one-star review in the Daily Mail. I am thrilled to have got so many one-stars in the Daily Mail. Every time I get one star in the Daily Mail I really know that I am doing something roundly right.

During the day all last week I worked with Hofesh Shechter and Ramin Gray on *Nuclear War*.

They seem galvanized by my text.

Think it sits beautifully in actor Ann Firbank's mouth. I love hearing an eighty-one-year-old woman talking so explicitly about sex and death. Some of the images that the dancers and Ramin and Hofesh made in response were beautiful.

There was a new dancer to us, a Norwegian dancer living in Norway called Hilde, who was, frankly, a genius. She had a fearless imagination and a commitment to testing herself that was astonishing. For a while I could see the piece as a two-hander between Hilde and Ann.

Hofesh is starting to find performers he is happy working with.

Ramin and Hofesh keep surprising me. Pushing the piece in directions I hadn't anticipated.

Sometimes this makes me feel as though the whole thing is a fucking disaster because I have missed the point of their intentions with my text quite completely. Normally it makes me feel as though we might make something that surprises audiences too.

There is a possibility of it going on at the Royal Court. I think this would be a far, far happier place for the piece than Sadler's Wells. It would remove it from the burden of expectations that a new Hofesh Shechter at Sadler's Wells would have.

I had a bracing lunch with Alex Poots who asked me to write a piece for the Manchester International Festival next year. I am sad that I won't have time. I simply won't have time.

I liked him though. He combined the tough hew of a Scot with the patter of somebody raised in the music industry. Also he played trumpet on the Blue Nile's second album *Hats*. Anybody who played on *Hats* is doing something fine by me.

And the week finished by seeing Ivo van Hove's startling *A View from the Bridge* at the Young Vic. It was arresting, alert, visceral and simple.

He turned the whole play into a Samurai story. It was like Ozu. It was like Kurosawa. It was astonishing.

14th April

I spent the day back at my writing desk for what felt like the first time in ages. I was working from home and the kids are on Easter holiday so it was difficult to concentrate.

Over the weekend a cap came off my tooth. Although the root has been clipped so it doesn't hurt. I've spent much of writing time flicking my tongue in the gap caused by the cap's disappearance and actually on Twitter.

I did though finish a draft of my film for Daria Martin.

I say 'my' film but I don't feel much authorship over it.

Probably the same level of authorship as her DOP might. This suits me just fine.

I was trying to crystallize the thoughts we've had, and that we've had with Joseph Alford, into language.

It was an enjoyable process. Forcing myself to allow the film to be framed by narrative rather than driven by it. So that images elide and sit in counterpoint with one another. And the images sit in counterpoint with the language.

While I seem to obsess about narrative clarity in the two plays I've got in rehearsal this year, in this screenplay for Daria and *Nuclear War* I am excited by the idea of my script being starting points for the creativity of others and for them being built on counterpoint and juxtaposition as much as they are by urgent narrative drive.

Last night I went to Theatre503 near Clapham Junction. I'd been asked by this important small theatre to choose and present a play by an emerging writer that I loved. I chose Monsay Whitney's *Hand to Mouth*.

I first came across Monsay when she was in Sean Holmes's production of *Saved,* at the Lyric Hammersmith in 2011. We shared a District Line back east together after a show one night and she told me that she wanted to write a play.

I got her a place on the Young Writers group at the Lyric and she wrote *Hand to Mouth* as part of the course.

503 were looking to lend my name to give to writers who otherwise might not have had a level of prestige or attention.

I loved Monsay's play. It is carved out of the same traditions that Andrea Dunbar and Shelagh Delaney wrote in. Young working-class female writers writing in opposition to the male and middle-class orthodoxy. It is fired by an extraordinary sense of optimism. At a time when we are governed by people who define their sense of self and try to define our sense of self by encouraging us to see the worst in each other, this is a play which searches for the human in the criminal. It is angry and poetic and very, very funny.

It has lines in it that I wish I'd written. Which for me is always the test of a play I love. It has a deep commitment to the stage as a form for telling stories.

And Monsay is an extraordinary woman. She peppers tenderness with volatility. She comes from traveller stock out of Harringay. She is a single mother living in a council flat in Tottenham. She has flourishes of deep articulacy.

The play read with real force and comedy. It was far funnier than I remembered it being. She's written a beautiful new last scene.

Afterwards one of the actors approached me to thank me for supporting a play which was written with a real working-class London voice. He said nobody was putting voices like hers on stage any more.

I think he's right. Prohibitive fees are making acting training an increasingly middle-class luxury. At the same time there has been a commitment to excavating middle-class crises at the Royal Court – the theatre that sets the temperature for how new plays are produced and this commitment has become a defining paradigm. The voices of the poor are marginalized again.

I did a post-show chat with Monsay in which she talked wisely and with passion about why and how she wrote the play. She has a proclivity to be self-deprecating which she needs to shake because it will stop her from achieving the things she might achieve and writing the plays she might write. We reach the level that secretly we feel we are entitled to reach.

I really want *Hand to Mouth* to get a life.

I'll write to Vicky Featherstone about it.

It is the kind of play the Court should be doing.

It's the kind of play the Court was opened for.

15th April

I spent the bulk of my writing day removing all the adverbs from my draft of *The Cherry Orchard*. This was my main response when I re-read the script a couple of months after delivery. Adverbs are flourishes which are redundant and every sentence in the play is better off with the adverbs removed.

Went to see *The Weir* in the West End. It was fascinating. Still a beautiful play born out of real humour and genuine horror and sadness. Still the ghosts were profoundly unsettling. Josie Rourke, carved from the same directorial rock as Ian Rickson who directed the play's premier fifteen years ago, made a production which was loyal in its attempt to realize Conor McPherson's vision and so weirdly felt like a recreation of Ian's production. There is a real space for contemporary reimaginings of modern classics.

16th April

I went to the Young Vic to get interviewed by a journalist from the music website The Quietus and it was a bit like being Paul interviewed by Annalisa. It was schizophrenic. Very, very odd.

Then spent a day with Marianne Elliott and Katy Rudd on Americanism in *The Curious Incident of the Dog in the Night-Time*. Managed to find pretty strong solutions to all of the linguistic glitches the American producers raised with the exception of the police giving Christopher 'a caution'. The US equivalent would be to book him, which is not only unimaginable in the mouth of a Swindon copper but also a verb not a noun.

Spent an hour and a half talking to US students from the University of Roehampton. Many of them on the grad school writing program at Penn State. This is like a machine for television writers. They are expected to leave school and graduate into the TV drama industry. It makes my piss freeze.

Then went with Marianne to see *Faust* at the Royal Opera House. The tickets cost £215 each. The opera was conventional and tedious and unimaginative and boring.

We left at the interval and went to the pub to talk about the circumstances in which we might sell our soul.

For sex, for money, for youth, for power, for beauty.

In an irrational unthinking moment of avarice.

In circumstances in which we were encouraged to not think about the consequences.

If we were encouraged that the consequences weren't real.

If the Devil told us he didn't exist.

If the ninteenth century was the age of coal and steam, and the twentieth the age of oil, I think the twenty-first is the age of Coltan. We know completely the consequences of the Coltan trade in Congo and of the smart phone factories in China and yet the addiction of the stroke against the screen is so acute that we ignore our own culpability.

We envisaged our daughters meeting for a drink at our age. Unable to go outside for fear of ecological catastrophe and violence caused by water rioters. They would realize that we had caused that. We are in effect selling their souls for our gratification. We are living in a Faustian age.

We carry out atrocious acts without being aware we are carrying them out. So blind are we to the consequences of actions caused by simply pursuing our way of life. The banality of evil is played out on broader cultural level than we might ever have thought possible.

At the same time there is the Conor McPherson possibility of telling tales of fairies on our roads and ghosts on our stairs and paedophile zombies in our graveyards.

To synthesize both these political and psychological horrors would be a thing.

26th April

It's not out of the question that I've lost a week's worth of diary entries. This is a technological fuck-up caused by writing the diary on three different computers.

I've spent the week making notes on *Faraway Lands*, the play that I'll write for Ivo van Hove.

I always spend a time while writing each play doing research work of a sort. I identify sources I want to read or excavate or look at. Films or plays or poems or images or pieces of music that in some way are thematically connected to the play that I'm writing. And make notes on these things.

This week I've re-read Raymond Carver's last collection of poems, *A New Path to the Waterfall*. The poems don't stand up as richly as the stories. He's attempting to synthesize the two literary forms – crystallizing moments of epiphany in simple form, but they are fundamentally descriptive and the metaphors are often thin and unsurprising. Or they seem so to me now. I loved them when I was in my twenties. But the sixth part of the book – those poems looking at his response to the news of his mortal illness – are powerful. His need to say farewell to Tess Gallagher, the poet he lived with for the last eleven years of his life and who he married in his last months and travelled Europe with. The images of watching her through windows. The images of boats coming to take him away. His sense of fear and his sense of love. That remains powerful.

His last poem was read at my dad's funeral.

I've also been looking at the films of Ozu. The trilogy of films *Late Spring*, *Early Summer* and *Tokyo Story*. This had the opposite effect. I watched *Tokyo Story* in my twenties and found it dull and was bewildered that it was seen as such a masterpiece.

But my God I understood these films this week. The stillness of his camera. The way he filmed actors giving dialogue directly to the camera. His portrayal of families. Their complicatedness. The capacity of cruelty in children. The capacity of sadness in the elderly as they watch their children growing up, knowing that they will experience regret and disappointment. The constant, unspoken presence of the end of the Second World War, of Hiroshima, of the prison camps.

It felt like a provocation watching these films. They made me want to write simpler stories. They made me want to shy away from structural bombast and write something clear and touching. To write more plays like *On the Shore of the Wide World*. To write simpler, more truthful stories.

I saw two plays this week. Marius von Mayenburg's *Eldorado* – a shattering play about how an imminent apocalypse encroaches on the lives of the bourgeoisie in an unnamed Western city. Written with wit and formal and linguistic bravery and scarred through with arresting images it inspired me in entirely the opposite way to Ozu. It makes me want to be more ferocious and want to be bolder and more daring.

I went to see it because Amanda Hale, who was in both *Pornography* and *Wastwater*, was in it. She's a beautiful, brilliant actress who combines intellect and instinct in poised tension.

I like the contradiction that existed in the gap between my response to Ozu and Mayenburg. I like not knowing what I want to do next.

I want *Faraway Lands* to be as simple as I can but aware of the imminence of catastrophe. A simple, clear story about death and grief. About two cities that came out of the water. About the end of liberalism and the end of capitalism.

Then last night I went to see Scott Graham's production of Bryony Lavery's *The Believers*. Scott's production was beautiful and the work he did with the designer Jon Bausor made it my favourite Frantic Assembly show. It was the most theatrically daring. It was the most artistically ambitious.

Did re-writes on *The Cherry Orchard*. Always cutting adverbs. Always clarifying the story. Always clarifying the back-story. Always making the language more direct.

Did re-writes on *Empathy Heartbreak* – the film I'm writing for Daria Martin. It is the most descriptive screenplay that I've written. She liked the images I'd created.

Wrote my speech about Chris Thorpe for the Stückemarkt at the Theatertreffen. I wrote about the importance of avoiding being established. I need younger writers, other writers, to stimulate and challenge and provoke me into not settling, into not being an establishment. In art the established is effectively the inert. Once you're an establishment you've stopped.

Met with film director Clio Barnard. We talked about making *Port* in 2016 for 300,000 quid. To make it as quickly and with as much guerilla spirit as we can. To encourage her to work outside her comfort zone.

Met with the performance artist Emma Smith who wanted me to get her contacts in the fringes of orthodox theatre in order to look at the relationship between rehearsal and performance. She talked fascinatingly about how particle physicists and ancient cultures and French philosophers alike are moving towards shared conclusions – we share matter, we are more unified than we are separated. We are more absence than we are distinct presence.

She also said something remarkable that I think will inform *Faraway Lands*. Apparently archaeological exploration of the changes in the voice boxes in early humans suggests that the human voice box was built originally to sing rather than to talk.

In our earliest culture we communicated by singing to one another before we spoke to one another.

We understand song in a more primal way than we can understand language.

The more I work in theatre shaping language the more I realize that the words are the least important part of any theatrical experience.

Met with the young director George Want. I encouraged him to dismiss the idea he has been taught at Birkbeck that the playwright in theatre is the primary artist. There is no such thing as a primary artist. Of course there isn't. Theatre is a collaboration. While I think that British theatre is built on the idea that where there is nothing the playwright makes something. But my experience of writing is more of a crystallization of ideas found in other forms, carved out of a culture rather imagined out of an ether.

If I find the other instalments I'll insert them anyway.

28th April

I watched Terence Davies's first trilogy of films this morning as a means into *Faraway Lands.*

They astonish me. With their remarkable sense of stillness and the grip of death.

They're not films about homosexuality. They're films about love and loneliness and death.

The image of the framed flower – contained on a windowsill – recurs.

Beauty framed and contained by humans.

Seems like a political image somehow.

His economic fascination is born out of that. He is fascinated by how poverty contains and restrains the beautiful potential of the human animal.

But the cantata of memory through the film, the way sound and image overlap to evoke what it is to remember, is simply astonishing.

I think the British underestimate their capacity for bravery and determination and poetry in their film history. He is a really, really great filmmaker.

I think *Faraway Lands* can be bold with the playing of time.
I think it can be bold with differing perspectives. Different characters have different perspectives on memory and things. Bolder than I've been.

Told through the lens of the character of Willem.

And then I went to the Lyric Hammersmith to watch a run of *Show 5*.

It was frustrating because the cacophony of the show prevented me from getting access to it.

The actors need to hold their nerve more. They need to realize that what they are doing has value. When they don't, then they come out of the scene. They giggle. They giggle in a way that if they did in a naturalistic play, then the writer and director would be furious.

They lack faith in the seriousness of their work and they shouldn't because when they do it feels like an 'in' joke.

Sean Holmes read Tim Etchells, the Artistic Director of Forced Entertainment and a huge influence on Sebastian Nübling, talking about risk and investment in performance. He suggested that actors need to invest in the seriousness of what they are doing and so allow themselves to risk their safety properly. In that way audiences will risk investment in the performance.

When the Secret Theatre actors giggle they pull away from all risk.

Also read John Berger's *and our faces, my heart, brief as photos*.

A gentle and profound exploration of death and how we live with it.

Suggesting that we can live in a time separate to the time of our body – the time of our consciousness. That the human being is unique in inhabiting these two time frames and this capacity is what defines humanity.

It is a beautiful and inspiring book.

29th April

A day with Terence Davies. *Distant Voices, Still Lives* and *The Long Day Closes*.

Distant Voices is a shattering film but I prefer *The Terence Davies Trilogy.*

The Trilogy stopped my heart with its depiction of death as whiteness. With its depiction of love and violence.

Distant Voices has those things too but it is in some way softer.

The music used to celebrate the lives and the human capacity to live in the face of everything, especially in the second half of the film feels sentimental to my taste at times.

Although the war is real enough. And the rage of the father.

He films people crying better than others I know.

I always say the only people who cry in a theatre should be the audience. But maybe I'm wrong about that. Maybe crying is dramatically useful not to make an audience sad but to pique their fascination and their sense of the oddness of being a human.

When I watch people cry in Terence Davies's films I don't feel sorry for them. I wonder at how odd the human animal is, framed in the light, singing bravely on its way to death. Contained like flowers in a vase.

The Long Day Closes has less savagery. It is more elegiac. It is built around love for the central protagonist, Bud.

I think Bud does carry a loneliness.

Sitting as he does between the institutions of family, school and the possibility of cinema.

I thought how the juxtaposition of image and sound including dialogue is key to what distinguishes cinema from theatre. We see and hear at different speeds.

I loved that about his films.

It captures memory with accuracy and the synchronicity of experiences.

I need to find the drive of Willem in *Faraway Lands*. I need to figure out what he wants. What stops him from getting it? What he does to get it. And what he needs rather than wants.

That will release everything.

30th April

Met with Mike Knowles at Blacks this morning. He's a friend from primary school now working in television drama. He wants me to write something for him. It would be nice to work with him and with Andrew Lincoln and Stephen Mangan, two great actors who are working in the company with him. But I told him I was busy with work until the end of 2016 and that is oddly true.

And I don't know if I want to go back into the shitty cesspool of television with its flattery and promises.

And then spent a few hours with producer Camilla Bray and Marianne Elliott talking about *Waterfall*. We went for a meeting at the British Film Institute, the funding body most likely to give us money to make the film. The women we met there were the first women over forty who have read it who haven't been working on it.

They were extraordinarily keen. One of them cried with enthusiasm. They seemed determined to have the film made. I'd never had a meeting like it. Not one where the enthusiasm was so palpable.

We talked for a while about how to capture euphoria in the film. Marianne said that there needs to be a moment that astonishes us and takes us completely by surprise.

I think there is a truth in that. But it can't be a random surprise. When surprise is not intrinsically born out of the controlling ideas of the story, then, rather than seeming exciting, it seems illogical.

They key is to identify the controlling idea of the film and allow that to be crystallized in the desires of the protagonist and their objectives. They need to get what they really want. They need to get what they need. They need to realize they are getting it. We need to realize it too.

I think the controlling idea in *Waterfall* is a celebration of the fact that even the English have the capacity to transgress and be true to themselves in even the most conservative of times.

To nearly lose it and then get it. At the moment Emily doesn't nearly lose what she most needs, which is Christopher and a route out of the island. And so when she gets it the stakes seem lower. She needs to nearly give up on it and then not.

I think.

Good to spend a day with them both.

The extent to which this appears to be a thing that may actually be happening is, I confess, rather surprising to me. That definitely now means it won't get made.

2nd May

Worked on collating notes for *Waterfall* and then had lunch with Anna Brewer from Methuen Drama in a lovely restaurant in an area of

London, north of King's Cross that has been only recently redeveloped. It's extraordinary. Like a fold of the city has been opened up. A spacious open square north of the train station that doesn't feel contrived but in some way seems to have grown organically from the railway station and the canal system.

Then I went to see two plays.

To the Royal Court to watch *Pests* with Clio Barnard. Vivienne Franzman's play was a beautiful, harrowing two-hander about heroin addiction. It was startlingly perceptive about the poisonous nature of addiction. Written with real feeling and insight and the most imaginative use of language I can remember seeing in a play since *Disco Pigs*. Sinead Matthews was quite, quite brilliant in it as well. It was just an amazing bit of work.

I love the Theatre Upstairs. I've not been there often enough.

It's such an intimate, supple space. It allows real intimacy.

Also it struck me that what is startling about the history of the Court is the history of acting there. As much as the history of writing the history of great acting performance there is impressive and Sinead Matthews in *Pests* adds to that history.

It also struck me that it was the first play that I've ever seen that had an honest description of a first period. How odd that such an innate and biological experience for fifty percent of the world population is never written about.

And then up to Watford to see James Grieve's production for Paines Plough of Mike Bartlett's *An Intervention.* This is a remarkable play too. Another two-hander about addiction that draws a beautiful line betwen military intervention and personal intervention. It interrogates the humanity or prurience of sticking your nose into other people's business. It is written to be played by two actors of any age and gender, and is light and funny and intelligent at the same time.

It was thrilling to see a play of such intelligence and formal inventiveness staged at the Watford Palace Theatre. And to see an audience react to it openly and with enthusiasm. This is exactly what Paines Plough is for and why it is so important.

I did find myself thinking about the commercial potential of the play which is unlike me and odd but it is true. As the economic climate changes and shifts and money is taken out of the arts, then the opportunity of having a play that might make the company a bit of money would be reckless to ignore.

3rd May

A day spent reading the notes that I'd made on John Berger and Russell Shorto. Gripped by a sense that I've not done enough work. That there's too much uncertainty around the world of the play.

The challenge of synthesizing it into action and character in situation.

This is always the agony with a play. To move the thing from a series of hunches or impressions or thoughts or feelings towards a concrete sense of character in action over time.

I need to hold my nerve. I need to apply the old rules. What does a character want? What stops them from getting what they want and what do they do to overcome those obstacles to get it?

To make the impressionistic external. To give it dramatic shape and open it up for interpretation.

Reading the Berger reassures me that there is something about characters' existence in space and time that is primal and fundamental.

Questions of naturalism or realism or abstraction are just shadings edging towards the same question of what it is to be human.

I always get afraid of this bit. It is always during this bit that the play is made.

6th May

I spent the bulk of the morning with Daria Martin and Joseph Alford refining the film which now has the title *In the World of Interiors*.

We read the script.

I think it reads okay.

Occasionally the screen directions verge on description of inner state rather than externalizing inner state through action or visual description.

Hearing Joseph read them out loud made me realize how flawed this is.

I'd never clocked that with screen directions before.

Daria has a fascination with precision of language. The work is to get the language absolutely accurate. This is unusual for me. I write in an attempt to capture an energy and sometimes this can result in chaotic chronology or inchoate grammar.

It was like working on a translation or a version but on my own script.

It may be the end of my work on the piece now.

7th May

I went up to Westminster College to meet sixth form students working on *Motortown*. They were bright and sparky and alive and surprised me.

Their questions were blunt and very astute. About why I wrote and what frustration was like and what failure was like and who was the most famous person on my phone.

They asked me about my new play and in answering it I realized that it's not good enough.

The story needs to be crystallized in a sentence that makes the audience want to hear.

So there's this guy. . . .

His brother dies.
He goes back home.
He goes to find the love of his life.
He left him because their love wasn't perfect.
He tells him he should never have left him.
Love, like democracy or a human life, is never perfect.
They don't reconcile.
He stays with his sister for one night.
He goes back home.

I spent the afternoon re-reading the notes.

Tomorrow I will organize the notes into sub-headings: characters, locations, observations and then, most crucially, events – in an attempt to give the thing a shape.

8th May

The process of *Faraway Lands* is continuing in much the same way as a lot of my plays have been made.

First there was a period of mulling, which in this case goes back as long ago as the trip I took with Mark Eitzel to Amsterdam last winter. During this time I did very little work. But allowed ideas about death and grief and love and Europe and cities and liberalism to settle somewhere in my head. Not worrying about noting down ideas so much as allowing the accidents of memory and intuition to edit them for me.

Then there is normally a period of some kind of more active research. I watched the Ozu and the Terence Davies and read the Berger and the Shorto searching for some kind of clues as to the shape that I might make.

And now I am re-reading over those notes and trying to allow them to crystallize into some kind of dramatic shape.

Some kind of form.

So yesterday I went through the notes and searched for the events that I was drawn to. And the characters. Rather than themes or thoughts or impressions, it felt important to me to think in more concrete terms.

Theatre is abstraction made concrete. In whatever form that takes. It is an attempt to give thoughts or feelings or impressions a concrete shape over time.

In my past the best way I have found of crystallizing those thoughts in that concrete way is through character in situation in progression, i.e.narrative.

That is the work I'm doing now on *Faraway Lands*.

Went to Brighton in the afternoon to see Dmitry Krymov's *Opus No. 7* at the Brighton Festival. It had moments of arresting beauty. Some images were startling. But it was fundamentally illustrative. There were two pieces juxtaposed together. One a history of Jewish culture filtered through the ghost of the Holocaust, called *Genealogy*. It culminates with the birth of Jesus. A second called *Shostakovich* was a study of the compromises Shostakovich was forced to make under Stalin.

Some of the images, a wailing wall blown into our faces, a ballet of pianos that looked like a tank battle, were arresting and extraordinary. But there was little space for interpretation or contradiction. What else can be said about the Holocaust other than that it was a catastrophe? What else can be said about Stalin other than he was brutal?

There are other things to say but I don't think Krymov said them.

It was good though to see Hofesh and Ramin. We talked about *Nuclear War*. I suggested to them that what should happen now is that the pair of them should work on making responses to my text. I think I need to step back from it and allow them the freedom to respond in a way that is creative and surprising and then come back and see their responses.

I find it too hard to respond in abstraction to something that I have already suggested in language.

They need to respond in that way and I need to respond to their responses.

It was good to see them.

I feel buoyed that this might work.

And also that if I can offer anything to the work it is to ensure that there are always the gaps and the doubts and the contradictions that Krymov's work lacked.

It strikes me that in making this piece, like in making all pieces, the key is to find a space for the audience to explore. A wound for them to stick their finger into.

14th May

Shattered on return from Berlin.

A few days missed from having been at the Stückemarkt in this year's Theatertreffen as a juror. I chose Chris Thorpe to represent me as a theatre writer I admire.

It was a surprisingly calm few days in terms of partying but good to see good friends.

The work was fascinating. Chris's production went well although its linguistic density and the stasis of the aesthetic alienated some people. I did a really smart Q&A with him. My only regret being that he was effortlessly, immeasurably cooler and smarter than I was.

In fact he was inspiring. His description of the importance of writers in a culture was ferocious and eloquent. We need writers, storyteller, to help us through the mess of our lives. Now more than ever they have more importance than most jobs. He perceived his job as being fundamental to our culture. As long as we've lived in cultures we've had storytellers. They help us understand our sense of who we are.

But the context of the Stückemarkt was interesting. This year they invited a devising company and director and a playwright in place of what has, in the past, been seven playwrights. I was accosted by Tobias Weis at the Schaubühne for giving my name to the active dismantling of one of the key playwriting institutions.

It felt like the kind of conversations we were having in Britain seven years ago.

Surely the notion of what a playwright is is changeable. It shifts and mutates. It is inspired by other forms and inspires other forms. This doesn't mean it will disappear or that our work is over. But we need to remain alert to our responsibilities to not turn our art into a routine.

It was inspiring too to meet the Belgian artist Miet Warlop and talk to her about her work. She was chosen to bring her work *Mystery Magnet* by Katie Mitchell.

She makes explosive expansive explorations of colour and form. *Mystery Magnet* seemed to me to be a carnival-esque study of sexuality and terror. All without language. It was thrilling to watch. Thrilling to watch theatre, a form I know in some ways, being used with such an energy of exploration.

She called herself an artist. She makes living art. Art in a theatre space.

It struck me that the shiftable mutable nature of nouns in context was illustrated by this week.

Such shifts are part of what makes language alive.

Theatres should engage in them not be afraid of them.

Saw Ostermeier's *The Little Foxes*. It was surprising. Beautifully directed, it exuded class and poise but also wealth and conservatism. I hadn't anticipated thinking of Ostermeier as a conservative.

Apparently in Germany this is how he's received. I knew that but thought it more indicative of the taste of German theatres. Not actually a truth about his work.

Carmen Disruption will close at the end of this season. It is a failure in the terms established by the theatre and the first word reached me that people in Germany are starting to think that my relationship with Nübling is tired.

16th May

I finished a pass on the first draft of *Faraway Lands*. I've enjoyed this week's writing hugely. It has meant that I've been absent from this diary too much.

Every moment that I've been able to grab I've wanted to work on the piece.

The way I've written this play is typical of a lot of my plays. A protracted period of mulling where it sits in the back of my head is followed by an intensive period of research. With this play I watched the Ozu movies and the Davies movies and read Berger and Shorto. Made notes on all those things.

I write up the notes. Bringing them all together in a forty page document.

I decide upon a structure. In this case seven letters over the course of seven days. I work through the notes and allocate relevant parts of the notes to relevant scenes (or in this case letters) from the play.

I write up the scenes.

With *Faraway Lands* this was really fun. I found myself discovering things about Willem. I found myself inventing things. It felt a playful write. It felt inventive.

I sent it to Mark.

I re-read it on Sunday. It needs a lot of work.

It is about twice as long as it should be. I need to really decide on what the main controlling idea is and focus everything around that idea. Cutting anything extraneous. Or sharpening it so that it is relevant.

At the moment it lacks a moment of epiphany. I need to decide on what Willem learns. The final scene with Isaac, his ex-boyfriend who he contacts and who has no interest in him at all, this needs to land with more force. He needs to learn something astonishing there. Or in the scene with his sister.

And maybe the two scenes need to feed into one another.

I wonder if it is in some way related to Willem's instinct to walk away when things don't work. I think this is the metaphor I need to thread through it. Politically it resonates and can be pinged out. And this is how he lost Isaac and what his sister asks of him. He should go back to his folks. His confrontation with Isaac leads him to know that. He can't though. He just can't.

Saw van Hove's *A View from the Bridge* with Oscar again on Saturday. And took my sister-in-law Emma and her husband Pete to *Birdland* on Saturday night. I think *Birdland* stands up as a production fairly well next to *Bridge*. *Bridge* is astonishing. A shattering piece of direction.

It is truthful and imaginative and bold but massively, massively humane at one and the same time.

The cast in *Birdland* were really rocking. Andrew in particular was amazing. He was alert and listening and alive. There was a fire in them and they were really playing with each other. It felt joyful. Properly joyful.

19th May

Went to Clapham to meet the new cast of *The Curious Incident of the Dog in the Night-Time*. I talked too much and don't think I said anything useful. If I tried to reiterate anything to them it's that the play only ever worked because it was born out of love and a sense of play and trust and that is the only way in which the play can work. The more successful the play becomes as it returns to the West End and tours nationally and then it opens in Broadway the more likely it is that we will lose that sense of play and the more urgent it is that we don't.

I enjoyed a question that one of the cast had about doubling. They asked how deliberate was the decision to employ doubling on my part.

I think it's fundamental.

This is one of those plays that for a lot of people it is the first time they've ever been in a theatre. The definite employment of doubling means that it acknowledges the imagined and the make-believe. In a culture where drama has become defined as being innately televisual, so that we see imaginary worlds meticulously created, it seems fundamental that an element of *The Curious Incident of the Dog in the Night-Time* is the celebration of the imaginary.

Lunch with the writer Eve Leigh. She gave me good notes on *Faraway Lands*.

And then I did a redraft.

I cut 3,000 words. All those things I was talking about I tried to address.

Tomorrow the actor Nick Sidi will read it to me. Nick is Marianne Elliott's husband. He has been in more of my plays than any other actor I think. I trust him completely.

There will be more work to do.

20th May

I saw Mike Bartlett's *King Charles III*. It is a bracing idea. To go toe-to-toe with Shakespeare in form and content. Imagining England in a future as the kingdom is put under peril and a man loses his sense of self. Written in verse.

It has been rapturously received as the best new play in a generation. This is brilliant news for Mike who is a fine writer and a great man.

I saw the play too late in the run. It didn't astonish me enough. I was too familiar with the concept for it to surprise me. I was expecting too much and in the end I didn't learn enough about myself in experiencing the play. I think this is what I go to the theatre for. Not to learn about other worlds but to learn about myself.

In the tiny, rather comfortable quiet room in the offices of the Young Vic I sat with Nick Sidi and he read me *Faraway Lands*.

There were bits that read really beautifully and that I was happy with.

Other bits lacked a real punch. I think I need to build it more around the rejection by Isaac. What did Willem invest in him? How did his rejection destroy him?

Also it was far too long.

21st May

I am writing these entries some time after the fact. I threw myself into re-working *Faraway Lands*. I changed the name to *Song from Far Away*. I like this name. It is Ivo's preferred name. But it also makes me think that we're writing a series of songs from the extraordinary Caryl Churchill play. As though we've turned this shard of dystopia into a song cycle and written the songs for it. I like that idea hugely.

Last night Polly was rifling through a box of old letters in the office that we share. She found a letter that was sent to me in May 1993, twenty-two years ago, by my agent Mel Kenyon. I'd sent her a copy of the first play I wrote after leaving university, a play called *Jerusalem's Love*. This remains one of my only plays never to be produced in any form. It wasn't produced when I was a student or by an amateur theatre company. The letter Mel wrote was encouraging and nuanced. She writes that real care about how she found the writing in the play 'strong and atmospheric'. She points out that the play lacked a dramatic drive. It did. She explains that it is for this reason that she can't take on the play or place it. She encourages me to send her the next play.

It was astonishing finding the letter again. I remember receiving the letter for the first time. Her care and encouragement galvanized me. Five years later I sent her *Bluebird* and she did take me on her list. Since then she has been a constant source of encouragement, dramaturgical rigour, legal representation and tenacious advocacy. She works with the same passion for all of her clients.

When I was starting off, after I left university, I was skint and working in a café and writing in as much spare time as I could. My parents were worried that I was wasting my life. They told me as much. They told me I was kidding myself if I thought I was going to make it as a writer.

I needed determination to keep going. Mel's letter gave me that determination. It took five years of trying to get from *Jerusalem's Love* to *Bluebird*.

There were two other champions in those days. Ella Wildridge, the dramaturg at the Traverse Theatre met me for a coffee. And Jack Bradley who later went on to be the Literary Manager of the National Theatre but was then the Literary Manager of the Soho Theatre Company read *Jeruslaem's Love* and enjoyed it. He invited me to London to workshop the play. I couldn't afford the train fare.

Their encouragement galvanized me. I realized that the day after I quit would have been the day that I would have made it if only I hadn't decided to quit. Having realized that I couldn't quit, clearly.

I photographed the letter and tweeted it. It was re-tweeted 250 times within five minutes.

I had breakfast with photographer Kevin Cummins, his publisher Kevin Conroy and film producer Todd Eckert. We have been kicking around an idea of me writing a film for Kevin Cummins to direct about The Smiths.

I crystallized my ideas into a document for them. The nature of writing these ideas and formulating them in documents and then sending them into the ether, which may only result in a meeting somewhere, is odd and bewildering.

It was a good meeting though. Let's see what happens. Possibly very little.

22nd May

Mark Eitzel is over in the UK. I met him this morning and with him re-worked the material from *Song from Far Away*. Tightened it all over the loss of Isaac. Built it all around the irony of Willem being a character that could never articulate his feelings. And who alienated people around him because he could never articulate his feelings. Writing a series of letters to his dead brother and songs articulating the experience of alienating everybody because he couldn't articulate his feelings.

We read through the text together. And discussed moments when he may write music.

It was a really joyful morning.

It was really special. One of the great mornings of my career.

Just to riff and batter ideas around with a songwriter I revere and have revered all my adult life. I remember playing my childhood friend Róisín Murphy one of Mark's albums with American Music Club. We were seventeen. She's gone on to be a singer of real success. She told me that if I ever made a record it would sound like Mark Eitzel. And now I'm working with him.

It's funny how present songwriters are becoming in my working life. Morrissey and Marr and Mark Eitzel and Nick Cave. The artists who most defined my sense of self, those artists whose writing made me feel less afraid, have come back into focus.

2nd June

I've been to the Isle of Man for half-term holiday with the family. It was invaluable going there while working on *Waterfall*. *Waterfall* is set on the island. I was inspired to write about the place after years of holidaying there with my family. It was startling to be reminded of the smallness of the place. The weirdness of that isolation. The physical geography being both beautiful and alienating at one and the same time.

How hard it would be to keep a secret here! I re-read the script three times while I was there.

We went to Channel 4 to talk about it today. The building has been the building in which more of my creativity has been rejected and dismissed than any other building over the last decade (other than perhaps White City). It makes me shrink into myself. It makes me feel smaller.

But the meeting went well.

They asked me why I thought it was cinematic. It made me think about the difference between cinema and theatre and television as a dramatic form. Cinema demands a story that we give ourselves to completely. It demands that we leave our worlds behind us. We can't watch the cinema while putting the kids to bed or making a cup of tea for our partners. We need to go into a building and abandon our world into darkness.

We need to make stories that invite that. Worlds that are huge enough. Psychologies that are compelling enough. Pictures that are astonishing enough. It is distinguished from theatre because it demands an absolute abandonment of the real world. The reality of a human form in a room, regardless of how remarkable or unreal the behaviour of that human is always renders theatre an engagement with an event rather than an abandonment into a fantasy. Those people are actually in the room. We don't cut away and refocus and refract. We are there with them. In the real room with them. Cinema is different in its fantasy.

While I was away *Birdland* finished.

I saw the last two shows. I found them beautiful. The acting was astonishing. The stage design excited me, although it alienated others. As an attempt to dramatize the existential hell of a sub-prime world of dislocated sense of self it made sense to me.

When we build our sense of selves around money, then all we are left with is a hollow self-reflective world and *Birdland* felt to me to be about that.

It made me feel I might finally understand those last two scenes. Those last two scenes I think I wrote without really understanding them.

How do we make sense of death when we only believe the individual to be the central concern of our sense of self?

If there is no such thing as society, then how the fuck do we deal with what it is to die?

3rd June

I spent the day refining *Song from Far Away* and doing my final touches to *The Cherry Orchard* and emptying my inbox.

Working through Katie's final notes, what is clear is for this most exquisitely pictorial of directors an absolute clarity and believability of story and world is imperative. We're almost there. Cut all the guff. Make the corners clean. Make the actions clear. Make the worlds cogent.

Then to the Almeida to meet the suntanned and sunglassed Rupert Goold and his dramaturg Jenny Worton and the songwriter Tom Gray. We talked about trying to find a way into making a musical adaptation of the biopic film about John Lennon, *Nowhere Boy*. I wrote a draft about two years ago and now Rupert has taken over as Artistic Director at the Almeida he is keen to try to find a way to stage the play. I think it may be impossible to really capture a central unifying commanding idea shared between four authors. The question I need to ask is whether I want to be the man who puts the shelves up or really drive the idea.

In my first draft, a couple of years ago, I wrote a series of scenes in which we start with Mark Chapman assassinating Lennon and then follow the stages of his death like the stages of the cross and interweave those scenes with the scenes from the play. I think it still works as a gesture. I think I am so drawn to the idea that we parallel Lennon's birth with his death that I'll find it difficult to move away from that.

Partly because it's playful and funny and theatrical but also because the question of how we live with what we will be, and then how we live with death, seems to obsess me.

This duality of birth and death is so central to all my thinking about drama that to move away from it will mean either that I leave the project or that I am employed as the carpenter.

I think I'd be happy to be the carpenter on the thing.

4ᵗʰ June

I met with the actor Nick Sidi again and he read the latest draft of *Song from Far Away*.

It was much better. Tighter. Sadder. Having Willem as a character who finds articulating feeling impossible works beautifully. The arc of the story is clearer. The political metaphor is clearer. This is a play about somebody's dead brother whispering into his ear that there is something wrong with his heart.

It all hung together with more force and clarity.

I sent it off.

The euphoria of the moment when a play on some level articulates that which you hope it will articulate never stops exciting me.

It feels like a weird alchemy. It feels in some way magical.

And the odd thing about writing for theatre is that it is impossible to quantify or properly describe. How to know when what you're doing works or when it's just shit? That is impossible. It is tantalizing. I kind of love it.

It also leaves me with a vertiginous sense of uncertainty having sent the thing to Ivo and Wouter. I will live in dread for hours now. The dread of uncertainty and the possibility that they will hate what I've written. It is impossible to know. That's what makes it joyful. And that's what makes it alive. And also what makes it fucking horrible.

I will live in paranoid terror until they respond to what I've written. And then for some time after that.

The play exists in the gap between the writer and the reader. That gap is impossible to quantify or describe or anticipate.

So much of the best work on the redraft has been on cutting. Carving the thing away. To give it space to breathe. There may be more to cut in time. The challenge, too, will be in finding how the music sings.

I watched the last night of *Birdland* thinking that I'll never write anything as good as that again. This is a feeling I often get when a play closes. But *Song from Far Away* works. It is a smaller, slighter form of a play and it is more ruminative or sadder but I think it has something.

I had lunch with my friends Jon and NoraLee Sedmak on Monday. Jon and NoraLee are commited and significant theatre donors. They are fascinating people and over the past five years we have become good friends.

I told NoraLee that I suspect what I need to do next is write more slowly. Maybe take more time. Maybe write with a greater sense of uncertainty about what I'm writing. To start a play and not know where it's going or what it is.

It strikes me just now this second that I need to do two things. I need to write a major role for a male actor at the National Theatre and a major role for a female actor for the Royal Court. This will be an inversion of the relationship between the gender of my protagonists and the two major theatres in London. I've written major women roles for the National/Royal Exchange and major male roles for the Court. It might be fun to switch those things around.

5th June

I met with Matt Wilde, a theatre director who has started making films and very much wants to make a film of *One Minute*. He was passionate and sincere and I told him that he had my blessing but frankly the film and television world is rendered perilous by the amount of money involved.

It is difficult to the point of impossibility to really make work that comes out of formal adventure.

I met an academic who is writing about *Birdland*. The conversation made me realize just how extraordinary Andrew Scott is. Some of the gear changes he took, some of the decisions he made were simply astonishing. I rang him to tell him. I got his voicemail. Left a message.

Lunch with playwright Chris Thorpe talking about his new play. He described his work as being purely linguistic. The decisions he makes are linguistic ones. He builds his rhythm and shape from linguistic connections.

He has a compelling, elastic, instinctive mind that makes me want to think harder to keep up with him. His new work has the potential to be great. Certainly the line-writing is shattering.

Chris gave me notes on the play whose title we have decided should be *Song from Far Away*. He was keen I find space to let Mark's music in and I think he is right about that.

He noticed one speech when he thought I'd found out something good from the internet – the description of what happens to a body after it dies. He could feel me doing my online research. It brought him out of the piece. He said it's the kind of thing he does all the time. He is of course absolutely right.

Maybe when writers did their research in the British Library there was an innately greater sense of something organic.

And then I came back to the office. All I wrote today was a speech for Voirrey, my mother-in-law, who is leaving her family home after twenty-five years.

I tried to capture how much that house meant to me. It is a place I often think of when I think of Polly.

It struck me that the process of writing, even on a fifteen minute speech – conceiving an idea, researching the idea, structuring and shaping and articulating the idea and then refining it is EXACTLY the same process as that which goes into writing a play.

I left it just as tired. It feels like something physical. That process. It feels like a reach.

6th June

I spent the morning rewriting *Waterfall*.

I never do re-writes on plays to the level that I do on screenplays. Partly this is because of the nature of the industry. There is much more money involved in film and television and so more people have a vested interest in the script. Partly because it is a more speculative, uncertain process. It's possible to see, in a room, the impact of a script. Screenwrting, it strikes me, is more like taking a punt on an imaginary world. Rather than writing into the solidities of an actor in a space at a time.

I find it draining because the likelihood of the film getting made is slight. Everybody works around it with a sense of optimism but it's an ill-founded optimism. And so the ferociously precise re-writes take on a futile hue.

Like carrying out hairline surgery on somebody very, very, very, very nearly dead.

But it's interesting for all that.

I learn from it.

What's interesting is the extent to which film demands archetypal narratives. So in a love story, like *Waterfall,* it's important that our couple really look like they might lose each other and then don't.

That is what audiences invest in.

I read a comment on Twitter that Tim Etchells retweeted. Somebody was promising that in their next novel there would be no characters and no action.

The more I work in drama the more I think that the human is the story-telling animal. We make sense of our selves in space over time through the stories that we tell. We draw from our imagination and our memory to help us make sense of ourselves. And this capacity is what has led us to thrive in so many cultures and environments over such a short space of time. This is how we have thrived as an animal. This is how the species survived in drought and under attack and in famine and fire. By communicating to each other how we lived through other anxieties through the stories that we tell.

The kind of stories we write now aren't necessarily about finding potatoes or fishing or how to fight lions, but they have the same job.

They help us survive dangers. The dangers of violence and loneliness and greed and arid government.

The point, surely, is not to dismiss this but actually to embrace it and feel emboldened by it. To take responsibility for the stories we tell, not to stop telling them.

We should be aware of the subliminal political mechanics of narrative – how gendered they are and how charged with ideologies and value systems – but that doesn't necessarily demand that we stop telling stories at all.

There is something profound in the experience of being a human that deserves to be contextualized in time and space, and that process of contextualization is best crystallized, I think, in the form of the story.

Not because it defers to the capitalist experience, not because it sells a script, not because Aristotle or Robert McKee or David Mamet insist on it. But because it is profoundly rooted in the experience of the human animal.

9th June

Spent the day working on *Waterfall*. Trying to clarify the pictures in my head.

Read Kieślowski and Piesiewicz's scripts for their *Three Colors* films as a way of teaching myself about screenwriting.

They're a fascinating read. It strikes me, looking at their work, that the function of a screenplay is entirely different to the function of a stage play. The function of a stage play is to prompt a response from a room of actors and directors and designers who are alert and sharing a space. In this way it is an active document.

The function of a screenplay is to evoke a film for a funder or a director or an actor. In this way it is entirely descriptive.

There is no way any contemporary playwright worth their commissioning fee would write for stage in the way Kieślowski and Piesiewicz write for screen. It would seem prescriptive and old fashioned.

Similarly there is no way anybody would write for screen in the way say Sarah Kane writes for stage with *4.48 Psychosis* or Martin Crimp with *Attempts on Her Life*. It would seem bewildering and impenetrable.

It's taken me a decade to really get my head around this.

I'm not sure I love screenwriting any more for having had this insight.

I went in the evening to see the young director Jude Christian's production of *Punk Rock* at RADA. It wasn't wholly successful – some of the acting was uneven and some of the concepts weren't wholly integrated in the drama of the piece. But at its best it was bold and imaginative and vibrant. Some of the acting was beautiful.

Some of the writing made me cringe inside. It's been five years since that play premiered and seven years since I wrote it. Some of the ideas are woefully over-egged. Some of the motifs clumsily repeated. I just kept wanting them to say less.

It strikes me there is a sexual despair at the heart of my writing that is more acute than the political despair. These school shooters, like their peers the suicide bombers, just need to watch less porn and go and get fucked.

Don't we all though, eh?

10th June

Spent the day mainly re-working *Waterfall*. Trying to master the whole notion of the descriptive screen direction. Drawing solace from Kieślowski. Trying to get it right.

All the while galvanized and inspired and provoked and thrilled by Swans's new album *To Be Kind*. That Michael Gira, at 60, is making work so frightening and ambitious is inspiring.

11ᵗʰ June

Met with Jack Bradley, the former National Theatre Literary Manager who is now working as an Associate of West End Producer Sonia Friedman. Jack has always been a significant figure in my career. His encouragement, when he was Literary Manager at Soho Theatre Company, in the early nineties, and was the first professional figure in London to read and reply to my plays, meant the world. His time at the National Theatre as Literary Manager there coincided with *On the Shore* and *Harper Regan* and he invited me to be Writer in Residence there for a year.

It was good to see him and to talk about whether the West End can seriously sustain new work.

He was optimistic about the future of commercial theatre.

For now, though, I can't imagine taking a commission. I think if I tried to write something commercial I'd fail. I prefer imagining the architecture of my favourite theatres and writing for them. Imagining the proscenium at the Royal Court or the space at the Exchange. And if, by some bewildering fluke, somebody seems to find commercial potential by accident, then I'm happy, like with *Dog* and *Doll's House,* for them to take it into town.

Back to *Waterfall* re-writes for a while. I find it difficult, I realize, to write about writing in this diary. I suspect this is largely because it's uninteresting. But also because it's unconscious. I just get my head down and go. Try to avoid internet distraction. Try to avoid doubt and self-fear. Try to write with energy.

I did write a few new scenes in *Waterfall* though. Some big open ones that felt more like they were scenes from plays. Tried to open up my lungs a bit with Emily and Christopher, the two protagonists. Tried to allow them to cut into each other's hearts a touch.

Then lunch with Selina Cartmell, the English director who will direct *Punk Rock* at the Lyric in Belfast in the summer. She probed gently around the edges of the play. It was good to talk to her. It's bold of the new Artistic Director at the Lyric Belfast to open up his new season with an English play about English schoolkids. A contemporary play at that.

I wouldn't be at all surprised if he really struggles to sell it.

But his bravery is laudable at least.

12ᵗʰ June

I had a meeting this morning with the filmmaker Paul Greengrass. We met at the Soho Hotel. I've always disliked the Soho Hotel. It's like Soho House but noisier. My anxiety about the environment exacerbated my nervousness at meeting one of the most successful and actually really great living British film directors.

Paul, though, was avuncular, charming and interested in me and who I am and what I've done. We shared stories of our mutual dissatisfaction with the idiocy and unpredictability of television commissioning editors and bonded over our reluctance to kowtow to morons and our love of football.

He enthused about working with New York producer Scott Rudin. We kicked about ideas surrounding the possible adaptation of David Ignatius's *The Director*. I left the meeting enthused and charged by the possibilities in the adaptation.

I think I could learn a lot from him.

Headed down to Clapham Common to watch a good run of the new cast of *The Curious Incident of the Dog in the Night-Time*. I worry about the possibility of it getting sentimental. Keep giving the same notes all the fucking time nowadays. Play the action not the feeling, ask the question, listen, the most important word is often the last one in a given line.

Again and again these four notes seem to pinpoint areas of uncertainty in actors' performance.

Went to the Almeida to see Robert Icke's production of Anne Washburn's *Mr Burns*. It was a remarkable night in the theatre. Vivid and energetically staged. It troubled me that its take on humanity had a cynicism but as time has gone on I've warmed to it more and more.

The new Artistic Director Rupert Goold, working with Rob Icke as his Associate, have re-invented the Almeida. Its audience was youthful and alert. It feels like a place in which difficult theatre can be found.

13th June

Up to Newcastle for a workshop at Northern Stage.

On the way up and down I completed a draft of *Waterfall*. It feels as though it's really turned a corner. I need to re-read it. But it felt like a good day's work.

The workshop was with twenty-three writers and actors and performers. Northern Stage is a beautiful theatre in the heart of Newcastle. It has a fine history of combative, imaginative work, especially under its last Artistic Director, Erica Whyman. The energy, at a time when Newcastle Council have removed all funding from the arts, continues under Lorne Campbell.

I interrogated the difference between human beings and other animals with the group in an attempt to cut to the quick of the question about what it is to be human.

It was fascinating to hear from a trainee psychotherapist in the group that one of the key physiological differences is that the human cortex develops after birth. Most mammals are born with the cortex fully grown. But the human cortex only reaches full growth at 6 years. Until then it is being shaped and refined and defined by interaction with other humans. We are social animals defined not, this person suggests, by any innate identity but an identity moulded and refined through the interaction of other people.

I fucked the timings up on the workshop. I spent too much time cracking jokes and going on intellectual rambles. But it was good and they seemed energized and responded to it.

Newcastle has a dignity to it and a beauty but it looks fucked. The more I travel out of London the more I realize there are two countries in England.

From sitting in the affluence of Soho Hotel to striding down the main drags of Newcastle defined by Wetherspoons, Money Shops and boarded-up shop windows, the extent to which England cleaved in the wake of the financial collapse of 2008, and the governmental responses to it, is startling.

It reminded me of my idea of going on a week-long holiday across the North with Sarah Frankcom for my next Royal Exchange play.

It struck me I should try and really write something huge for that place. Something sweeping and big and formally bold and about this rift.

20th June

I've lost a week.
Somehow I don't know how.

It was a week spent refining *Waterfall*. I'm proud of it. I think it evokes a world more completely than previous drafts did and I think the narrative is more compelling. It is now completely dominated by Christopher and Emily. The role of Emily is now, I think, a huge role. In my head I was trying to write something that could be sent to Emily Watson and that she wouldn't say 'no' to and I think this film could be sent to her and she wouldn't think, necessarily, that it was shit.

I delivered it this afternoon. Now it is entirely out of my hands.

I think the extent to which I do keep my head down when I'm writing in this detail has distracted me from my diary. I think when I'm at that stage it does become more all-consuming. I shut everything else out. I become autistic in my drive to get the work done.

Well.

It's done now.

My sense that I need to write more expansively about England was exacerbated by trips to Guildford and Birmingham. London is in a different country to those cities now. It is a country built around the movement of money, and money is moving with giddy energy through it. It leads us to better restaurants and a club life and better suits and all that. The rest of the country can't compete as a money market and the dissipated infrastructure leaves the place battered. But it may be that it's in battered places that real life and proper creativity are found. The future may be more bleak for London in some ways than for the rest of the country.

Guildford, away from the promise of a trip to Polly's mum's house, is defined by empty multi-purpose office space. What do people do in those offices? What are they having meetings about? Everybody looked like they were in the CID. Slightly shit smart clothes and a simmering undercurrent of violence.

I went to speak to a bunch of lively, engaged, engaging sixth formers and enjoyed that hugely.

On Thursday I was up at the University of Birmingham talking to students there and reading from my plays. I read from *Bluebird*, a play that I wrote in 1997. That was odd – moments when phrases resonated with my centre of self and could have been put in *Waterfall*; other moments of inertia and dramatic imprecision. *Sea Wall*. Always a crowd-pleaser and *Song from Far Away*, which read nicely. I was happy with it.

I wrote to Mark Eitzel to see how he would feel about actually being IN *Song from Far Away*. It strikes me that it could be beautiful. It could elevate it into something more remarkable. Something that could sit in a lot of theatres. He could ghost it. He could write more music.

I spoke with Karl Hyde. Our conversation made me feel the shape of *Fatherland*. I wonder about four individual stories interweaving over an imaginary 24-hour period. Intersecting. And a chorus sitting against the individual voices.

I wondered about sending Rob Icke or the Gate Theatre *Carmen Disruption*. I wonder if that play will ever be done in the UK.

Maybe, in simple terms, it doesn't work.

21st June

I delivered *Waterfall*. Hit the deadline. I think it's interesting.

In the evening I went to see Punchdrunk's *The Drowned Man*. A huge immersive site-specific exploration of the *Woyzeck* myth in a disused shop depository in Paddington. It infuriated me. The audience donning masks were left to wander freely through what was unarguably an exquisitely crafted world. But I felt that I was always in the room next door to where the good stuff was happening. The more I travelled the more I realized I wasn't. Nothing was happening. It was a piece designed to tantalize. It lacked substance entirely. It assimilated the surface mythology of David Lynch's movies. But had no proper interrogation of nightmare or horror or what it is to be.

It felt like I was wandering round a warehouse full of people entirely missing the point of David Lynch.

I got home drunk and tweeted about it, which I regretted immediately. Tweeting negative thoughts about other people's work is redundant. I've never done it before and felt wretched for doing so.

It's interesting why the show made me so angry.

It is unquestionably beautifully designed. The performers work with some real grace. It is unarguably an event. You enter in the same way as you enter a music festival or a rave. There is an unarguable gesture to it that is in some ways compelling.

But I kept having that feeling that I was being cheated. I was reminded of Johnny Rotten in his last Sex Pistols gig. 'Ever get the feeling you've been cheated?'

Finally I think that this is because there was such an absence of story.

I am astonished how often I am returning to the need for story as a theme in these diaries. I hadn't anticipated doing so.

But, without a unifying idea that was big enough to contain the piece, it seemed ultimately empty.

And that seemed in some way cynical. It felt as though they were aspiring to the status of the next Cirque du Soleil. Global branding selling itself as art. This is probably massively unfair. But that is what it felt like to me.

22nd June

Over the weekend I saw Nick Payne's exquisite *Incognito* at the Bush Theatre. A beautifully made piece about the intangible nature of human identity. The impossibility of mapping the human soul through brain-mapping. Themes refrained in Peter Brook's utterly fucking exquisite *The Valley of Astonishment* at the Young Vic last night. How can we place where the human essence is? How can we shave a bit of it off a brain?

Watched *Butch Cassidy and the Sundance Kid* on Sunday night while reading the William Goldman script. Goldman's script is dynamic and descriptive. Dennis Kelly said to me when I asked him what the difference was between screenplays and stage plays, 'Well, a screenplay is a piece of prose'.

Goldman writes the shots. He writes the camera movements.

I've started a playwriting workshop with ten-year-old kids at my kids' primary school, Chisenhale. Lively groups who take some settling but have made beautiful ideas. Really smart. We did some excellent hot-seating of characters they made. They loved that. It was inspiring the work they've come up with.

I find the days in between finishing work and starting the next work odd. They are kind of limbo days. I need to start work on *Kasimir and Karoline* and will do so tomorrow.

Yesterday I mainly taught ten-year-olds and ate meals with playwrights.

It was excellent seeing both Alice Birch, a young writer of startling promise who has just won the George Devine Award, and Dennis Kelly, who is probably the playwright experiencing the same oddities of a theatrical life as me.

We were talking about another writer. How for years he had a partner who didn't believe he could write. That relationship ended. He has fallen in love with a woman who has real faith in him. And now he is writing brilliantly.

I've never had any partner other than Polly. It made me think that her faith in my work has been more empowering than I ever acknowledge.

I'd never seen Peter Brook's work until last night. It was poised and simple and elegantly made and beautifully acted.

I loved it.

He writes about death with the wisdom and graciousness that only the very elderly could conjure. He writes with optimism about the magic of what people can be. That love and optimism infuse the piece.

24th June

A second session with the kids at Chisenhale. They were more
focused. They were more committed. They did work on their
characters and on second characters, and we did some talking about
the difference between human beings and other animals.

This is the question with which I start every workshop.

They talked about curiosity and fingers and thumbs. Which is
fundamentally the whole point of being human. Being curious and
having fingers and thumbs.

Then we did work on their characters' desires.

I met with the academic Jacqueline Bolton. Jacqueline is based at the
University of Lincoln and has published more work on my writing than
any other academic. We talked about *Harper Regan*. The sudden
interjection of racist diatribe in that play: what its function is. It was a
play carved out of my horror that Israel, a country formed out of the
worst war crime in history – should behave towards their Palestinian
neighbours with the brutality of war criminals. The speeches that
pepper the play are designed to undermine convention. To shock
audiences into being alert to the possibility of thought.

Went to the dentist's.

Made some tea.

And went to the first preview of *The Curious Incident of the Dog in the
Night-Time* at the Gielgud Theatre. It's a beautiful theatre. Next to the
Apollo it is spacious and elegantly maintained. The toilets are lovely.
The bar is lovely. The backstage isn't held together with Gaffa tape. It
is a terrific building. In beautiful condition.

The show works. I noticed things about it last night I'd not before. A
really smart cast with Nick Tennant as Ed, an astonishing Graham
Butler as Christopher, Sarah Woodward as Siobhan and Emily Joyce

as Judy. They need to speak up. They need to not underestimate the size of the theatre and so the need for attacking the top of scenes. They need to understand the technical challenges of playing against that soundtrack. But they grew into their performance and by the second half were just extraordinary.

The nuance of Graham Butler's decisions was particularly impressive. His Christopher was wittier than others, less gentle, less low-status. He had an exasperation and arrogance that did evoke John Cleese at times. It was funny and moving. The space created by the gap between his performance and the loneliness of the character was evoked by the comic decisions he made. Comedy exists when a character is not aware – and never aware – of their own sadness and that is what Graham Butler brought to Christopher.

If the audience in the first half seemed slightly perturbed by the formal decisions in a play like this playing in the West End, then by the second half they were on their feet. There was a remarkable sense of celebration and delight.

I'm proud of the democracy of that play. It was a play I wrote so that I could take my youngest son Stanley to see something I'd been part of making. Last night it felt as though the mission was in some way accomplished.

Had a whiskey at Blacks on my way home. It's been six months that show has been offstage. It means a lot to have it back.

25th June

Back in Chisenhale Primary School. Doing some really good work with the kids now. I think I might like this group as people as much as any group I've worked with at the school. They're crackling with imagination. They're a little lively. They struggle to concentrate and to listen but their ideas are fizzing.

And then emptied my inbox. Half my life I spend emptying my inbox nowadays.

In the past people would collect writers' correspondences. They would be letters. Beautifully formed. Elegant. Pithy. Extraordinary. I just rattle off badly spelt emails. And I feel fine doing exactly that.

Form follows function.

26th June

Up to York to talk at the Drama Barn to undergraduate students in the university's drama society. This was where I staged my first plays. I acted in *Asylum*, the play I wrote with Jonathan Stroud, now a successful teenagers novelist, here in May 1990. And *Frank's Wild Years,* the monologue I wrote when I was seventeen inspired by the Tom Waits song, was on the same bill. *Duke* and *Good Rocking Tonight* were staged there. I played guitar in Jimmy P & The Telopines, the Elvis cover band formed to play on *Good Rocking Tonight* in the Drama Barn. It was an extraordinary thing to go back. There was a real rush of nostalgia.

The re-opening of old wounds that inspires us to create. That Oliver Sacks theory came to mind. His notion that creativity comes from the same place as nostalgia – the need to complete the interrupted or repair the broken. I experienced so many interruptions at the Drama Barn. So many unfinished conversations. So many ideas cracked.

It was lovely to go back and patronize young people.

I talked for two hours with the chair of the drama society and with a brilliant man called Ian Stuart who was the founding member of the drama society. Three generations nattering. It felt really quite special.

It was odd to be back in York. The town seemed more specific than I remember. I remember it being a place to live. At the time it felt like a generic English town. There felt nothing remarkable about the place. On returning, the extent to which it remains defined by its medieval past was weirdly legible. For me, at that time, it was pubs and shops selling beans, and the campus.

Spent the train journey home doing cuts on *The Curious Incident of the Dog in the Night-Time*. Maybe shaved three pages in total. Marianne won't implement them. She urges me to do these things with a sense of urgency. I do them. Then she doesn't implement them. It's a good job I love her so much.

27th June

Brutal treatment in Moorfields this morning. Too much iodine and I could barely walk down the road.

Spent my time there reading the literal of *Kasimir and Karoline*. Walter Meierjohann, the new Artistic Director of the new Home Theatre in Manchester who has asked me to write the version, has an instinct to relocate it in Manchester. I think it's the right instinct. I don't want to riddle it with anachronisms but there are little nudges that could be done.

I'd update the music. Get rid of the setting of a 1929 Oktoberfest. I think the idea of peppering the language with the desolate clichés of those people so battered by an economy they've lost touch with how they really feel is a good one. Soap opera speak. Polluted by language.

30th June

Started work on *Kasimir and Karoline*. Working through it from the beginning. Replacing the band playing old Munich folk songs with one playing old rock and roll standards. Making the stage more alive. Cutting the breaks in between scenes so that they run into one another to make more orthodox scenes. Making the language as full and as florid as possible.

1st July

A day locked in a recording studio in the middle of Wardour Street with Mark Haddon. We did ten radio interviews about the return of *The Curious Incident of the Dog in the Night-Time*. The journalists all promised not to ask about the Apollo roof collapsing and then all asked about it. It was odd and hypnotic answering the same questions again and again. Trying to make the answers seem fresh and alert. Mark has been answering the same questions for ten years.

He did say that before he wrote *The Curious Incident of the Dog in the Night-Time*, in an attempt to write an adult novel, he'd completed three full novels that he threw away. The idea of discarding an entire piece of work is bewildering to me. It's the reason I find writing for television so battering – the notion that months can go into creating something that then is redundant.

This, though, is how Mark works. He's done it with several plays as well as with the novels.

After ten interviews I'd almost lost the ability to speak with any kind of cogency at all. I found it difficult to not have conversations that were in some way performative. It felt like I was in a loop of interview.

2nd July

The day of the performance of the kids' plays from Chisenhale. I met Matt Barker who'd been in *The Curious Incident of the Dog in the Night-Time*, Nitin Kundra from *Harper Regan*, Charlotte Randle from *Birdland* and Kat Pearce from *Port* in a cafe on Grove Road and we had a coffee and went up to the school.

It felt like a treat to be working with those actors.

We settled ourselves in the room in the school in which I've been working with the kids and one at a time they came in to present their scenes to us.

They were variously nervous and cocky and giddy, and the actors were bemused and charmed and inspired by them. Collectively we battered the scenes into some kind of shape and the actors were encouraged to play broad-brush strokes, hit primary numbers, smack the ball in the centre of the bat and play it large and, largely, they did.

We went up to the classroom where we performed and read the scenes to the class. There were ripples of giggles as the kids used 'bitch' in their scenes. There was real concentration and real listening.

This year the cumulative effect of the scenes was surprisingly bleak. The key note of these eleven-year-olds' plays was dramatic. There were four scenes about orphaned kids. There were two uses of the word 'bitch'. Occasionally it became a bit too much like episodes of *Eastenders* but not that often. There were scenes set in Chicago between an artist and his step brother baseball player, a scene at a Bow graveside between a mother and her son at the point of leaving for America, a scene between two orphaned girls as the elder tried to stop the younger from fantasizing about their mum; a scene set in Tokyo between a shoplifter and her victim; a scene set in the government offices in Cebu as an orphaned kid persuades a government employee to steal a file on corrupt government plans; and a scene between two kids at a party.

The class received them in raptures.

The actors loved it.

Went in the evening to see *The Curious Incident of the Dog in the Night-Time* again. It was more contained, more truthful this time. The audience stood. The actors listened. The time was tighter. The cuts worked. It's in good nick. Nick Tennant's Ed, Christopher's dad, was particularly truthful. It was one of my favourite Ed performances. He avoided emoting. It was simple and practical and clear.

3rd July

A meeting with Alex Poots and Karl Hyde and Scott Graham to try to persuade Alex to commission our piece on fatherhood for the 2017 Manchester International Festival. Alex is lively, alert company. We talked about the resonances between the idea of a search for fathers and the idea that as a culture we have lost touch with our past. Alex was keen to push us into considering Europe as a continent isolating itself into intolerance. He was keen to get us to think about unusual spaces. And to try to push the form of what a play might be.

All of which seemed exciting and releasing to me. He was edging us towards creating something immersive. If we could combine the architectural imagination of the best immersive theatre with a real substance and a real content, we could make something rare.

Had a meeting with Bart Van den Eynde the dramaturg from Toneelgroep Amsterdam this evening about *Song from Far Away*. He was very, very warm about the play. He loved a lot of it. Ivo did too it seems and Jan Versweyveld, Ivo's designer, very much.

He was keen for me to cut the dates and may be right about that. He was keen for me to tighten the characters of Mina and Willem's dad and make them more surprising. I think I can do that. The sense of relief that they don't hate the play was profound. It always is.

Bart's a smart reader and I trust him. Ivo is simply a great director.

We talked about the idea that Mark might perform in the play. Bart seemed intrigued. I think it could work.

In the evening I went with Oscar and Polly to see *Show 5* at the Lyric by Secret Theatre. It was as brave and fearless as anything I've seen all year. Nadia Albina played The Protagonist. Her name was drawn from the hat. She was fearless and ferocious. She exhausted herself. Her performance as Juliet in the show's re-telling of the balcony scene was remarkable. As raw a *Romeo and Juliet* as I've seen.

4th July

Travelled to Barcelona for the Obrador at the tiny Sala Beckett Theater. Every year I run a week-long workshop with writers from throughout the world hosted by this small hotbed of Catalan new writing. The impact of the theatre in the city is profound. They have generated in the city the idea that theatre might be made of new plays.

I'm working with two Catalan writers who write together as well as writers from Spain, two from France, Germany, Argentina, Uruguay, Chile and Britain.

They've written plays in response to the provocation I set them that they should build work on a consideration of what might happen in the future of their cultures. Their work is good this year. More defined by clear character and dramatic action than it often is. Funnier.

I met them in the evening.

We had some beers and went to watch Colombia play Brazil in the quarterfinals of the World Cup. Brazil won an enthralling match.

15th July

I want this week to take some time out to write about the workshop that I'm running at the Obrador run by Sala Beckett.

I hope that by writing about the work I do there in more detail it might inspire other practitioners – teachers, writers, directors – to use some of my exercises or approaches.

Over the past fifteen years the process of teaching has been important to me. Teaching runs in my family like other professions run in other families. Some people come from families of policemen, some from families of criminals. I come from a family of teachers.

The process of teaching has illuminated my work. It has allowed me to take control of my own process. It has allowed me to be conscious of what I'm doing and to take ownership over a process that otherwise may remain instinctive. I think artists can only survive for a limited period on instinct alone. Teaching has allowed me to avoid that limitation.

I first taught at the Obrador in 2009. Each year has been bracing. Sometimes it has been difficult. What I have learned most from working at the Obrador is that those assumptions that have informed my work about what writing is and what theatre is are not innate at all. But rather they are culturally specific and defined by having been raised in Britain at the end of the twentieth century with all its cacophony of capitalism and affluence and terror. It has also been a consequence of being trained at the Royal Court Theatre with its mixed influence of European and American dramaturgy and its sense that the work of theatre is fundamentally dramatic rather than epic, and that narrative matters and that the function of the actor is to pretend to be another human being.

These are notions that have been interrogated again and again in recent decades in other cultures. It has been a challenge and provocation to work with writers from France or Germany or Latin America or the Iberian Peninsula in recent years who have engaged more fully with notions of post-dramatic theatre or have been more inspired by Brechtian notions of epic theatre.

I return again and again to the dramatic form rather than the epic or the post-dramatic but my work has been informed and changed by the provocations of writers operating from other assumptions. Nowhere is it more provoked or challenged than in the Obrador.

Every year the writers have to write plays inspired by a question that Tony Casares, the Sala Beckett's Artistic Director, asks me to set for the groups. This year the writers have written plays in response to the following:

We live in an age obsessed by the one thing it can never understand: the future.

Perhaps there is something about our consciousness that means this was always the case. As animals we can understand that our lives have a future. Even if scientists prefer to think of time as a dimension rather than something moving forwards in a linear direction, this movement forward continues to define how the human animal experiences its world. Time appears to move forward. Entropy seems to rise. We seem to get older. We have the capacity to remember. We have a need to live in the moment. We have no idea what is going to happen next.

The older I get the more fixated I get about this. Partly this is related to the fact that death is more palpable to me now, in my forties, than it has ever been. Partly it's related to being a parent of three children. I think about their future often. Their future sits exactly at one of those nexus between my personal life and my political world that breeds stories for me. For me plays come out of an attempt to explain something that I don't understand and that grips my heart. Increasingly all notions of a future seem to do this.

I also think that, in the West at least, we have built a culture around fantasies of a future.

Economically we live tantalized by the possibility of recovery or the terror of further collapse. We build industries around an obsessive need to improve and progress and live tainted by the possibility of regression.

Ecologically our future sits over us like a shadow – the defining trauma of our culture, has, it seems, yet to happen. We know that it will. We don't know what form it will take.

Culturally we are tantalized by the next technological shift into a utopia that can seem as awful as it is seductive. What will come next from Apple? What will Google know next? What will we soon be able to capture and share on YouTube or Twitter?

Politically we are inspired and terrified by what might happen next. As we face our collective future we wonder if optimism is idealistic and self-deluded or the only useful and pragmatic and responsible way of reclaiming political agency. Is pessimism the only intelligent position or is a self-indulgence of the wealthy that serves no political purpose at all?

*

I would like the writers to write short plays informed by the question 'What will happen next?'

These plays should be informed, in whatever way the writers choose, by the cultures and countries they are living in. I'd like them to think about some form of future. This might be a political future. It might be an economic or a technological or an ecological future. It might be a personal future. It might be built around an interrogation of the very notion of a future in the first place.

The plays could be set in this future but they needn't be. They should just be informed by a consideration of what might happen next.

The plays might be set in their own countries but they needn't be. They should just be born out of a brief time of thinking about what the future holds for them or threatens them with or promises them or means to them.

The plays should last between fifteen and twenty minutes in length. They can take whatever dramatic form the writer chooses to take and use any number of actors.

*

What has surprised me in recent years, as opposed to the years immediately after the economic ruptures of 2008, is how increasingly writers are drawn to creating plays in which there are characters and there is a notion of time and there are narratives. As though there is an attempt to understand the ruptures of our culture through story telling.

I always start the workshop with the same exercise.

I ask the writers to close their eyes and I talk them through the story of their lives. I ask them to think about what they know about the conditions of their own birth. What they've heard about what they were like as a baby. Their earliest sensory memories. I ask them to think about early childhood and their families and their school, and then guide them through recalling their memories of school and changing schools and adolescence and sexuality and love and the workplace and teaching and writing and reading and drama and theatre and the mess and the complications of their life. I ask them to keep their eyes closed. I try to take my time.

I allow them about twenty minutes to do this.

Then I give them a sheet of A3 paper and ask them to draw the map of their life. Including the details they can remember as though they were drawing a map to help somebody get from the start of their life to the moment of the workshop.

They can include roundabouts where they got stuck in their life, roadworks, crossroads and motorways. They can put pictures on the side of the maps to illustrate the key events in their personal lives and the key memories of the political world.

I think of plays as being maps of behaviour, so practising cartography skills is helpful.

They share the maps with one other person and it is the job of this person to remember the map and to guide the rest of the group through the maps.

It's a bonding exercise. Its a way of allowing the group to get to know one another in a way which is intimate and private but also safe because they are held in the hands of their partner rather than the whole group. It is also an exercise that incorporates elements of the making of theatre. The idea that we depend on one another, that we give maps to each other when we make plays and trust one another to pay attention to the maps and follow them well. Our collaborators. Our audiences.

It also has parallels with the process of writing. Each map is distinct and particular and part of the joy of the process is to see the initial reactions to the exercise when the maps are revealed. Writers, in making maps, use their technique in application to a subject and in doing so reveal what is best described as their style. Each is individual and particular. This is what happens when people make art. We apply our technique to our subject revealing our style. It is the same in playwriting. It is revealed in this exercise.

The maps this year were more abstract than in previous years. They were less linguistic. They were more expressionistic. This might have been because I didn't clarify the exercise properly.

More likely though it is that the notion of the exercise is charged with very culturally specific assumptions. Maybe I work from the assumption that it is possible to draw a map of a life. Maybe I assume it is possible to draw a life in one line moving forwards in time and that this idea is predicated on the assumption that time moves forward; that life exists chronologically is a culturally specific notion. Maybe it's only in Anglo-American cultures that we experience and understand life to be lived with a narrative. The boldest, most expressionistic response to the exercise came from the Chilean writer, a writer carved out of the Latin American indigenous cultures who removed himself from his own map and certainly wasn't interested in asking questions about when events in his life took place or where they took place.

It may be that this philosophical paradigm may be a rift in the group for the rest of the week.

I also played volleyball with the group. I've done this every Obrador. We play a simple game of 'keepy-uppy'. I took this from Elyse Dodgson in the Royal Court international department while working with her in Mexico City. It is a game where the group have to work together to try to get a record score.

I like it because it's playful and silly and physical in a workshop that may otherwise be overly cerebral. I like it too because it demands collaboration and instils a spirit of teamwork when the group may otherwise atomize and work in isolation.

6th July

Before the writers come to the Obrador I ask them to prepare materials to bring in. I ask them to bring in one photographic image, one news story and one piece of music. This year, in line with the theme of the workshop, I asked them to choose materials that in some way refract their culture through the prism of what the future might hold.

This morning the writers shared their materials.

Collectively they created a kind of collage of notions of the future. Their work ranged from an analysis of the shifting nature of global geo-economics to a sweet story of a woman who met her estranged father when he drove her in a taxi through Buenos Aires. In Uruguay the government isolated technical experts who resisted their attempts to bypass them in state-run industries. In Lyon a primary school teacher forced the girls in his school to cover themselves in plastic bags when on a hot day they wore short skirts to school. In Barcelona a government official's son was battered into a coma when people attending a party at which he was dealing drugs found out who his father was. In Britain a generation was lost in the face of political structures that bypassed them while economic structures blurred their lines between the workplace and their home. In Chile European settlers in indigenous areas had their house burned to the ground and were burned to death within it.

Together they created a collage of a global culture in a state of transition and anxiety.

7th July

The work today involved asking how they as dramatists can articulate their responses to the gap between the personal maps of their lives and the collage of their state in the global world. Drama exists in the tension between how we live as individuals and how we live in the world.

I asked them to do an exercise that I always do when I write my plays. With the particular application of considering the future I asked them to write for five minutes about what made them angry, five minutes on what made them frightened, five minutes on what gave them hope and five minutes on what they would be too ashamed to share with the rest of the group.

These emotions of fear, anger, hope and shame are primal and generate material.

I ask them to write without thinking and time their writing so that they are forced to reveal their unconscious in some way. I tell them that nobody will read what they've written so they can be fearless.

In order to look at how we might dramatize their responses to their world in flux, I asked the group to read Martin Crimp's brief, astonishing *Face to the Wall*. We read the play as a whole class and then in small groups they had to list all the decisions that Crimp made in the writing of the play. They fed their lists back to me and I had to force them to turn their observations into specific decisions that writers make in the creation of their plays. The exercise demands that they are scientific and specific in their thinking. I have to encourage them, trained as they often are in philosophical university departments, to think not about why writers do what they do but *how*. This can be tough for those with a good academic training. I'm not interested in why writers make decisions in this exercise but in what decisions they make. I'm not interested in the why but the how.

Eventually, as a group we compiled this list:

Why is the writer writing the play?
What does the writer think about the world?
What does the writer think about the traditions of playwriting that they write in?

Are there characters?
If there are . . .
   What is their gender?
   What is their name?
   What is their relationship to one another?
   What is their off-stage life?

What are the actors (personae) doing?
Who are they doing it to?
What are they saying?
Who are they saying it to?

What else can we hear?
Who says what? How evenly is language distributed?
Who does what? How evenly is action distributed?
Who is in which scene?

How long is the play?
(How) is it divided?
Into how many parts?
How long are these parts?

What happens before the play starts?
How is this revealed or recounted?
How reliable is the revelation or recounting/recounter?
How cogent is it?
When does the story start?
How is the story released chronologically?

What happens IN the play?
When does the action start?
In what order does the action of the play happen chronologically?

Is there language in the play?
What order are the utterances in?
What language is the play written in?
What words are used?
What register do the characters speak in?
(How) is the play punctuated?
Are there silences and pauses and beats?
Are words repeated?
How long are the phrases and sentences and speeches?

How does the writer sign the play?

It is an incomplete list but a starting point as I try to get them to think like thieves and to read like thieves, not like academics.

8th July

After a very promising game of volleyball we started work.

In the past at the Obrador I've used the morning sessions to offer feedback on the writers' plays. This always felt a bit reductive. I hate teaching sessions where the writers offer critiques to one another. It becomes an ego fest, a bunfight or a nervous tentative inability to publicly exchange thoughts that are better shared over lunch or coffee or beer. So for the last few years I've changed it.

Now I ask the writers of the previous evening's play readings to ask questions to the rest of the group. This may include the question, 'What did you think of my play?' but doesn't necessarily have to. Instead they get to control the agenda.

This morning the two Catalan writers Nao Albet and Marcel Borràs who write together asked the group if they ever submitted work that they weren't proud of. Some of them have. This was largely to meet deadlines. A few years ago the Lyonnais writer Samuel Gallet suggested that the worst thing about British playwriting was that it was possible to make a living in Britain from writing for theatre.

As it is possible it becomes an imperative.

This, to an extent, dominates those moments when writers submit work to festivals or deadlines or to satisfy commissions that they fundamentally don't believe in. Writing processes and aesthetics are defined by the conditions in which work is made.

The writer from Spain, Lola Fernández de Sevilla, suggested that she sometimes took on too many commissions out of a need to keep working and found that overwhelming. I related to that fear completely.

They asked too how writers dealt with the hell of watching directors destroy their work. Of the ten writers in the group, nine of them it seems direct their own plays. This, too, is a product of the cultures and industries in which they are working.

I would miss the possibility of discovery. I'd miss the possibility that somebody could find more in my play than I would ever know is there. The playwright Robert Holman once suggested to me that nobody knows a writer's play more than the writer. I don't know if I believe that. I am amazed by how often directors discover things in my play that I had no idea were there. I would miss that if I directed my own plays.

The Uruguayan writer, Luciana Lagisquet, asked the group if they believed there was such a thing as feminine or masculine writing. This split the group right down the middle. I think there may be feminine dramaturgy, there may be structures that resonate more with a feminine mentality than with a masculine sensibility. It is rendered problematic because men who read with a masculine dramaturgy run so many theatres. I think the active protagonist, the direct dialogue may be masculine traits. I also think that it is possible for men to write feminine plays and women to write masculine plays if those adjectives accurately describe trends in dramaturgy.

The German writer Michel Decar asked if it was possible to imagine a civilization without capitalism any more. The discussion on this was rangy and felt. Brad Birch from the UK offered a compelling description of the difference between capitalism and trade. There was no agreement about whether or not capitalism dignified the West and rendered it peaceful or was a rift driving through our consciousness like a bolt.

In the afternoon we started a workshop I have always done as a means of investigating dramatic action.

I base my thinking on the assertion that plays are necessarily considerations of what it is to be human. It is possible to write a poem about a lake or a song about a tree but it is not possible to write a play about anything other than human beings. I asked the group to write for one minute about what it is to be a human being. Then to share their answers with a small group of three.

They talked about the fact that the human animal has a consciousness that is wide and expansive and can consider universes. But that we don't know about animal consciousness, so it is ludicrous to try to define it or assume what they experience. They talked about how there is a tension between the scale of the human imagination and the reality of the human body, and how this can lead itself to deceptions of difference and a belief that we are not animal. They talked about the rational mind. They talked about fear of death and about language. We are the linguistic animals.

It always fascinates me this discussion. It fascinates me that the answers I receive about this question from groups – that range from ten-year-old children to life prisoners to the world's leading emerging writers – only ever really reflect the make up of the group, not any tangible truth.

So this group talked about the mind and consciousness. But not about the opposable digit – that simple physiological phenomenon that allows the human to manipulate tools so that it can live in a wide array of physical geography. The chief exec of Coca-Cola in London talked about the human being on the top of the food chain when I had this discussion there. No animal eats the human for food. Of course he did. He's the chief executive of Coca-Cola in London. A ten-year-old a few years ago whose parents were black and white said that other animals were more multi-coloured than humans.

I have always been drawn to considerations of consciousness. I like the idea that the human is conscious of its own consciousness. And that this plays out over two axes. That of time and that of space. We know to a shattering degree where we are. And to a shattering degree when we are. We can imagine a past before not only our own lives but also that of our parents, our cultures, our species. And we can imagine our future.

Specifically we can imagine our deaths. And this imagination leads us to want to live a life according to our will. This will – this desire – defines us as an animal. We want things under the shadow of our own mortality and the behaviour we use as we overcome obstacles to get what we want defines our personality.

It is a very traditional Anglo-Saxon philosophy. It is steeped in a dramaturgical tradition formed at the Royal Court. It has helped me write.

Aristotle said that beginning playwrights labour under the illusion that their work should involve the writing of beautiful speeches or the creation of characters with interesting pasts. It doesn't. It involves the mapping of behaviour.

The playwright needs to look unerringly into the heart of their characters and ask what they want as they sit under the shadow of their death – what stops them from getting what they want – and then map their behaviour as they try to get it. This has always informed my writing.

Raymond Carver said that you don't need to be an intellectual to be a writer. You don't need to be the cleverest kid in your class or the cleverest kid in your street. All you need is the capacity to stand and stare open-mouthed in wonder at the world. I think the playwright stands and stares open-mouthed in wonder at the things people do.

I finished by asking the group to think of one thing they wanted before the end of the day, one thing they wanted before the end of the year and one before they die. When they can keep this specific and they can be simple and clear, it allows us to have a relationship with their personality that is based on interpretation and so is in some way deeper than if it had been based on description.

I sometimes think that this is how theatre works.

An audience deciphers and interprets the behaviour of characters in an attempt to empathize with them.

This is what theatre is for. It exists to exercise our empathy. It is an empathy machine.

9th July

The questions this morning from last night's writers were fascinating and more pragmatic perhaps. Pauline from Lyon asked the writers what their dream career would be, what their ideal working day would involve. We talked about the difficulties and possibilities of making a career in the individual countries. We talked about how much money writers earned for a commission and how the commission fee was staggered. We talked about other ways writers could earn money. How commissions are offered. What other jobs the writers did.

It has been clear to me for the past five years of doing the Obrador that the conditions in which writers work, in this sense, in the UK are privileged. We are more likely to get commissions than any other country in the world. There are more theatres producing new writing than in any other country in the world. The commissioning fees are standardized, not hierarchical, so that a beginning writer is paid as much as an established writer. It is much more likely that a play written in the UK by a new writer will be produced rather than given a public reading.

We talked about who writers are writing for. Some said they were writing for themselves. Some said for the audience. Some said that they were writing to punish lovers or parents. I liked very much what Michel Decar, the German playwright, said. He was writing the plays that he wished somebody else had written so he could sit in the imaginary audience of the theatre he was writing for, with the actors he was writing for, on the stage in his mind's eye imagining he was waiting for the play that he wished somebody else had written so that he could see it.

We talked about writing coming from pain and from fear.

I told them about Oliver Sacks's notion that creativity comes from nostalgia. This makes sense to me. Certainly the feeling of writing feels very similar to the experience of nostalgia. That odd rush of euphoria and melancholy. That is exactly how it feels when I write.

Hugo from Chile asked about the importance of comedy in the other writers' work. All of the writers agreed that its function – to tickle and tickle and tickle the audience in order to set up a good smack round their chops – was fundamental.

This is why, I think, much to Sebastian Nübling's despair, I like laughter in my audiences. It suggests the audience is ready to listen.

Luciana talked about the role of the Fool in the Medieval Court. The Fool alone was allowed to say whatever he wanted without risk of execution. This, she argues, is the role of the artist. To say whatever he or she wants, to reveal truths, to mock the unmockable and speak the unspeakable without fear of execution. At least in our countries.

It's odd to me that I think, as a teacher, I could teach nearly any element of playwriting. Character, action, situation, theme, but the one thing I don't think I could teach, or really offer notes on, is how to make writing funnier. It is beyond my articulacy. I think my plays have some great gags in. I think even the darkest plays have very funny bits. But I don't think I could tell another writer how to make comedy.

I spent time this afternoon doing work that I have done in my workshops for the past fifteen years.

I started by reading the second scene of *Birdland*. We read it twice so that those writers for whom English was a second language could be sure to have understood the scene. Then we read it again playing a game I call 'Tactics!' Whenever the readers or the group think that a character has changed tactics in their attempt to get what they want they have to shout out, at the top of their voices, 'TACTICS!' and identify what the character is doing.

I force them to articulate the tactic using a transitive verb. If they are not able to do that I won't accept the tactic. So 'making her feel guilty' would become 'inculpate'. They needed to find verbs that would grammatically complete the phrase 'Paul … Annalisa'. It's a way of reading, of training the mind to think transitively. It is, I think, the root of Anglo-Saxon dramaturgy.

The list we compiled from reading the first page of that scene closely was:

Negates
Mocks
Teases
Threatens
Intimidates
Teaches
Lectures

Entices
Enchants
Fights
Insults
Patronizes
Confronts
Belittles
Diminishes
Dismisses
Destabilizes
Charms
Flatters
Disorientates
Softens
Provokes
Challenges
Impresses
Surprises
Compliments
Undermines
Overwhelms
Annihilates
Peacocks
Impresses

Eventually they enjoyed the challenge of thinking transitively. It is imperative to my writing. I use the approach as a redrafting tool. But also to calibrate my thinking about what a scene is for. If I can't, finally, apply a transitive verb like this to a line of dialogue, then I cut it or change it so that I can.

After lunch I did two warm-up exercises.

I played them a Bach cello suite and asked them to write an automatic monologue that was in the first person and started with the word 'I . . .' I then played them 'Fortress/Deer Park' by The Fall and asked them to write an automatic response to that piece that was in the second person and started 'You . . .'

I then did more structured work.

I asked them to think of a character they wanted to write about. This could be a character they were already working on or a character from one of the exercises or from another play.

I did some exercises I defined and refined at the Royal Court.

I gave them ten minutes to write a list of fifty-one things that the character can remember. The tension of writing against the clock releases the unconscious I think. The attempt to get fifty-one means that the writers are writing without thinking. I then gave them ten minutes to write a list of twenty-one things a character can remember.

I have used these exercises myself all the time. I use them because writing against the clock and trying to attain that list forces me to reach for things that surprise me. I've done them on all my plays, I think.

I then ask them to choose three verbs at random from the list of transitive verbs we established.

And to write those verbs down.

To think of a place where the character on which they were working feels frightened and to write that down.

To imagine another character who is not frightened by the same place and to write down that character's name. I always think that when two characters have a different relationship to the space it gives the scene a charge that is energetic. It also frees the dramatist from exposition – it creates behavioural differences that audiences enjoy interpreting.

I ask eight questions about the relationship between those characters.

How long have they known one another? In what capacity? What do they openly like about one another? What do they openly dislike? What do they secretly like about one another? What do they secretly dislike? What do they get from one another? What do they want that they don't currently get?

I ask these questions to allow the writers to fully imagine the relationships between the characters. But also to generate material that may be used in dialogue. I use this exercise when writing my own plays. You can find the movement to secrets being revealed in a lot of the plays as relationships move forward.

There is a writing exercise that serves a similar purpose that I didn't get a chance to do with them. I give myself five minutes to write as many things as I can about what my character knows about themselves that nobody else knows. Five minutes to write as many things as the character knows about themselves and other people in the play also know. Five minutes on things that the other characters in the play know about the character but that the character doesn't, and five minutes on things that I know about the character but that neither the character nor anybody else knows.

After the writers completed these exercises, now they had a clearer sense of their characters and the muscle of their scenes, I ask them to start writing.

I divided the time of writing into three. Giving the writers seven minutes to get their protagonist to act in the way prescribed by the first of their chosen three transitive verbs. If they have chosen 'flatters', then the first seven minutes of writing will involve the first character flattering the second.

Then after seven minutes I ask the writers to shift gears and get the characters to act in a way prescribed by their second chosen verb. So the character 'flattering' in the first seven minutes might now start 'threatening'. They write for seven minutes based on this gesture.

And then finally to get them to act in a way prescribed by the third chosen verb. So the character that started flattering another character and then threatening them will now start perhaps 'mocking'.

It is important that the second character in the scene is not inert but rather *acts in response* to the actions of the first character.

The notion is that scenes built around behaviour put audiences in a position of interpreting and so they have to give more of themselves. We finished the scenes by the end of the workshop.

The random nature of the gear changes built on the randomly chosen verbs creates a life and unpredictability in the scenes.

10th July

The questions this morning were these.

Brad Birch, from Britain, asked the group how the working classes were represented in their theatres. This involved a consideration of how they were represented in the artistic workforce or the workforce of the theatre in general. Or how they were represented in the theatre audience. Or how they were represented in the content and worlds of the lives on stage in the plays.

The conversation was rangy and passionate. At its heart was the notion that the working class may have shifted. That in European countries the move away from manufacturing economies towards the service industry meant that the working class no longer necessarily involved physical labour. That earnings were no longer representative of class. A plumber can earn far more than a university teacher. That it was increasingly rare for people to do the same work as their parents and grandparents. That the working position most likely to be inherited was that of unemployment rather than employment.

It was asked why it was important for the theatre to represent all social strata. Was that its responsibility? Did it have a responsibility to entertain or to provoke and inspire? Was it patronizing to assume the working classes needed enlightening? Shouldn't people have the right to do what they want with their spare time?

Is there a danger that putting on plays that concern themselves with the lives of the poor for theatre audiences dominated by people wealthier than the characters in the fiction becomes in some way pornographic? Certainly at times *Country Music* at the Royal Court felt to me like I'd peddled poverty porn. After Charles Spencer's four-star review came out in the Telegraph there were certainly a lot of Telegraph readers in attendance watching the broken life of a Gravesend car thief.

I think the only reason theatre has a responsibility to represent the working class is because otherwise the gesture that theatre makes thins. When the same type of people are making theatre as watching it, and the stories or worlds being told are tailored to those people, then the power in the action of the play towards the audience is polluted by the notion that it is in some way an action of congratulation or affirmation. The gesture becomes a celebration that they all belong to the same world.

Xavier from Paris asked if the dramaturgy of his short play, written as it was without characters or narrative or action, was successful. The consensus seemed to be that work that is abstracted in this way – work that the Germans have described as 'post-dramatic' – becomes dependent on contrast and juxtaposition. It is dependent on the musicality of the piece and the use of time. Theatre is a time-based medium. Narrative is a powerful way of controlling time, predicated as it is on the notion that the audience wants to know what happens next.

To remove narrative doesn't remove the extent to which theatre is bound to time. Time moves forward. If the writer wants to remove story, then they need to control the time of their play with much more musical rigour.

The writer needs to be aware, too, of the importance of allowing contrasting and contradictory voices. So that the piece doesn't become a description of what the writer wants to say. Voices need to counterpoint against one another. Xavier's piece felt a little too overtly that it was articulating in language what he wanted to say.

Theatre is a space for uncertainty, it strikes me, not for certainty.

Xavier asked us, too, if theatre can change the world. I think it does. In the way that Edward Bond compared it to the changing of a tile in a mosaic. Every personality of every individual can be compared to a mosaic, he said. Every work of art they experience changes only one tile of that mosaic. But in changing one tile it changes the entire mosaic irrevocably. In that sense it changes the whole person. The artist needs to take responsibility for how she changes those tiles.

Brad Birch also clarified that for him the theatre may be a place to interrogate ideas or to worry away at them. But not to generate ideas. Because theatre, like all art, is built upon troubling and rendering uncertain, not upon persuading or changing.

Lola asked the group where they write. I write in an office in a former art deco furrier factory on the New North Road with a view overlooking a block of social housing. My ideal working day would involve cycling to work in the morning. Working from 9.30–10.30 on my emails. Reading. Then writing from 1–6 and coming home.

It rarely works out like this. I have to go to meetings. I have to go to workshops. I have to go to rehearsals. I get distracted by the internet. I get distracted by the world. I should buy the computer program *Freedom* to block the internet and social network from my computer while I'm writing. Often I find myself dawdling or surfing or shitting about with irrelevant bullshit. And then I am left having to race to get work done.

But I think I've done a lot of work in recent years. I need to acknowledge that sometimes freneticism has generated material. Maybe if my time was more structured I would write less. Also, something that Graham Whybrow, the former Literary Manager at the Royal Court and the man who remains the most important mentor in my career, told me: a writer's working day needs only to involve four hours' work.

If I could protect those four hours every day, then I would be fine.

Maybe I should only take meetings after 2. Actually as I write that, I realize it's a really good idea.

I might try it.

Fuck.

Yeah.

I can, though, write anywhere. I can write in my kitchen. Here in the Barcelona seminar room. In the cluttered room at home. I go into a tunnel where I can't see the world around me. It's tunnel vision.

Lola also asked the group if there were themes they return to.

Two years ago *A Doll's House* and *The Curious Incident of the Dog in the Night-Time* were in rehearsal at the same time. I noticed that both plays had the same line in them: 'I could never spend the night in a stranger's house'. Possibly this was because I am a lazy writer. But rather I think that it's because both texts, generated by other writers and responding to specific sources – Mark Haddon's novel and Henrik Ibsen's play – resonated in some way with what I found myself returning to as a writer.

I write again and again about characters needing to leave home but terrified of its impossibility; or struggling to live away from home; or having left home being unable to ever return.

These are themes that I return to obsessively.

I return also to considerations of how possible it is to empathize with others in a world atomized by technology and economics.

These twin themes run like seams in my work.

And recurring lines of dialogue appear like a poker player's 'tells'. Just as Sarah Kane always has a character smelling a flower and describing it as lovely, or Robert Holman always writes of a single tear rolling down a character's cheek, so I am certain my thematic obsessions are revealed in repeated lines or stage directions. Other people can find them.

I did suggest that the writers one day sit and read all their plays in one go. It can be an illuminating experience. It can reveal clues as to who we are and what our themes are. It is a myth that a writer needs to reinvent themselves with every play or find a new subject or do something new.

The great writers return to the same questions obsessively. Having identified these themes, we can take ownership of them and so consciously find new ways into them.

In the afternoon I gave the writers a much freer exercise. I asked them to take something from the wall they'd created over the weekend – a map of somebody's life, an image, a news story – and I played them William Basinski's *Disintegration Loops* and asked them to create a response to the source material in the same room as the music was playing. Their response could take whatever form it had to. It could be a scene or a poem or a line of dialogue or a song. They had thirty minutes to write it in.

At the beginning of the week I had asked the writers to think of a writing exercise that they would set one another. They needed to think of their own strengths and weaknesses, and the strengths and weaknesses of their peers, and create an exercise as a prompt for them.

I gave them forty-five minutes to do this in.

Some of the exercises were quite entertaining. One writer asked another to write a monologue from the point of view of Diego Maradona, synthesized with Shakespeare's Richard III. Another asked a writer to write a speech in which every word began with the letter 'd'. One asked a writer to write a monologue from the perspective of a real person they hated but to excavate real empathy for that person. The writers came back galvanized and entertained and provoked.

11th July

A morning off for me as I sent the writers throughout Barcelona for a bit of tourism with three writing exercises.

They had to keep a sensory diary. Noticing three things they tasted, touched, smelt, three colours they saw and heard. They had to write a postcard from Barcelona that could only have been written in Barcelona to a real person who they knew in life but this would be a postcard they would never send. They had to do character exercises on somebody they observed around town. Noting three things the person knew about themselves that nobody else knew, three things that they and others knew about themselves, three things that others knew about them that the person didn't; and three things that the writers knew that nobody else knew.

Sometimes meetings with strangers initiate the possible scratches of possible ideas.

We met in the afternoon to attend an immersive exploration of the cultural and dramatic consequences of economic catastrophe in those countries, namely Portugal, Ireland, Italy, Greece and Spain, that have identified themselves as PIIGS. Those countries most battered by the economic collapse of 2008.

It was fun and exploratory if ultimately slightly forced in its technique. But it did inspire Michel Decar to ask a brilliant question. If we lived without newspapers, in a world with no information reaching us from outside, would we as individuals have noticed that the economic crash happened at all?

Certainly in London it would be hard to notice. London's wealth has increased exponentially as the cultures it affected by the consequence of its irresponsible monetarism suffered. We built skyscrapers. We opened new coffee bars. We ate new food. We drank champagne. Outside London they suffered as a consequence of the bonuses we paid ourselves.

12th July

I led the group through an exercise that David Lan led me through when I was twenty-seven. I was working with a group of emerging writers at the Royal Court for a week and he led us through a workshop on narrative.

Lan, before he was Artistic Director at the Young Vic, was a playwright and before that he was an anthropologist working on the narrative structures of aboriginal tales. He presented to us the hypothesis that in the entire history of world dramatic literature there had only ever been one story that had constantly been told and retold in different ways.

Inspired by his approach I ask the group to think of a film or a play the story of which they know very well. Then to take a piece of paper and then to tear it into five pieces and on each of the pieces to write one event, without which the story of the play would make no sense. They share their stories with each other and try to identify shared motifs or elements and in so doing to establish a template that might describe their stories.

We come back together as a group and see if we can identify things with each other.

The template the group this morning came up with was this:

A character exists in a place and in a series of relationships with other characters.
An event ruptures the world of the characters and, in the shock of revelation, leads them to change and to change each other.
The characters engage on a journey that may or may not be a physical journey that leads them to make a decision that means that *their* world can never return to how it was before.
The main character's situation crystallizes into either challenge or fight or conflict against an obstacle.
The character or the world of the play leads to a crisis that might be described as the downfall.
The character or characters face a final conflict that leads to the establishment of a new status quo.

I have refined David Lan's model, quoting from his introduction to his version of *The Cherry Orchard*. I tell the group that the following might describe every story told in Western dramatic literature.

A character exists in a culture. Something about the culture is causing the character to suffer. Something happens to make them realize they need to do something or get something to ease the suffering. They go on a journey, which may or may not be a physical journey, in their attempt to do or to get this thing. On their journey they confront obstacles, which they either do or do not succeed in overcoming. In their success or their failure either they learn something about themselves, in which case the story might be described as tragedy in classical terminology, or the audience learns something about them, which classical terminology would describe as comedy.

This leads to the idea that there may be seven endings to a story. A character gets what they want and what they need and learns something. A character gets what they want and what they need but learns nothing. A character gets what they want but not what they need and realizes this. A character gets what they want but not what they need and fails to realize. A character doesn't get what they want but they do get what they need and realize this difference. Or they do this but don't realize. A character gets neither what they want nor what they need and realizes this or they get neither and never realize.

The value of this is not in its truth because it's not true.

It is politically charged and arguably polluted by sexual and racial and economic politics.

Its value for me is in whether it's useful or not.

The amount of times when I have tested ideas for stories against this model and learnt something about either my work or the work of students I'm working with is countless. In the simplest terms it helps make my plays better and I use it to test all my ideas for story.

I finished my workshop with a study of Caryl Churchill's *Far Away*. In particular I wanted the group to look at how she uses structure in this play to disorientate, unnerve, frighten, alarm her audience in order to clarify the political proximity of the world she dramatizes.

The exercise is quite simple.

As a group we read the play. It's a short play and easy to read in fifteen minutes.

It's also a strange play. An astonishing play that I chose as my favourite play of the first decade of the twenty-first century when asked to choose one by Foyles Bookshop. It feels prescient in the way it predicted the irrationality of the War on Terror. It is astonishing in the breadth of its persona and political imagination condensed into three brief scenes.

The play normally divides the group. It always has. I remember when it was submitted to the Royal Court in 2000 it divided the script meeting. Some leading figures in British theatre were confused by it. They were too embarrassed to admit that they didn't GET the new Caryl Churchill play.

We talk about what the play means and why she wrote it and what she was doing to the audience.

For me this is a far more interesting question than what a writer is 'saying' to an audience or, for fuck's sake, 'teaching' an audience. Our responsibility as writers is NOT to teach an audience anything or even to say anything. It is to provoke, move, astonish, upset, alarm, and disorientate them. The function of theatre is to spread uncertainty. Because to be uncertain is human. To be certain is, on some level, always dishonest.

What is incredible about *Far Away* is how in such a short play she synthesizes so many elements of the playwright's craft to achieve the goal of frightening or alarming or confusing her audience. There is an extraordinary tension between the familiarity of characters and situation (a girl stays the night at her aunty's house, a couple fall in love at the workplace, a boy meets his mother-in-law) and the terror of a world that becomes unrecognizable in which animals, professions, ages are all mobilized in a global war.

Linguistically it is simple and clear with one or two moments of ferocious poetry:

'I think the stick was metal', 'If it's a party, why was there so much blood', 'What did you imagine you could see in the dark?'

But structurally it is fascinating. Like a Feydeau farce the play's first act is in one world (Harper's home), the second in another (the hat maker's of a fascist executioner regime) and then in the third act the second world is brought back into the first (warfare comes into Harper's house).

I ask the writers to list five events that happen in the personal life of the characters that we see on stage, five events that happen in their personal lives that happen off stage, and five events in the political world of the play.

I get them to tell me what they've identified and with them I build up a timeline of the play. This invariably illustrates the range of Churchill's imagination – how completely she has imagined the lives of her characters and the political catastrophe of her world that, as one writer once suggested to me in Amsterdam, retells the book of Genesis backwards. People are mobilized, then nations, professions, ages, animals, nature, elements, light, silence.

I then ask them where they would put the play. I don't explain the question or give them help but rather enjoy as they get it wrong until someone always guesses that the play can be told with eight marks on the timeline.

One for each scene.

A long one near the beginning. A long pause. Six short ones. A long pause. A long scene.

In this sense the play is revealed as being symmetrical. It is revealed as being dominated by absence as much as presence. And as having a centre that is blown to pieces. Atomized.

I sometimes play out the sound for the group to hear. One beat. Long silence. Six short beats. Long silence. A beat.

In that way the structural force of the decisions Churchill makes is revealed. She uses this symmetrical structure, defined by space and an atomized centre, to dramatize her theme.

She uses structure in a creative way to articulate idea.

And this, I suggest to the writers, is what structure is for. We don't need to read about structure in books. We don't need to understand the academic principles of structure. Structure involves simple considerations.

Having marshalled material into narrative we just need to ask ourselves: How many scenes are we going to divide the play up into? When will they start? When will they end? Where will they be set?

That's structure.

And if we can be playful and imaginative and musical rather than academic. If we can invent structures that best do what we want our plays to do, rather than simply fall into the structure that tells our story with clarity, then we'll just make better plays.

15th July

Back in London. Back in the office. Back on *The Funfair*. I'm rather enjoying myself. Making it a dirty exploration of a mythical Manchester. Basically basing it on The Smiths' celebration of the sex and violence of fairgrounds, *Rusholme Ruffians*. I've only just really realized that. But it's true.

16th July

More *Funfair*.

A cycle into town to be interviewed by Claudia Winkleman about *The Curious Incident of the Dog in the Night-Time*. It's odd the way interviewers invite us to repeat ourselves over and over. She was very lovely though. An enthusiasm that startled even me.

And then to the dentist to have hardcore shit scraped off my teeth.

17th July

A fucking ace meeting with Ben Power at the National this morning to talk mainly about *Threepenny Opera*. I'm not sure that rendering the play into something contemporary would work.

The song structure and the dramaturgy demand some beats that are just not based on any recognizable reality at all. And our audience will be so literate in the demanding verisimilitude of contemporary police precinct drama that to fudge it would be exposing.

But we came up with a plan to make a leaner, more dramatically cogent draft for now – leaving aside the issues of how contemporary it is or not.

Cycled in extraordinary sunshine to the Royal Court to see a double bill of plays by women presented by the RSC. Timberlake Wertenbaker's *The Ant and the Cicada* had moments of astonishing poetry and political insight.

It was counterpointed by Alice Birch's *Revolt. She said. Revolt again*. This was an utterly different experience. Wry and anarchic and funny and angry – built on listening. Built on doubt. A rough diamond of a play but something incredible about it. The penultimate scene was built around a beautifully made cacophony.

The counterpoint of the two plays was amazing. Like it existed on a hinge of the past of British theatre and its future.

Met Chris Thorpe there and sitting in the yard of the Royal Court he read me scenes from his new play.

A nightmare of incremental apocalypse, it is a shattering thing.

A dream. A nightmare. A thing of rare power.

25th July

In New York for the rehearsals of *The Curious Incident of the Dog in the Night-Time*. It opens at the beautiful Barrymore Theatre on Broadway in October.

I came out before rehearsals start properly on Monday in order to be there for the press launch. This was a bewildering occasion. We had to have our faces powdered for the camera and arrive 'hair ready'. It was a very strange way to meet the key cast members.

We did a series of odd and posed photos and then went round on a cycle of ten screen interviews for local websites and TV. The same questions being asked again and again.

I talked about how the play started. With Mark Haddon calling me out of the blue to ask me to have a crack at the adaptation. I talked about Marianne and how much I value her and her sense of imagination and of democracy. Her love of an audience carved out of her time at Granada TV. I talked about Christopher's bravery. For me this is a play about family not about illness. I think this is why the detective story model works.

Families are defined by secrets: the secrets parents keep from children and from each other and those children keep from parents. If the novel is a detective story about difference, I think the play is a detective story about families.

I think this is why it's also built around the outsider to the family – Siobhan, Christopher's teacher. She can see things the family can't. She sees things in Christopher the family doesn't. They see things in him through their relationship with her.

We all keep secrets from one another, in families, and all hanker to find out truths.

It felt like being in a weird circus. The pressure of the machine of
Broadway is an odd phenomenon. The struggle will be to hold on to
the initial joy and love in and for the book that we all worked from. Not
to be distracted by the people with money. Not to be worried by failure
but to revel in the love of exploration.

If we can do that and ignore the big machine of Broadway with its
puppyish eyes and gleeful enthusiasm, then I think that will be
infectious.

It might not. Who knows? We might close within a week. But fuck it,
we can have fun trying.

And learn something about our work and us.

It was fascinating watching Marianne direct and fascinating talking
about the play round a table.

Marianne directs with a sense of naughtiness.

She asks questions, which are clear and precise and encouraging, but
there is always a glimmer in her eye like she is doing something she's
not meant to be doing and that is utterly infectious. All theatre should
be carved from that sense of fun. Our role culturally is to misbehave
because misbehaviour throws assumptions into doubt and that, I
think, is the function of art. To make certainties uncertain by speaking
the unspeakable. That has to be done with an energy of misbehaviour.

It's fascinating watching her get the actors to exactly where she wants
them to go. Especially because she's re-creating a machine that works
so she knows completely how she will make and block the thing but
she allows the actors to find the psychological energy they need to
feel like they're discovering it for themselves.

It is the beautiful illusion of a democracy.

She gave the actors homework to do. She asked Enid Graham, the
actress playing Judy, to list all of the things that made her a bad

mother and to identify one thing of Christopher's she would take with her when she left.

It was revealing to realize the poisonous way in which Judy's sense of shame has rendered contacting Christopher impossible. Shame is a corrupting engine of behaviour. It ruins things. It also revealed just how normal a parent Judy is. Judy and Ed both parent like all of us parents do, with that mixture of awe, shame, failure, and frustration and joy.

It struck me in rehearsals that the key to the play is when people see dogs in the way that Christopher sees dogs. It is easy to forget that what drives Christopher to London is not his dad's betrayal or deceit about the mythical death of his mother but the fact that he thinks his dad could actually kill him because he killed Wellington. Most audiences assimilate the killing of Wellington as being an understandable action. Bad. But not heinous. And in the circumstances regrettable but human. A little crime.

But Christopher interprets it as an action that makes his dad a dangerous killer. He is really afraid that he will kill him. And when Judy understands that she becomes a better mother. And his father's apology at the end of the play is not about the letters but the promise that he would never do anything to hurt Christopher.

It's fascinating watching a play that I've seen staged so many times in this production being interpreted from the point of view of actors in rehearsal. They don't need to think about the bigger picture. It doesn't help them or the work as a whole to consider the entire production. Or the effect on the audience. That's not their job. It's Marianne's job. Their job is to pursue the truth of their behaviour on stage, in this case in their characters.

It's fascinating to watch emotionally articulate American actors wrestle with the emotional inarticulacy of their British characters. Ed finds it extremely hard to tell Christopher he's proud of him. Ian Barford, the actor playing him, spoke about how often he tells his kids he loves them. I'm the same. But watching him contain his emotions is extraordinary.

Bravery is what moves audiences. Not emotion.

I wonder if emotional guardedness is a characteristic of the working class. In the way that the Estonians inherit a cultural guardedness from their history of brutal repression. The working classes toughen up to show the fuckers that they've not got them down. They're not broken. And this makes emotional articulacy dangerous.

28th July

The first day of proper rehearsals in the expansive double rehearsal room on 42nd Street.

There were maybe fifty people gathered to hear an introduction to the play before rehearsals started. I spoke briefly to them.

I told them a story Mark Haddon told me about the first time Christopher Boone appeared in his imagination. Sos, Mark's wife, heard him typing in his room. She observed how, as he wrote, he started cackling to himself. Sos asked him two questions. Firstly, she asked him if real writers laughed at their own jokes. Secondly, she asked him what he was writing. Whatever it was, she said, he should keep writing it. It was *The Curious Incident of the Dog in the Night-Time*. Mark was laughing at the idea of somebody finding a dead dog in a garden with a garden fork sticking out of its side and wondering what would happen next. That image, and the dark comedy in that image, was the starting point of the novel.

What would happen if . . .? This is a remarkably potent question in the root of how stories are created.

We did some name games and then read the play.

There are still corners that need tightening. But not so many.

The cast read with a real sense of life. Alex Sharp, the Juilliard graduate playing Christopher, was astonishing in his frankness and his intelligence but it was an intelligence shared by the whole cast.

It strikes me that the story of Christopher finding the capacity to be brave in the face of impossible circumstances is one that resonates deeply in the US. Perhaps to an extent that is sentimental. In the metabolism of the country, perhaps, there is recognition of this narrative form that leads them to reject all others. When a story does what it is meant to do, it makes the people here feel heroic.

Perhaps this is a country born of the mythology of the capacity of the individual to be brave. This might lend itself to sentimentality and needs to be watched.

Especially if it allows characters to come out of focus. At the end of the read through, the whole room applauded.

There was something both saccharine and inspiring about this.

Heroism here in this sentimental country.

29th July

Spent the morning at The Standard Hotel in the East Village scraping through the last few pages of *Kasimir and Karoline*. Trying to keep an eye on the silences. Trying to keep it real, trying to keep it active. Trying to re-engage with the idea of it being an excavation of the notions of the future in a world rid of hope.

Some little changes. Tightening corners. Making everything seem smooth. And nothing wasted.

And then into *The Curious Incident of the Dog in the Night-Time* rehearsals.

The company spent most of the morning working with Scott Graham and Steven Hoggett of Frantic Assembly, the movement directors on the piece. They were trying to communicate with the important freshness of discovery that which they unarguably know works.

Went to the rehearsal room to hear the response of the 'homework' Marianne had set. She gives each member of the cast something to research. So one looked into old cars, one into rats, one into A levels or Swindon or Swindon Station or Paddington Station. I think this background knowledge gives the company a sense of ownership over the world.

It was fascinating to hear perceptions of the small towns of the UK from the perspective of New York City. Their relationships to the places are less sentimental. They had a keen understanding of the psycho-political geography of Swindon.

I kept having to stop myself from intervening. The point should not be for me to demonstrate how clever I am but for the actors to move forward.

Marianne measures a rehearsal room with real poise between the thought and the body and the word.

She did an exercise based on actions. Trying to encourage the cast to get into ways of thinking built on the transitive verb.

I joined in. I learnt a few things. People have transitive verbs they default to. These are often manifestation of their status. The assistant director, the mighty Katy Rudd, for example, found it difficult to improvise around high-status verbs. Also the verbs that worked best were based around shifts in status. Status transactions. Some verbs that were predicated on equal status interactions (to welcome, to tickle) worked less well than verbs where there was a shift in hierarchy (to seduce, to terrorize)

The transitive verb has been central to my thinking about drama for fifteen years. It isn't what the characters say or feel that counts but what they do. There is no finer measure of behaviour than the transitive verb.

Working with Marianne is like working with my big sister. My instinct to annoy her is rich and born entirely out of love.

6th August

A huge gap in my diary caused by my computer breaking down in Manhattan.

I had a fraught moment with Marianne on the third day of rehearsals. I expressed to her my concern that Alex, as Christopher, was smiling too much and was showing himself too keen to contact others. This, to me, feels like a sentimental betrayal of Christopher's condition and I told her and she was furious.

She was mainly furious about my timing of the intervention. She was very nervous about starting to really direct the actors. And she needs to be able to make mistakes and to follow instincts. There are so many people watching her in the room and so many people breathing down her neck in this city that the idea that I should add to this collective breath and pressure with my clumsy insistences exasperated her.

She was right.

I should have stepped back.

I do think Alex, at the moment, is being too sentimental. But it is imperative that actors make mistakes. It is fundamental.

I went to see Evan Cabnet's production of Theresa Rebeck's *Poor Behavior*. It was tight and well made. A play spitting with anger and straining against the conventions of comedy. We talked about this idea. Evan said something that James Macdonald had told him. The key to rehearsals is allowing actors to get it wrong for as long as possible.

I fucked up by the clumsy way I intervened and Marianne was right to be furious with me.

I apologized. We made friends.

Evan said that it's hard for directors to allow and encourage actors to fail in New York. Even though it is through failure that we learn most.

I suspect he's right.

This is a city in dire straits creatively, it strikes me. It is running on the fumes of earlier generations. Sam Shepard and Patti Smith and the Ramones and John Cage and Merce Cunningham and Bob Dylan. Their last breaths are the fumes the city inhales.

But it is corrupted.

There is no scope for failure. There is no space for risk. The greatest creative figures in the city are producers who are only interested, finally, in making money. They might have seen every play here for thirty years but their endgame is only ever financial.

Audiences are ancient. Decrepit. And two critics hold a paralysing grip on the place.

Subscription kills the audience so that it is only happy when it sees what it expects to see.

Artistic Directors are in their posts for too long. They kowtow to their subscribers and write letters of apology when they offend them.

So writers like Rebeck write into received forms. And when the forms are as defined as they are, then NOTHING dramatic can ever happen on stages here.

The big breathing corpse of Broadway lurks behind our every movement and even the best artists here know that if they fuck up too much they'll be shat out or spat out or both.

Theatre artists in the US should move to Detroit. Surprising things might happen there. Nothing creative will happen in New York until its economy collapses. The depressing thing is that soon, the same will be said of London.

That people like Annie Baker and Mark Schultz and Chris Shinn continue to try inspires me.

I made various notes for Marianne regarding various things.

Reminders about the presence of Ed having killed Wellington throughout.

And also to allow Ed to enjoy his capacity to take the piss out of Christopher when Christopher doesn't even notice.

Interestingly, the energy caused by Alex having to concentrate on building the train track making it difficult to engage with Siobhan is a useful energy for Christopher. All human interaction is an irritation for him.

I wanted Reverend Peters to have a greater ontological understanding – and not just be a buffoon.

I wondered who had told Christopher that his mum was in heaven. And whether Ed told the school that she was dead.

All these little notes and more were born out of returning to the play again after time away.

It struck me in rehearsals at one point as I watched a group of stage managers and actors try to build a train track that it is an odd thing to have a tribe of primates working hard to perfect the construction of, for example, a model train track, a central image in *The Curious Incident of the Dog in the Night-Time*, in order to help us tell stories about each other. We work hard on these things, not for protection or for food or for mating (at least not directly, indirectly it is for all these reasons), but to help to tell a story better.

We had a long chat about how the word metaphor IS a metaphor. All words are metaphors. Because they are shapes on a page or sounds that denote ideas. But the word metaphor means carrying something from one place to another but we don't pick things up and carry them in order to communicate meanings in metaphors.

We are, I wrote in my notebook at this point, the metaphorical animal.

I drank a lot with my brilliant New York friends.

Came back home.

This week and for the next few weeks I'm mainly looking after the kids.

But I did scrape away on re-writes of *Song from Far Away* and *The Cherry Orchard*.

The latter seems very wordy to me. I am nervous it is too late to trim.

And this morning had an Associates meeting at the Lyric. How do we sustain the spirit of the Secret Theatre Company after the year has finished and the theatre re-opened? We became excited by the idea of reconvening every autumn to make more work with different directors and in different ways.

Sean toyed with the idea of doing *Herons*. This would make me very proud.

I first met him at the Royal Court bar after he'd seen it.

That was fourteen years ago. I'd heard of him by reputation at the University of York because he was making the best theatre on campus and all the girls fancied him. But I'd never met him. He seemed stunned by the play. It was the start of a significant friendship.

7th August

Met with Mark Eitzel who is in London for August. We met for coffee in Shoreditch and then walked over to my office. I read him the latest draft of *Song from Far Away*. We scratched away more at it. Paring it right to the bone. Trying to release a layer. Trying to release the tragedy. Make the dad more complicated. Make the play less wordy. Make it less like a tourist guide to Amsterdam.

The spaces we carved out for songs seem right.

The melody he has written is astonishing. It is huge and wide and open.

He needs to get the lyrics right. So that they don't release a sentimental inner world. They need to juxtapose with the text. We think he had some breakthroughs. He needs to write a Broadway show tune about New York that nobody realizes until the end of the play is actually an annihilation of the protagonist's heart.

We went to see Jennifer Haley's *The Nether* at the Royal Court together. I liked it more than him. Watching Amanda Hale and Stanley Townsend go toe to toe was a real joy. A strange dystopia play about the release of the internet. A safe place for paedophiles to play. Or a place that defines their crimes as normalized.

It had a conventional dramaturgical structure that sat at odds with its searching subject matter.

I wonder if I'll write the play I've been toying with writing about porn. I could call it *Jihad* or *The War on Terror*, just as *Pornography* is about suicide bombing.

28th August

On the flight from Heathrow to JFK for the last days of rehearsal of *The Curious Incident of the Dog in the Night-Time*.
It is 2.23 UK time and 9.23 am NYC time.
I'm drunk.
Flights have a drinking time zone all of their own.
So I've had two glasses of Chardonnay and two glasses of sherry and two large gin and tonics and holy actual fuck what did the AA crew think they were going to do to me?

Yesterday was the first day of rehearsals for *The Cherry Orchard*.

In the last week of my holidays Katie Mitchell sent me a series of emails detailing thoughts that she had on my draft. While it was irritating to get the notes while I was on holiday, her thoughts were clear and strong.

Her thoughts shared a few impulses. To be as economic as we dare. To be as clear as we can. To be as rigorous as we can. To be as cogent as we can.

Sometimes I worry that I value the inchoate more than she does. Or that my sense of humour is cruder than hers. I wonder if I value contradiction more than she does. Or that I enjoy the actual fact of actors being in a theatre more than she does. I enjoy the presence of audiences. The truth of the fact of what is going on in the room.

She has a commitment to what she describes as a 'stable text'. Unlike a lot of directors I've worked with, she resists re-writing in the rehearsal room or throughout preview. Not altogether and not completely but her commitment to getting a disciplined and finished text before rehearsal starts manifests itself in the rigour of her reading and the rigour of her notes prior to this.

This play is important to her. She has directed three major productions of Chekhov in her career but never *The Cherry Orchard*. She describes it as the masterpiece of naturalism and it is hard to disagree with her. It is a shattering play. Sometimes I found working on it dispiriting because I knew I would never write anything so daring.

We met at the Jerwood Space for the first day of rehearsals on the day after my return from holidays and it was joyful to work with Katie again. 'Joyful' is a very Mitchell word. She is one of those people whose vocabulary it is easy to assimilate. It is so striking that is sinks into you.

We read the play together. Everybody in the room taking a line and reading the whole play. It was fine. It was clear and cogent. I was struck by the idea that Chekhov writes often of his characters talking through tears. What I think he means is that they're trying not to cry. The comedy in the play works in the same way. Audiences should be trying not to laugh.

The essence of comedy that Chekhov defined is that the characters are not aware of the horror of their lives. Katie told me she had no interest in the audience. Ever. Though when she directed *Wastwater* I've never seen a director watch the audience more rigorously in preview.

How, then, she will direct a comedy, the essence of which is dependent on that tension between character and an audience, is interesting.

We read through a lengthy and detailed breakdown of the past of the characters that she'd established. Her need for certainty and cogency makes sense. But sometimes there are spaces and gaps in the backstory of a play that are necessary because a writer has been negligent or has obfuscated or has been inconsistent, and that is part of our job because capturing humanity and the odd incoherent miraculous errors that our species makes is our job and sometimes demands the ignorance of academic rigour. But it does make it difficult to act.

She has an attuned radar for noticing when actors are imagining different worlds to one another and finds those differences exasperating.

She demands that her writers imagine the same worlds when they perform. She demands that they imagine the same backstory.

She asks the actors to excavate key themes from the play. For *The Cherry Orchard* she chose money, death and the sense of powerlessness one feels in the shifting sands of a world outside our control. She might have chosen unrequited love or the naïveté or dignity of optimism. Her choice of themes will manifest itself deeply in the tone and timbre of her production. She'll ask the actors to imagine moments from their lives that crystallized these themes and over the course of the week stage improvisations that dramatize these moments.

In these improvisations the actors can find a shared vocabulary of reference points to draw from as they rehearse and experience the emotional impact of the moments in the play.

I won't see these improvisations because I'm heading back to New York for the final runs of *The Curious Incident of the Dog in the Night-Time* in the rehearsal room.

Read *The Funfair*, my version of von Horváth's *Kasimir and Karoline* on the way into town. It was largely fine and visceral and clear but a bit sweary.

29th August

Met Bart Van den Eynde at my hotel to talk about *Song from Far Away*. He will work as Ivo's dramaturge on the production. His notes were searching and supportive.

He still doesn't think I've cracked the dad yet.

We go again.

Mark has written the most beautiful song for it. He had the idea that the song should be written from the point of view of Pauli, the main character's brother.

A song written to save his elder brother's life that he never sings to him but which somehow he hears in a gay bar in Amsterdam.

Saw a run of *The Curious Incident of the Dog in the Night-Time*. The cast were calm and clear and they revealed a sadness to the play which was inspiring.

I sent Marianne and Katy these notes:

I think it's in great nick. Beautifully honed and measured. Very funny and very moving.

It's very transitive and active and that is all I ever really look for. It means the world.

You are, both of you, extraordinary and I'm very grateful.

I have a smattering of observations or thoughts and one or two linguistic thoughts.

Ignore at will.

These are all about washes or touches or graces of things. Don't misinterpret them as being radical rethinks and I am as likely to be massively wrong as I am likely to be remotely perceptive.

They tend to be covered by the headings 'enjoy how fucking funny Christopher is because he can't tell and the audience breathes in your enjoyment' and 'allow him to tickle you with his funny, wonderful mind because when you do it's infectious and lets us in'.

I am slightly aware that piss-taking as a means of communicating love might be a very English habit but I think it's a useful way to release tiny elements of love in the play.

I said at lunch that the tone of Mrs Shears discovering Wellington is better than I've ever seen it. It really feels like a woman is honestly discovering her dead dog.

One of the consequences of this is that there is a very dark tone established early. Which I like. But I also wonder if it means that there could be more work done to discover some humour or lightness to act in counterpoint to this.

I think this was my main thought today and I found myself listing several areas where this could be done.

I think Frankie's enjoyment of Christopher is truthful and brilliant and as good as I've seen it and I urge her to continue. She lets us into the story of a boy with a remarkable mind and this, after that dark opening, is an urgent thing. She's stunning.

I wonder though if others might share it.

Is the Duty Sergeant perhaps as tickled by Christopher's behaviour as he is pissed off with him? Compared to the usual scrotes he deals with, Christopher might be quite funny?

I'm talking a tiny wash not a big change.

I think this is a general thing for Ian. He can enjoy taking the piss out of Christopher more. Partly because it relieves the exhaustion of dealing with his son and partly because taking the piss out of his son (with his lines like 'terrific', 'could you?') is a way of communicating his love for him.

It strikes me that this capacity to communicate love through mockery is a very English trope. Perhaps the biggest difference between English and American behaviour. The American people have a beautiful directness which infects their instincts when acting.

I think even Reverend Peters can enjoy C a bit more and C can enjoy, a touch more, his victory over Rev P.

Mr Thompson's 'who ARE you' can similarly be tickled.

Tickled is a recurring word in my thoughts on allowing enjoyment of Christopher into the world.

PLEASE CHANGE BISCUITS TO COOKIES.

Siobhan's 'I wouldn't' on being asked about dog killing could be more tickled.

I like the idea that Christopher uses 'looney person' to Mrs A and 'lunatic' to Shiv – because, and this was a new thought for me today, I think C can enjoy being naughty and transgressive a TOUCH more. So he chooses 'looney person' because he knows it's naughty and wouldn't do that to Shiv. It interested me how naughty Christopher sometimes is and that there might be scope for enjoying that wash of transgression.

I wonder if Ed might enjoy the battle with Mrs G over the A level and enjoy his victory and if this might charge the scene a wash more.

Ed's 'yes mate you probably would' and 'I noticed' can afford a wash of irony and affectionate piss take.

When Shiv reads 'I was really confused', it's ace when she sounds genuinely baffled not sad.

'So I went into his bedroom' can revel in his naughtiness of the transgression a touch more.

I know this is a perennial one with me but I do love when 'and that was when I started spending a lot of time with Roger' has an ironic combative edge to it. Like she is savaging Judy a touch – I know we might disagree on this and I'm happy to defer.

'Shit buddy, we're not exactly low maintenance' can have a wash of irony – sharing a self-deprecating joke to bond with his son.

I thought that after the Wellington confession Alex lost the action on both the numbers and his turning from one possible host to another – he lost the urgency of the decision 'oh fuck what am I going to do?!?!'

I'd rather the map lady with the umbrella said 'I've not got time for this' than 'ok we're done here'.

I think the Station Policeman at Swindon can have a wash of entertained baffledness about him. Again comparing him to the drunks and the junkies he might otherwise be dealing with – Christopher is quite funny and he can enjoy that a bit more.

I could cut five lines from Swindon station policeman with my eyes closed if you wanted me to.

'Thanks a bundle' is better than 'thanks a pissing bundle'.

'Get out' is better than 'beat it' from a-z woman.

It should always be a-zed not a-zee.

Please make the Mini a Mini Cooper.

Only Mike Noble has ever happily played the joke Judy: god! c: Reverend Peter IS going to invigilate. It's a shit joke but it's there somewhere. Like C confused by God as a response offers the olive tree 'yes, God might be irrelevant but to be fair to you, Mum, as it goes, Reverend Peters IS going to invigilate'.

Should the line in the nighttime packing be from Judy 'it's four o'clock IN THE MORNING' not just 'it's four o'clock'.

In Ian's last two scenes he needs to contain his emotions a touch more. Having excavated a beautiful sense of loneliness and need he can police that by making sure that his actions are always those of a parent. He can be more 'effective' Dad and less 'bruised animal'.

Yeah, he over-compensated for the A* reveal so that felt almost like he was disappointed. It should be entirely factual.

I think he tends to over-romanticize his list of ambitions for his future at the end and I always like it when he makes it as dryly functional as he can.

I loved it.

Thank you.

That's all.

Too tired to really write more.

The show is in good shape before it goes into preview.

We'll see how tech treats it but I love seeing runs in the rehearsal room. They exercise our imaginations.

Met Mark Brokaw who will direct *Heisenberg* next year.

It was a good meeting. He was searching and clear thinking. We talked about the imaginative space afforded by a rehearsal room aesthetic.

There is an honesty to it that demands the audience invest their imagination in what they're seeing and so invest themselves. It is a kind of aesthetic that I discovered working with Ramin Gray on *Motortown* and with Sean Holmes on *Pornography* and it infected a lot of my work with Sean on *Morning* and then the Secret Theatre Company. Keep the stage bare as much as possible. Make the props real as much as possible.

It also means that nothing is foreshadowed. A mimetic set mediates the audience's response to the theatre and suggests to them what the play is about to be and what might happen. The conventions of set design establish expectation. Removing set design removes this expectation. So that the story is revealed absolutely in the present tense.

Back to rehearsal.

Marianne worked notes with clarity and force.

I'm exhausted. Never recovered from the amount of booze I drank on the flight. I must remember that complementary alcohol is not necessarily compulsory alcohol.

And in The Standard this time round there is a door adjoining my room to my neighbouring room which means I hear every word my neighbours are saying. So I work too hard and don't sleep.

Fucked really.

1st September

Back in London. I met Michael Longhurst this morning. He is a director whose work I have enjoyed immensely over recent years. His production of Nick Payne's *Constellations* was particularly beautiful.

I found out over the last month that the Almeida will stage *Carmen Disruption* and that he will direct it. I'm as thrilled as I am surprised.

We talked about the detail of British acting. How great British actors bring a sense of conviction and truth that sometimes German actors lack and how the smaller more intimate space of the Almeida can release this detail beautifully.

He talked too though about how the choric form and the music and the possibility of movement might bring a unity to the performers, so that this play about the search for love in a time of dislocation is graced by the possibility of experiences being shared, however atomized the lives on stage are.

The speed of going from meeting him to the marketing department of the theatre where we talked about copy and looked at images was remarkable.

This is a production that is happening and is happening soon.

Walked back to my office.

On the way I bumped into Ben Wallers. Ben was the singer with *The Country Teasers*, the band I was in for ten years. I've not seen him for maybe six years. It was beautiful seeing him. Like an odd gift of coincidence. If I hadn't delayed my departure from the Almeida to go to the toilet I wouldn't have seen him. If I hadn't walked instead of going on my bicycle I wouldn't have seen him.

It took my breath away. He greeted me with the beautiful exclamation, 'I KNEW this would happen one day!'

He looks older. I do too. This is because we're ageing. Our bodies ageing at a different speed to our sense of self. Or at least at a more concrete, identifiable speed.

Finished the first draft of *The Funfair* and delivered it. Horváth's play is a beautiful bruised cry for love from a culture on the cusp of the catastrophe of racism born out of poverty. At a time when UKIP gain power in the UK, when nationalism is spreading throughout Europe, the play seems timely somehow.

I edited out the swearing. Tried to clarify the storytelling.

I like swearing in life and in plays. I think swearing dignifies us. It cuts to the quick of the urgency of a human situation.

But in first drafts of my plays sometimes I swear too much. This is because I'm pushing myself into a heightened extreme energy in order to construct and enter into the vitality of the play.

The swearing becomes a kind of scaffold. I need it in order to make the thing live. I then need to take it away in order to let it live by itself.

2nd September

Moorfields in the morning. They tested my eyes and the vision in my left eye is stable, so they decided to take me off injections for a while. They'll keep checking me but I don't need to be injected for at least two months.

I left euphoric.

Spent the afternoon implementing Bart's notes on *Song from Far Away*.

They're good notes. Forcing me to reach deeper into the characters and the world. Forcing me to articulate more fully but through more simple imagery.

I tried my best.

In the evening I went to the Young Vic to see Benedict Andrews's *A Streetcar Named Desire*. Andrews is a house director at Berlin's Schaubühne and the production combined the classical form of the Schaubuhne's work with a slightly punk spirit.

It was beautifully framed.

Every image looked beautiful. The soundtrack had Swans in it, which can only be good.

But I missed the roughness and real danger of Sean's production.

3rd Septembr

Back to *The Cherry Orchard* rehearsals. Katie working through the events of the Fourth Act with head-teacherly rigour. The cast are engaged and excited by her incision. The first thing she said to me when I walked in the room was, very sweetly, to ask me not really to say anything.

She is marshalling the company through their intentions and events and she wants to take them in the direction she wants to go.

I don't mind in any way. This is her production. It's her work. I am just there to help get the words right.

There is a gap between the kind of chaotic instinct necessary in order to write something and the precision and rigour of her reading that can sometimes lead to the inaccuracies and errors in my work being exposed. Sometimes I chose the wrong word or wrong phrase because I like the rhythm. I like the dance in the mouth of the word 'transcontinental' when Yasha talks about the express train but it is an invention and Katie spots it and decides it is wrong and she's right to do so.

It made me feel foolish. But I got over my anxieties and worked with her to make the draft as clean but as precise as we can.

As often as not this involved removing adverbs.

The amount of time she spends thoroughly excavating every detail of the off-stage world so that it is shared and agreed upon is fascinating. Since working with Ramin Gray on *Motortown* the value of this work has been thrown into the air for me.

What interests me are the things that people do to each other. How much of a shared imagining of an offstage world they need to do this, I'm not sure of. But the cast seems engaged and motivated.

Then back to *Song from Far Away*.

Back to those notes.

Back to trying to reach as far as I can.

I am quite utterly fucked.

4th September

To Belfast to see Selina Cartmell's production of *Punk Rock*. Worked on *Song from Far Away* on the flight.

Was met at the airport by a charming man, Philip Crawford, the head of creative learning at the Lyric.

My visit to Belfast was important to me. This was the town my grandmother, Granma as we call her, now ninety-three years old, was born. This was the town my mum was born in.

Philip gave me a small tour of the city. To the docks to see where the Titanic was built. And then up the Shankill Road, bewilderingly smattered with Union Flags and murals of the Queen and down the Falls, bewilderingly smattered with republican flags and murals of IRA folklore heroes.

The two roads run adjacent to one another. Right next to each other.

The iconography is familiar from my childhood. Growing up in the eighties the echoes of IRA bombs were heard in Stockport. It was especially odd knowing that my family was from here to know it was a place of terrorism.

But the centre of the terrorist activity is small. The pubs where killings were planned are tiny and overt. The head of Sinn Féin. The Shankill Road Orange Order. That such a small area sits in the middle of an otherwise quiet and actually apparently affluent city was just odd. That quiet affluence abutting the most iconic terrorist hotbed of Britain's twentieth century.

Philip dropped me off outside 25 Rathcool Street where, ninety-three years ago, my Granma was born into what would become a family of seven girls. A tiny terraced house. I walked through the city, over the River Lagan to 125 Sunnyside Street where my mum was born. A slightly bigger house with a garden but still an odd place in which to imagine my mother's birth or a family of seven girls living.

And then to the theatre. A confident modern reimagining of a theatre space looking out over the river. The building was rightly nominated for architectural awards. I had a Greek salad and ran a workshop.

I did my usual stuff about dramatic action with a mixed group in terms of age of fundamentally emerging writers. It went well. We looked at dramatic action. Talked about humanity. Listened to Sonic Youth. They were alert and grateful and it was good.

I worked for three and half hours with them.

One day I am going to invent a different workshop from that one. But for now it seems to work. And it requires no planning.

I am such a lazy fucker.

Dinner with Jimmy Fay, the new Artistic Director. He is a funny, confident Dublin man. He and Sean remind me of each other. They often direct the same plays. They have the same earthiness and the same confidence. A confidence which sometimes masks a vulnerability.

We talked about the difficulties of running a theatre in a fundamentally conservative city. And of our experiences with Edward Bond.

Punk Rock has had great reviews and small audiences.

It was a terrific production.

Occasionally one of the actors would revel in his own lines to a ludicrous degree. Taking huge pauses. Killing the thing. But mostly they listened, picked up the cues, played the action.

There was a frenetic physical energy to the thing that crystallized in Frantic Assembly-style scene changes. These were high punk and high octane and I loved them.

Selina had William deliver the final speech to the audience. Removing the actor and imagining the audience to be Dr Harvey. This works beautifully. The house lights up.

We become culpable. It's an arresting moment.

The cast was young and buzzy.

Graham Whybrow, the former Literary Manager at the Royal Court and one of the most defining influences on my thinking about theatre, came up from Dublin where he is now working. It was fucking great to see him.

We failed to find somewhere to have a late drink and so went home.

5th September

Long sleep. Midday return flight.

Back to the office.

I finished the rewrites on *Song from Far Away* and sent them in.

I think they work.

Had a bit of a battle with Mark Eitzel over email when I suggested that the song might be sung a cappella. This appalled him. He got edgy and suspicious that it was an idea from somebody else.

I was just struggling with how we can get Willem to the piano.

Mark's defensive because he's anxious because he is so deeply outside his comfort zone.

He is going to spend a week working with Eelco Smits, the actor playing Willem, in New York, to teach him the song.

There, I hope, he can learn to trust these people a bit.

8th September

Back in *The Cherry Orchard*.

I thought I would try to share some of my impressions on working with Katie Mitchell.

She emailed me over the weekend asking me to look at a particular phrase of Lopakhin's in the middle of Act One as he tells Lyubov of his plans for the destruction of the cherry orchard. In my version he started his speech:

'I've got some good news. I think you'll be delighted.'

She wanted it to be a gentler introduction to the speech. As though Alexander had not intended to tell his plan until that very moment. I finally had the line 'I wish I could say something to make all this easier'. As though his speech is a response to his desire, not the real intended purpose of his visit.

That kind of calibration and re-calibration and angling and re-angling is the essence of my work on the piece. The precision of Katie's thinking forces me to return to my text again and again.

She texted me when I was on my way to tell me the day was going to be really boring because she was going to be working on intentions all day. She presented it as a caution that I would have a boring day. But underneath it was an anxiety about my presence.

This is rational and fine. I think, of all the directors I've worked with, Katie is the most anxious about having writers in the room.

This is because she leads the rehearsal room with more determination than any other director I've worked with. Or at least she's the most unapologetic about it.

She has a very clear vision of what her production will be. She doesn't want that being distracted by the meanderings of a self-concerned writer.

Over recent years I've become more and more sympathetic to this idea. I've enjoyed, since The Curious Incident of the Dog in the

Night-Time, thinking of my presence in the rehearsal room being like that of the sound or lighting designer. I'm the language designer.

I go in to focus and refocus language in the way they might go into focus their thinking about lighting or sound.

I reassured Katie of that and was allowed to stay for the day.

So I sat with lips buttoned as she worked though four or five pages of the play over the course of the day working out the intentions for all of the actors' characters that fill up the time in between events.

It's worth trying to define some terms here. I've got this wrong before and will get it wrong again.

So Katie gave each act of the play a heading. Like a chapter heading or the type of heading Brecht gave his scenes, describing the central action of each act. The family and household welcome back the estate owner in a time of crisis to the house where her son died, for example.

And the choice of these titles defines areas she is interested in nudging the play towards.

As she said herself, the artifact of this play is a hundred and ten years old. For a hundred and ten years it has been played and replayed, read and re-read in cultures and countries throughout the world. There is no point trying to establish a definite version in any form other than the text actually written in Russian by Chekhov. But plays aren't intended to be read. They are gestures that are intended to trigger an evening in the theatre.

And as soon as that is agreed upon, then we enter into the area of version and interpretation. Of course, even before that is agreed upon because the very gesture of reading is interpretive. Nobody has a real understanding of what Chekhov was trying to suggest. Even *he* would never have done that because writers don't. Our work is too instinctive or intuitive to allow us that luxury.

Once the process of making an evening of theatre has started, then all notions of received or established or proper or conventional productions should be abandoned. Because they don't work like that. Every decision made by every collaborator in the creation of a night in the theatre is a product of that collaborator's cultural moment and intentionally or unintentionally corrupted and defined by it.

This is what the making of theatre necessarily involves.

Katie has landed on the house in *The Cherry Orchard* being a house of grief. The defining event for her is the death of Lyubov's son, Grisha. This is a grief that the family can't shake. The play sits poised between their grief and the arrival of revolution.

This reading of the play manifests itself in the titles she gives each act.

She then divides the acts up into events. I still find it very hard to define exactly what an event is. But I think it is when something happens that changes the thinking or immediate intentions of the characters. This can be something one of them says or it can be something leaving or entering a room. Or it can be something somebody does.

The first week's rehearsal is often spent defining the events as well as building improvisations round what she has decided are the key themes in the play.

Her interpretation of the role of optimism in the play defines the key themes. So everything is slanted into her reading. This is entirely as it should be.

The second or third week is spent working through the events deciding what the characters' intentions are.

Each actor has to suggest their intentions of what they're playing between the events. Katie acts as a kind of chair. She refines and will actively recalibrate these intentions, sometimes forcibly so. She knows absolutely what she thinks the characters' intentions are and while she will listen to actors, she has very little interest in creating any illusion of democracy. Often actors are praised if their suggestions accord with hers and corrected if they don't.

She sits round the table with her actors to do this. It feels like a university seminar. But a very intense one.

Each actor has responsibility for his or her own intentions.

Katie, like a symphony conductor, has responsibility for measuring all of their intentions.

It is a remarkable feat of intellect.

Sometimes it seems arid to me. Sometimes it seems to lack the play and spirit of naughtiness that I love in Marianne's room or the provocation of chaos that I love in Sebastian's room. After a day fundamentally calibrating the intentions on four pages of text, I left exhausted. My brain befuddled. I was happy I'd done a few useful re-writes but the work battered me.

It didn't, though, batter the actors. Katie casts carefully and often returns to work with familiar actors because she knows they trust her process and don't undermine or distract her. I was astonished by the company's intellectual energy.

They tussled with her. They took her corrections. They loved this astonishing depth of interrogation.

And it is astonishing.

The actors are left in no uncertainty as to what they are doing at any point in the play. Everything has been thoroughly interrogated.

It perhaps means that after such a rigorous process it becomes harder to discover new things about the scenes through the action of playing them.

Instead the actors are encouraged to use the intentions as a sort of road map. They have to return to what they have agreed on.

Perhaps the play comes as actors find ways they can explore the landing of their intentions. And perhaps in another director's work such exploration can lead productions to be off kilter.

What this process definitely empowers an actor with is a sense of being in the same room as each other. Their offstage pictures are as close as possible to one another. Their memories are shared and agreed upon.

They know what the other actors are thinking.

Today the actors seemed to love it.

Katie spoke to the company about cues and the audience, or the fourth wall.

She told them that they will be cued onto the stage from about four feet off stage so that by the time they cross the threshold of the stage, they are already playing their intention fully. She hates the indiscipline of actors getting into character on the edge of the stage and won't abide it.

She also asks the actors to pay no attention to the audience. The audience can distract actors from their intention as they try to please or flatter or entertain or frighten or move them. She thinks this work to be irrelevant.

Actually I think she says this. I don't think she *does* think that. Rather, I think she thinks this as being *her* responsibility and not something for the actors to take ownership of. So she asks them to pretend the audience isn't there. She asks them to have low audience-consciousness and warns the actors that she will correct them if she thinks they are getting too aware of the audience. They need to trust her she told them. If you don't pay heed to an audience, then all you can pay heed to is the director and she needs absolute trust from them as they do this to her.

I was fascinated by how often characters' intentions in between events involved 'convincing other characters'. To convince characters they are on top of their emotions. To convince other characters they are unafraid. Perhaps this is because convincing is an easy line to play and doesn't involve much precision of thought on behalf of the actor. But I actually think it's more that because Chekhov's intellectual preoccupation was in the performative nature of being alive.

We have these personas that we play to each other in order to stay sane. Chekhov wrote about that instinct with more wisdom than anybody else.

There are moments looking at my version when I know completely that I have failed. Hundreds of writers in hundreds of cultures for a hundred and ten years have tried to articulate what Chekhov is trying to say with some kind of clarity. Some of them concern themselves with accurately translating the Russian. I was less concerned with that. I was just fascinated by trying to capture the energy of behaviour that he wrote about and dramatized more beautifully than most other writers. This involved moving away from the clunk of 'translatorese' and finding a language that sat happily in the actors' mouths. Specifically English actors' mouths.

There are moments looking at my version when I am appalled by how wildly I have failed.

Sometimes when the actors get on their feet, I realize I might have nearly got it right. Mostly I've got it wrong.

Good! Failure!

9th September

Went to the Gielgud Theatre and did a public Q&A with Mark Haddon. They didn't get a moderator so we interviewed each other. It brought out my inner Michael Parkinson. It was hard thinking of a question for Mark about *The Curious Incident of the Dog in the Night-Time* that he's never been asked.

We set it as a challenge to the audience to think of a question he's not been asked in the twelve years since the book's publication.

One of the audience succeeded. She asked how the book would have been different if Christopher was a girl. Neither of us really knew what to say with any confidence. The extent to which autistic behaviour is masculine is fascinating. The notion that all men sit somewhere on the autistic spectrum.

Mostly we just told the jokes we'd told before but that's what you do in Q&As to an extent. I feel a metabolic need to make people laugh in them. The entertainer in me is in all British people.

It'll be posted on line.

Mark and I went to Blacks for dinner. Had a fantastic bottle of red wine and great food and talked a lot.

I like Mark deeply. We share affinities to do with age and gender and sexuality. But I kind of find myself wanting to look after him. Absurd in somebody older than me and who is frankly a fucking grown up. But it is great sometimes just to talk about process with other writers and I think maybe it's that his process, with its incumbent self-doubt and stopping and starting over and over again, makes me worry about him.

I'm more robust. I mull. I plan. I start work.

10th September

A morning flight to JFK. Suddenly the idea of having a play on Broadway caught me completely by surprise.

I decided not to drink too much on the flight. Watched most of *The Sting*. Slept through the end of it. A good three hours' sleep. Went to the hotel. Had a bath.

Andrew Scott is in New York. He texted and we met for burgers and beer and it was the first time I've seen him since *Birdland* finished.

He was an explosion of energy and light and came with me to the play.

There was a queue round the block. A thousand people came to see the play. It was tremendously strange.

And a good preview. Messy. Loose. All things that can be worked on. Some horrendous technical clangers involving something called a 'midi'. Cues were slow. The stage felt cavernous and distant but, as is often the case with previews when a show is put in front of an audience for the first time, it had a mania to it that was compelling.

The audience stood as one at the end and roared approval for the cast. They listened with attention and didn't seem alienated by the oddness of the world, the idea of Swindon, the swearing, the strange stagecraft that sits so at odds with the orthodoxies of commercial theatre . . . Anything.

They were completely behind it.

Afterwards everybody was buzzy. Stunned by the reaction. Optimistic. Marianne was slightly frenetic. Anxious. Determined. I never worry working with her because her standards are higher than everybody's and her capacity to imagine what a show might be and take it there is remarkable.

11ᵗʰ September

Had breakfast with Jonathan Berry. He directed *On the Shore* and *Punk Rock* and *Port* in fringe theatres in Chicago. He's in New York assisting on Kenneth Lonergan's *This Is Our Youth*. We enjoyed contrasting Chicago with New York. We agreed that Chicago is a theatre city while New York is a money city. The former concerned with making theatre, the latter with the infectious nature of success.

Met Marianne in a cafe across the street from the theatre to give her my thoughts on last night and chew over cuts. The waiter asked us if we were working on the show across the road. He had an infectious interest. It felt like the kind of thing that may not have happened in a West End cafe. It is in this sense, the sense that there is a part of this city built round these old playhouses, that New York reveals itself to be a theatre city.

It was fascinating watching Marianne give notes. Whereas Katie Mitchell creates an atmosphere of concentration and rigour, Marianne creates a sense of play. She hides any anxieties about the show last night, works briskly through notes, demonstrates suggestions in a way that has charming self-mockery. Allows her cast the opportunity to respond to what they have experienced.

Then into the theatre to work through changes.

I find these days a strange contradiction of the fascinating and the tedious.

Sitting in the dark, the designers perch in headphones behind banks of astonishingly futuristic-looking computer screens, working with patience and clarity and chatting about their lives. Marianne running the room. She gives notes to actors privately. So I watch her without hearing her. I might have an idea for a note only to find that Marianne is whispering the same note to the actors without me having to mention it.

So a scene is run. There is a flurry of private conversations I can't hear for what seems like ages, then the scene is run again and on nine times out of ten with Marianne it is invariably better. To the extent that it's like she's a bit psychic.

The clock always ticking. The pressure always building.

Today Marianne lost her temper with the cast. Told them that she had high standards for them and she wasn't going to let them not reach those standards. It was an extraordinarily uncharacteristic moment. You could feel the whole room crackle to attention. She has a reserve of respect and love with them. They stepped up and were better.

15th September

There is often a moment as a play works through technical rehearsals and previews when the sheer number of people employed to realize an idea I had, years before such work starts, takes me by surprise. People selling tickets, building sets, running theatre houses, drawing up contracts, learning lines. Watching stage management teams work or set builders work is humbling. The level of commitment that these people have to making my idea for a play become an actual play is astonishing. Some of them become friends, some remain strangers. Their collective work reels me a little.

Previews have been good. The queues round the block, although actually indicative of poorly planned theatre architecture, are kind of amazing to witness. Friday and Saturday audiences in New York, like in the West End or the Royal Exchange, are traditionally cooler. Midweek audiences tend to have a more engaged attitude to theatre. The weekend audiences are just coming for a big night out and they may just as well be going to see a new film or eat in a new restaurant. They're harder to reach and to impress but we got them in the end. We left them cheering Alex Sharp's Christopher like he was a rock star or a football player.

His face, excited and shy and humble is lovely to watch.

It is fascinating working with Marianne at the same time as working with Katie.

I don't think I prefer one to the other. I think they are both significant artists and I value them both as friends. But the differences in their approaches fascinate me.

Marianne works with just as much tenacity. Giving the same note five, six or seven times if it's not landing until it does. She mocks herself more openly. And creates a sense of loyalty that is palpable.

She builds her work around actions – using that as a clear marker for calibre of acting. She asks often what an actor imagines a character to be thinking at a particular moment as a means of excavating their performance in order to release something.

She employs a team, Steven Hoggett and Scott Graham as movement directors, Katy Rudd and Benjamin Klein as Associate Directors, and divides notes amongst them.

I find that my notes again and again seem to be about calibrating jokes. Partly I wonder if this is because the American sense of humour is so different to the British that the actors are struggling to find some laughs that are there. Partly I wonder if the discipline of comic acting is in some way differently valued in the US. It is steeped into the metabolism of the English actor. The tradition that stems back to Elizabethan theatre in which comedy was used as a means of softening an audience in order to land an idea is less celebrated in the great plays of the USA. Perhaps this is a more earnest country.

I spent some time, initially at the request of the producer, looking at the swearing in the play. There's actually not that much of it. Maybe nine fucks and nine shits. I looked at each line and tried to imagine the line without them and ended up removing about half of them. Often the lines with the swearing removed had a powerful directness that the swearing actually softened.

I spoke to my friend Raphael Martin who is the Literary Manager at Soho Rep about the work we were doing this morning. He was staggered that we were still working so thoroughly.

It feels right to be doing so though. It feels like it is part of a persistent search to leave the company in a position where they can grow and own the thing.

Of course all the usual problems apply, and the usual solutions. The actors work best when they listen to one another. When their actions are clear and committed. When they pick up their cues.

When they play like that and play with each other, then they create an incredible energy which is utterly infectious and which leads audiences to lean into them.

Marianne pays generous attention to the audience without softening the work. She is concerned about volume levels. About people getting access to the world and the characters of the play. About people getting the jokes and the audiences in the cheap seats seeing the actors' faces.

Alex Sharp was thrown by the third preview. His performance was actually clear and strong but he found it excruciating. This happens often in previews. Nearly always there is a preview when an actor thinks they've given an awful performance but actually it has had a real clarity and force to it. Actors find it difficult to measure their own work. The stage actor, as an artist, can necessarily never see his or her own work. This can confuse and debilitate them. They need support. They deserve it.

Mainly they are confused or disorientated by a surprising audience reaction. They need to concentrate on the work, not on how it's being perceived. But when there are a thousand strangers in the room looking at you, this can be disorientating.

There are moments when the weight of expectation on this show is clear to me. I'm aware that much of the National Theatre's budgeting rests on at least a small success here for *The Curious Incident of the Dog in the Night-Time*. That this fundamentally is down to two things – a good review in the New York Times and a Tony nomination – seems arbitrary and stupid and contradicts everything I've ever worked for in theatre. I never wrote for awards or commercial success and don't give a shit about reviews. I care about actors and audiences and the possibility of communication between them and the idea that strangers might gather to share an experience.

But the weight of it is so profound here in the city that it is distracting.

I guess if it is a commercial hit – if it runs for a year here and two more in the West End, then financially for me and my family it is a life changer. That is entirely out of our hands of course. It is dependent on the whims and vicissitudes and decisions of others. But it is nevertheless a powerful distraction.

We have to ignore it.

Stick to the work.

Allow the idiotic others to concern themselves with their decisions and frivolities because it doesn't matter.

17th September

Despite a theatre culture that appears buckled and an accelerating gentrification process that might rip the heart out of the city, there is something stunning about being in New York. I walked on Sunday with Christian Parker down the Hudson to Battery Park and up through Wall Street to Broadway. To remember standing at the foot of the World Trade Center as a teenager was astonishing. I was struck by how the defining act of terrorism of my lifetime happened so close to the water.

There are remnants in that area of the oldest part of the city. There are traces of the first who landed here. To look out over the East Side from my hotel room and see its expansion from those little churches downtown is bracing. The force of the grid of streets that gaze down the major avenues, all the way down to the bay, miles and miles of city, is unarguable.

Yesterday in rehearsal I re-inserted a speech that two previews earlier I had cut. In the speech Christopher describes to Siobhan his father's behaviour as he stays in his house, refusing to talk to him. We cut it to make this scene, very near the end of the play, as lean as possible. I realized after a few shows that it's absence made the last two scenes confusing. The problem with the scene wasn't the speech, but the position of the speech. It needed to build to the scene's conclusion, not trail off after it had peaked.

It was fascinating watching Alex Sharp wrestle with the logic of the speech's position. Fundamentally watching him try to learn the lines. I'd not watched an actor learn lines in such a concentrated way. He did it by building a logical and rigorous path from one sentence to another so that the only thing he could say at that given moment was that which I'd asked him to say.

It seemed to illustrate something fundamental to the playwright's craft. The job, at moments like this, isn't to write beautiful sentences but to map behaviour with absolute precision and to release that behaviour in words that are as simple and clear as you can make them. Whenever an actor drops a line in my plays, I know that it is probably because I've not done my job properly.

The audiences here have been far more ecstatic and open than I had anticipated. They are younger than I thought they would be. Will Frears suggested to me that actually it is easier and more accessible to get a ticket for a Broadway show than to get a ticket for a show downtown. The audiences in the subscription theatres actually are older than audiences in commercial theatres. They are also more attentive than I expected them to be. And the cumulative build of the play sweeps them away. I met an audience member last night who said to me 'secretly the audiences here are hungry for something different'.

Every other play on Broadway leads with a star. We lead with a kid straight out of drama school. Who happens to be extraordinary. Every other play looks the same and is structured in the same way and has the same relationship to naturalism. *The Curious Incident of the Dog in the Night-Time*, for all its democracy, has a formal boldness that is playful and alive. It is utterly theatrical. It could not have been made on film or TV. Every other play follows the structure I identified in the Theresa Rebeck play. Confronted with something palpably fresh the audiences have lapped it up. I was dreading they would reject it. They've roared approval.

Last night as Alex led us through the way Christopher solved his maths problem they were on their feet in the aisles, thumping the air. It was like a rock concert to Pythagoras's Theorem. It was fucking moving and fucking exciting.

Back to London.

Back to *The Cherry Orchard*.

23rd September

The physical exhaustion of travelling to and from New York is draining me more forcefully than I'd anticipated.

So my entries have become more erratic.

What has been fascinating this last week has been watching Katie stage the ideas that she and the company have defined in their table work. Carefully the actors reveal the circumstances and events and intentions in their acting.

It is a rigorous method and one so cleanly defined (despite me not really knowing the difference between when something IS an event and when it isn't) that when Katie was poorly for a day, her assistant director Matthew could step up effortlessly to cover her and know exactly what she would be looking for.

If I had one reservation it would be that while actors think about intention, circumstance, event, they don't always allow themselves to think about language. I guess the work is to make sure the language is carrying the intention as fully as possible and not just getting in the way of whatever the actor is thinking in their head.

It can lead to clumsy blocking where actors huddle around the subject of their intention and I wonder how Katie will calibrate this. I admire the commitment she has to naturalism. I even rather like that this can lead to moments when we don't see any actors' faces at all.

I have enjoyed changing my seat in the rehearsal room watching the acting as though watching in the round the rehearsals of a play that will be performed end on.

As rehearsals progress I oscillate between relishing the idea that we have set all the action in Grisha's nursery, Katie taking her lead from a psychologist she met rather than Chekhov, and wondering if we haven't maybe missed layers of complication that Chekhov washed into the play with his multiplicity and musicality of locations.

I think, finally, both positions might be true. We do lose something of Chekhov's music. But it becomes an incisive vision imagined by Katie Mitchell and I cherish her authorship, finally, as much as I cherish his.

There is an obsession in British rehearsal rooms with capturing the author's voice or realizing his imagination or getting inside her head. This misses the point of how theatre actually works so roundly that it is almost ludicrous.

Theatrical experiences are never pure articulations of any kind of authorial voice. The author's intentions, as revealed in their plays, are only ever starting gestures towards an evening in the theatre. This gesture will be refracted through the prisms of theatre architecture, social geography, audience make up, audience size, design, casting and rehearsal. In a translation it is refracted through the prism of the translator and when a version has been written from a literal translation through the prism of the writer of the version.

It is pointless wishing this weren't so because it simply is. Otherwise we would be reading novels. So the best we can do is acknowledge this refraction and celebrate our right as theatre artists to attack our work with confidence. Katie's description of the piece as a 'hundred and ten year old document' is as accurate a description of the play as it is entertainingly unsentimental.

Chekhov offered us a gesture written in Russian that, published, has survived and it has led to evenings in the theatre in every theatre culture in the world and has never fallen into obscurity. We are responding to his document. Katie as fearlessly as I have seen her. If this 'misses the point' of Chekhov or fails to serve his vision, then so be it. We're not here to serve visions of people who died a century ago and that we can only dream of glimpsing because they spoke a language that we can't speak. We're here to create something alive and present tense.

24th September

A workshop at the West Yorkshire Playhouse yesterday.

A jumpy old train up to Leeds. All that city's brown stone tinted grey evoked by the brutal lyricism of David Peace.

A neat small group of searching thinkers and then back home again.

Read *Carmen Disruption* on the train in preparation for next year.

It struck me that I can make it better. Make the chorus cleaner in its function. Make the beginning and the end better.

Build the chorus around the senses. Make their lines shorter.

It made me wonder if Sebastian's encouraging me to write a looser text was a mistake.

I should have stepped up to take dramaturgical control. And now I can do this I can make the play better.

25th September

Back in *The Cherry Orchard* rehearsals. Katie is off work for the week so Matthew, her assistant, is leading the rehearsals.

It is maybe the sickest rehearsal room I have ever worked in. Everybody seems to be ill.

But Matthew is leading Katie's methodology with clarity. Perhaps he's a bit nervous. He sometimes seems hesitant. I wonder if that is the real essence of direction – creating the myth of democracy and the illusion of certainty.

I watched some scenes and they looked extraordinary. Tremendously alert and moving and funny and sad.

I made some cuts. Sometimes I think Chekhov was writing into the conventions of a theatre culture and the extent to which his plays were defined by that culture is legible. So he uses a lot of exposition because there were forty-five-minute breaks between acts, for example.

I found myself pruning that exposition. Making the script as lean as possible.

Contemporary audiences are so much more alert to their reading of situations. They don't need exposition. They read things so quickly.

29th September

Another flight to New York and again my scattergun schedule has slightly battered my body clock and led me to lose track of this diary.

In London *The Cherry Orchard* rehearsals continue apace. Although as the week came to its end Katie's absence from the room became more telling.

It's not that Matthew and Cat, Katie's other assistant, didn't do good work because they did. But there was a sense that the work was consolidating rather than moving the piece forward. I think she'll return this week to push the actors further.

Cuts kept coming in from Broadway. I feel amateurish in that I find it difficult to make judgement calls on cuts and changes just from a script. Surely this should in some sense be my job. But I feel the need to be in the room, to hear lines spoken and scenes played in order to really calibrate decisions relating to re-writing. The writing doesn't exist on paper, but in the space coming out of an actor's mouth.

Preparation for *Carmen Disruption* has started. It seems, rather brilliantly, that Lizzie Clachan will design it. This will be the fourth show of mine that Lizzie has designed. She's one of my oldest friends. I've known her twenty-two years. She used to live with Polly when the two of them were students at Edinburgh College of Art and we have two large canvasses by her in our house. She's Oscar's godmother. She is also an artist of rare and real imagination. Every piece is something fresh for her. A work of art, sprung from an intelligent and creative response to what the play is trying to do.

She is at the vanguard of an exciting time in British theatre design.

For too long the dominance of the playwright's voice within the sometimes explicit and sometimes implicit hierarchy of artistic creation in British theatres led to a design aesthetic that was in some way representative or mimetic in its attempt to create worlds that a writer had imagined. In recent years a new, younger generation of designers, inspired perhaps by design aesthetics from European theatre cultures, have offered different ways into designing stage spaces for plays. They have been more expressionistic, more creative, more unapologetically artistic. There has been a fearlessness in the attempt to do more than simply build the world the writer sees in their mind's eye. Lizzie, with her background in the devised company Shunt's work, is definitive in this way. She has made sets that are exquisitely detailed or defiantly conceptual. I look forward hugely to seeing how she will react to the challenges and demands of the Carmen text.

1st October

I'm back in New York for the start of rehearsals of *Punk Rock* at the MCC. We've had two days.

The first day started with the same rigmarole of website interviews and photographs as did the first day of *The Curious Incident of the Dog in the Night-Time*. It's a bewildering way to meet the actors and the artistic team and the producers of the theatre. It is, I gather, the convention now in New York. Before we even start work there is a focus on selling the thing. My face felt strange smiling so fixedly for so many photographs. Talking with as much enthusiasm as I could muster about how excited I am to be back in New York and back working on the play.

And it is exciting, of course it is. In so many ways the play started in my unconscious in the USA. This was the country that graced the world with the school shooting in the first place. The play was generated by the killings in Columbine and Virginia Tech. Here places of education and potential fulfilled became places of murder. This horrifying, bewildering idea led me to write.

And here the Punk Rock that I obsessed about through my youth was generated. Patti Smith, Tom Verlaine, the Ramones. They all kicked their ideas around for the first time in the Lower East Side. Their drive to find form out of dislocation and shape out of anger inspired me through my adolescence and continues to.

I like the four men who run MCC. They seem though to be aware that they are running their theatre in the eye of the catastrophic storm of a theatre culture driven entirely out of money. Their commitment to my play seems palpable but Christ those guys are operating in an economy that makes fearlessness frightening.

The first couple of days of rehearsal have been oddly blissful.

The process has been very familiar. The cast, all young, bright eyed, enthusiastic and puppyish read the play with a real clarity and force.

Instinctively they play action not feeling. Instinctively they listen. And the play wasn't shit. At times it was alarming. Some of the gear changes worked. The way a character can play massively contrasting actions in the space of a very short space of time. Chadwick Meade moving from tenderness to rage. Lilly seducing and destroying. Cissy sassy as fuck and then fragile. Tanya ferocious and afraid. At times it feels over-written and I hope over the next few days to shave it back and shave it back until it is lean.

The more I write the more I realize that the thing that kills plays is words. And *Punk Rock* is a play about words. About characters searching to make sense of a world that terrifies them. Trying to contact one another in a world that atomizes them.

There is an instinct to keep the play contemporary. This involves some fascinating changes. I remember writing the play in 2007 inserting lines about a DVD library to make it more contemporary. Nowadays the notion of young people looking for DVDs to watch seems absurd. Young people download their films rather than watching them on discs. When I opened the play in 2007 the Large Hadron Collider wasn't working so I re-wrote to accomodate its failure. Seven years later it is working spectacularly so the re-write seems odd.

But it had a force, the play. The cumulative effect of it was legible.

And then we went back to the beginning and slowly re-read the thing. Stopping to talk about what we find as we go. It is informal and exploratory. I love the space for discussion because it gives me the space to read and discover the play. To discover new things about a text that I wrote seven years ago. To do this especially from the position of knowing that it has, in fact, worked and so I don't have to be anxious about it is a real relief.

The cast is smart and detailed. Today their capacity to listen was startling. They really heard Chadwick Meade's apocalyptic monologue. It affected them deeply.

To listen. To behave. To finish sentences. Again and again I reiterate this and again and again it yields.

I spoke at the Drama Bookshop last night. An audience of maybe forty people came. I read from *Bluebird* and *Motortown* and *Song from Far Away*. I enjoyed the process of reading my own stuff. I enjoyed exploring the rhythm of the thing.

Christian Parker interviewed me. It was kind of great. We talked about my obsessive need to return to the same themes. About the practice of distilling writing to fewer and fewer words. About the urgency of theatre and why it matters now.

I came to the Drama Bookshop ten years ago or more when on tour with the Country Teasers. I loved exploring the nooks of the shelves. To return now with a play on Broadway and another off-Broadway in rehearsal was utterly remarkable.

Dream come true stuff. Seriously.

4th October

I've been in rehearsals for *Punk Rock* for most of the week.

The production's director Trip Cullman's process this week has been familiar and reassuring.

We sit round the table. We read the scenes together, the actors reading their own lines. We interrogate the meaning of the play. The cast is inspiring because their youth is so infectious.

None of the bitterness or cynicism or irony of even the best older actors has crept into their work yet. They're open and so brilliantly enthusiastic that it has made for a remarkable room.

I've discovered things about the play that have surprised me. The sadness of Bennett's intellectual frustrations sitting under his rage, how right it feels that Chadwick is loved at home almost to the point of suffocation; Tanya's imaginative, joyful fantasy life and how it is punctured by Chadwick.

I talked to them about how William is losing all sense of when somebody is speaking in real life and when he is hallucinating. How this uncertainty drives him to despair. We talked about the sense of proprioception – the sense that allows humans to know when somebody is looking at them even when they can't see them and how in William this seems to have gone haywire.

I talked to them about Edward Bond's notion that plays take place in what he describes, I think, as 'accident time'. He talked to me one time about how he was clipped while driving down the motorway and his car went into a spin. In the time it took him to control his car he saw the world with more clarity than he ever thought possible. The colours were more vivid, the sounds clearer, the lines sharper. This he suggested is the atmosphere in which great scenes should be played. There are moments in *Punk Rock* when I think it is helpful to imagine the world of the play is taking place in this accident time. When Bennett is traumatizing Chadwick, when Chadwick describes the future instability of a world. At these points the characters' adrenaline is harder, their body temperatures higher, their breathing faster, their senses more alert than at other times. It is this perhaps that explains their inability to move or act.

Tomorrow night *The Curious Incident of the Dog in the Night-Time* opens on Broadway. Although it's a strange night because all the critics will already have seen the play. There is nothing riding on the performance. A great deal though rides on the reviews and a big shenanigan is made of the whole thing.

On the one hand it simply IS exciting. The energy of the thing intoxicates. The TV interviews that nobody will see. The red carpet. The posh frocks. The celebrities. This is all kind of crazy. On the other hand it sometimes feels like a perverse burlesque as the moneyed people of a corrupt theatre culture celebrate the monetization of an art form.

Grinning desperately we tell each other how exciting it all is.

It's fucked up.

I think *The Curious Incident of the Dog in the Night-Time* works beautifully but I think I can establish that for myself with my own judgement without depending on the preening of video cameras.

10th October

There was something disorientating about the opening night being nothing but a celebration of the work going into the play. In the US, unlike in the UK, the press has all been in to see the play before opening night. So the only people in the audience on the opening are glamorous guests and friends of the show.

I was grateful that Polly was there. And Mel. The two of them held my hands and took the piss out of me. They took the piss out of the party and allowed me to enjoy myself.

And I was grateful, too, that a handful of my favourite New York friends were there. Chris Shinn and Annie Baker, Christian Parker,

Annie MacRae, Keith Nobbs, Trip Cullman, G. T. Upchurch. We all sat together on a row.

The show was tight and received with real warmth. Although the microphone fucked up during the appendix which was frustrating. The gesture of the appendix, when Christopher tells the audience how he solved his maths problem, is normally celebratory. With a technological melt down it ended the show with an undertone of frustration. Critically this had no impact because the critics had already been.

We walked down 8th Avenue through the bustle of the peripheries of Times Square to the party on 42nd Street.

The party was an odd affair. I pottered around trying to make contact with my mates. I was taken away to do webcam interviews and found it difficult to really contact anybody after that.

The drink measures were tight. I missed all the food.

There were hundreds of people who I didn't know and I found myself wanting to hang out with the cast and failing to.

At about eleven o'clock Chris Harper came to find me. He told me the reviews were raves, across the board. The New York Times loved it. And the rest loved it more.

It was an odd moment. I was thrilled for Chris and Marianne and everybody who'd worked on the show. I was very glad that Chris had told me. He has supported the show throughout, not least after the ceiling collapse at the Apollo last December. He deserved this success.

But I still felt slightly corrupted by the whole phenomenon of building our response on this review alone.

The work that so many people had put in deserved reward. The randomness of it all coming down to one person's response was strange to the point of being mildly ugly. But we got away with it. And for the relief on Chris's face alone, it was worth it.

We got very, very drunk and went home.

Had a day off on Monday. I spent it with Polly. Eating lunch. Going to the astonishing Metropolitan Museum at the Cloisters – a megalomaniac folly of John D. Rockefeller, recreating a medieval cloister in the mountains of the north island. A stunning collection in a stunning place.

Then to see the movie *Pride* with Andrew Scott being brilliant.

It was a great day. One of my favourite days of the whole year.

On Tuesday it was the gala night. Thrown by fundraisers for the National and held at the elite and elegant Harvard Club on 44th Street, hosted by American Vogue editor Anna Wintour. A hundred donors paid up to 100,000 dollars a table towards the National Theatre for the privilege of sitting next to the artistic team and various glamorous guests.

Actors from the National Theatre's recent history all bustled together in fashionable suits.

I sat next to fascinating people. A prosecution attorney who'd spent much of her career prosecuting New York street gangs and somebody who'd made a lot of money in the music industry selling music on CDs in the early days of the CD.

While there was something odd about that opulence and something baffling about people spending quite that amount of money, the party was much more fun than the opening night. I got to spend more time with the cast and the relief of the New York Times review touched the whole theatre.

People congratulated me fully. As though the review confirmed what they had hoped to be true but were uncertain of until they'd been assured by Ben Brantley. Maybe that's not fair. The relief affected everybody. But I couldn't help feeling that even if he had trashed it the show was still as good as it was after his rapture.

I didn't need his confirmation to tell me it was so. But it seems others enjoyed it.

It's not so much the relief of the people working on the show that worries me as the warmth of people I'd never met before.

I found the whole thing confusing.

We did see the show for a last time. It was a great performance. Alex Sharp was stunning as Christopher and Frankie Faradany similarly stunning as Siobhan. That night on that big open stage it seemed a happy fit for the size of Mark Haddon's gesture.

Flew back the next day.

Having had a few moments where I allowed myself to enjoy the oddity of having a Broadway hit.

Came to see *The Curious Incident of the Dog in the Night-Time* at the Gielgud to catch up on the show. A packed audience dominated by school kids seemed like a buzzing counterpoint to the glamour of Broadway.

Abram Rooney played Christopher. He is Graham Butler's second. He gave a clear, lucid performance. I liked London school kids as an audience to the play. They were receptive and excited.

Meeting at Channel 4 this morning to talk about the idea of writing a film about The Smiths. A minefield of litigation or the opportunity to tell a story with some care and detail. I'll find out.

Late last night I wrote an essay for the Guardian about adapting *The Cherry Orchard*.

I wrote this:

Three years ago Katie Mitchell suggested to me that I would write a fairly good version of Anton Chekhov's *The Cherry Orchard*. I told her I would never dare.

The Cherry Orchard is my favourite play. It is a complex exploration of a culture on the cusp of disappearance, the Russian Aristocracy as it enters the final decade before the revolution. Chekhov is my favourite writer. In his plays and his short stories he excavated the human condition with more tenderness and honesty than anybody else I've read. Startling in his economy he sees into his characters and their capacity for contradiction and silliness and despair with a clarity that staggers me.

I didn't feel that I was good enough to write Chekhov into English. I didn't feel as though I was grown up enough.

Six months later I changed my mind. I still didn't feel grown up or skilled enough to write a version of *The Cherry Orchard* properly but I hadn't been able to shake the idea since she'd first placed it in my head. The idea of turning down such an opportunity troubled me more than my probable failure.

I have had three English language versions of other plays produced. All three of them have been at the Young Vic. In 2011 my version of Jon Fosse's *I Am the Wind* was staged there and in 2012 my version of Henrik Ibsen's *A Doll's House*.

The process for working on *The Cherry Orchard* was similar to my processes in both those versions. I don't speak Russian. The Oxford academic Helen Rappaport produced a thorough and invaluable literal translation of *The Cherry Orchard*, complete with lengthy footnotes. My task was to make her translation actable. To turn it into a text that sits happily in actors' mouths.

It is a process I find fascinating and that rewards me. When making my own plays I rarely think consciously about language. Rather the bulk of my conscious work concerns narrative or structure or theme. The actual line writing is done best I think when it is entirely instinctive. Sometimes I can't remember why I made particular word choices. This ignorance is often exposed by inquisitive actors in rehearsal rooms. This is how it should be.

With the writing of versions my sole concern, in the case of these three plays, has been linguistic. I have kept the characters the same and the structure the same and the story the same on all occasions. The judgement behind my word choices in *The Cherry Orchard* is entirely subjective and based on no linguistic consideration of original Russian syntax or grammar.

The politics and ethics surrounding this process of producing new English versions of texts written in other language has sparked much debate.

In his introduction to his compelling versions of Strindberg plays, Gregory Motton savages the culture of writers writing versions from literal translations. The subjective decisions the writers make ease the jaggedness and vitality of the original plays, he argues. The act of writing a version becomes necessarily a dilution. The esteemed Chekhovian translator Michael Frayn agrees. His widely produced versions are written from the Russian. Frayn is a fluent Russian speaker.

I admire Motton and Frayn hugely. I also think they are wrong.

I think their ideas are based on the odd assumption that it is in some way possible to make a pure translation. It isn't. Language shifts and mutates historically as well as geographically and to assume the possibility of a perfect translation is to ignore these shifts and changes.

It seems especially odd to suggest that a play text, out of any literary form, should be carved out of an attempt to accurately translate the original language of a writer writing a century ago. Playwriting, for me, is not a literary or linguistic pursuit and plays are not literary artefacts. I think of them instead as being starting points for a night in the theatre.

It bewilders me that a translator of a Chekhov play should concern herself with accurately replicating in English the Russian of the early last century even if this comes at the expense of the vitality, sensuality, pathos, rage and compassion of the spirit in which those plays were first made. When the concern with accuracy prevents interpretation or imagination on behalf of a director or an artistic team, then it is not just wrong-headed but damaging.

To offer an example: Chekhov's plays, like all plays, were written into the theatrical conventions of his time. He wrote four acts, which were performed with forty-five-minute intervals between acts. This lent itself to a literary style that became necessarily expositional. The audience needed reminding about what was going on. Our contemporary audience operates with different skills and needs and assumptions. To not address this and refine a text accordingly purely because it would be an inaccurate representation of the original source artefact seems bull-headed.

The Cherry Orchard has been translated into English on countless occasions. Since Stanislavski's first production of the play at Moscow Art Theatre in January 1904, it has never been out of production and has been performed all over the world. It could be argued that the last thing the world needs is another version of the play.

I think the reason it continues to be reimagined and restaged is because nobody has ever got it right. Nobody has every captured the depth and spirit of the play. Nobody has done this because nobody *can* because language doesn't work like that and language in theatre certainly doesn't.

Freed from the pursuit of achieving the impossible, writers have instead been inspired to calibrate Chekhov's work through their own standing ground. In recent years Anya Reiss in London and Annie Baker in New York have produced urgent contemporary versions of *Uncle Vanya*. John Donnelly's recent *The Seagull* felt driven by a faith in Chekhov as a theatre worker with a vital relationship to his audience. Filter Theatre Company's deconstruction of Christopher Hampton's *Three Sisters* was as engaging as Benedict Andrews's own version last year. I love Motton and Frayn's writing but I think they are wrong to disparage the work of Reiss, Baker, Donnelly, Andrews and hundreds of others when the work these writers have made has felt so alive and alert.

I have worked closely with Katie Mitchell on my version of *The Cherry Orchard*. It is a thousand words shorter than Rappaport's literal. It is refracted through concerns that Katie and I share. Ours is not an accurate representation of what Chekhov intended but is an honest refraction of what his play means to us.

The Cherry Orchard is a play that resonates now with as much force as it ever did. It made sense to both myself and Katie that it should be produced in the hundredth anniversary of the start of the First World War. The war was the first catastrophe that manifested the terror that Chekhov seemed to foretell for his characters. He dramatized a world shuddering with an uncertain sense that something awful was about to happen. The notion that England now is shuddering in the same sort of anticipation gripped both of our imaginations.

We were fascinated too by its consideration of grief. We have relocated the action of the play to more tightly excavate the grief caused by the death of a child. We have simplified the nomenclature of the play. We don't use anachronistic words or references to our own contemporary culture in the way that Benedict Andrews did with such joy in *Three Sisters* but we have tried to make a language that is simple and clear and economic.

We've done this not because we think it is a more accurate representation of the original Russian language. But because we are inspired by the play to make a night in the theatre that evokes the same sense of loss and tenderness and fear that reading Chekhov evokes in us.

I told the cast on the first day of rehearsals that I have probably failed in my version. I haven't captured the breadth of the play or its truth or comedy or sexiness (and it is a very sexy and funny play). I never could have done. Nobody could have done. No matter how brilliant their Russian. No matter how masterful their stagecraft. The nature of translation means that to think otherwise is folly. The nature of theatre means that to aspire to do so is slightly perverse.

Instead we try to make versions of versions of versions. That is the essence of our work and it defines our art form.

In my failure though I think we might come close to capturing something interesting. And I also think that we might continue the conversation so that in a very short space of time another writer will write another version of *The Cherry Orchard.* They will fail like I've failed. Their failure will inspire others. This is how it works and exactly how it should work. This is something to celebrate I think, not to chastise.

13th October

The first preview of *The Cherry Orchard* was stunning, I think. I've been so detached from it. But the decisions that Katie made were exquisite. Visually it was stunning. Vicki Mortimer's design captured the dilapidation and despair of the nursery in the heart of the Ranevskaya household. Gareth Fry's sound design was unsettling and beautiful. The cast acted with exquisite detail.

Katie builds her aesthetic around thinking of the audience as spectators looking in at a room that lives as though unaware that we are there.

This is in direct opposition to the nuanced concern for the audience that Marianne brings to her work or the anarchic spirit of combat that Sebastian brings to his. At times this meant that in an early preview there were issues of audibility. I had to work to hear what people were saying. Much of the time the actors wilfully acted upstage.

But it rewarded the effort.

The cumulative effect of the piece was remarkable.

I think she needs to find a way of communicating the movement of time through the piece.

I think she needs to be bolder in the distinctions between the acts.

I wonder if at times every element isn't working together to reinforce the gloominess of the world to a degree that suffocates the contradictions in the play.

I wonder if I could happily cut maybe five minutes.

But it had an impact on me and lingered in my consciousness for much of the weekend.

14th October

More than any director I've worked with Katie Mitchell has a distinct and clear vision in her head about what her show will look like. She works ferociously to have her actors and her artistic team realize that vision. This can mean that she is frustrated by the unreliability of the human animal. She hankers after a precision that can be ruptured by the instinctive and chaotic nature of just being human.

After the preview on Monday night she was frustrated by the unpredictability of the actors. She was angry at the idea that actors are 'organic'. 'It's not an organic process, it has to be forensic.'

This is a fascinating perspective. So different from mine in a lot of ways. I cherish the interaction between actors and a room. I cherish the liveness of the thing. She finds it maddening because it can lead to performances that are what she would describe as being 'unstable'.

Her vision has such clarity that I tend to think the only thing to do is to support her. Her eye for acting detail is so sharp that there are very few things that I notice that she won't already have seen.

So I tend not to give her acting notes. Feedback and suggestions from other people interrupt her thinking rather than recalibrate it, so I just stay quiet. And take solace in my role as 'language designer'.

I've enjoyed the previews. I think they have a powerful cumulative force. I love that the play is running at an hour and fifty minutes without an interval. I love the darkness of it and its spikiness.

Some people will find it cold. I don't.

There are issues of audibility still but Katie is working thoroughly to attack those. She talks of the audience as 'the other people in the room who we're sharing our work with'. I think in the last two shows that gesture of sharing needs to be further to the fore. At the moment the audience need to work to hear so that can lead them to work less on thought or emotional engagement.

I hope this will be overcome.

There is a moment where Charlotta crosses the nursery naked after swimming, puncturing the chatter of the male characters' attempts to interrogate the dignity of the human spirit. This is an invention of Katie's and not in the script. Last night David Lan raised an anxiety about how justified that was. I think he was maybe right to interrogate it but I love the moment. I love its defiance and its anarchy.

The musicality of the play floors me. Chekhov was masterful at orchestrating the cumulative effect of human behaviour. So that moments of silence or inarticulacy have a real power. I would love to master that. I would love to be able to write stillness and quiet with half the ferocious power that he has.

15th October

The final preview of *The Cherry Orchard*.

It was a fascinating show. The actors had been noted and noted about their audibility and last night I sat in one of the most difficult seats in the theatre in terms of actually hearing the thing. It was perfectly audible. There wasn't a word I couldn't hear.

Subsequently the audience connected to it more strongly. They laughed. At times their laughter was quite raucous.

And then something very interesting started to happen. The actors became increasingly conscious of the audience. And, while not exactly playing to them, they did start to lose a certain amount of focus on their intentions and their immediate circumstances and the temperature of the room and the time of day. I thought they really lost a sense of those defining themes of the play that had been excavated early on and a sense of what the heading of each act was.

They became aware of the audience at the expense of their work.

And the more aware they were, the more the audience engaged with them and so they became more aware still.

Katie was furious. It enraged her to have all the work that she'd put in dismantled by the flirtatious relationship between actor and audience.

For her the relationship with the audience should be very simple. They should feel as though they are peering into a world that is real and their experience should be that of the voyeur. She hates the idea that the actor would be aware of the audience and the audience aware of their awareness. She finds laughter intolerable.

She finds the fragility of the actor's stability in the heat of that relationship maddening.

In Britain the audience comes with the sense that they want to laugh. They come with the impulse that they must be entertained. This sits at odds with the expectations of theatre audiences in Germany and Holland and France, theatre environments that Katie feels more comfortable in. In those countries the audience are expecting serious, considered, angular cultural provocation.

I think this discomfort is what makes her an essential figure in English theatre and why her marginalization at the National Theatre was such a shame, and why her return to a major London stage directing a classic play is imperative.

I was reminded last night about the initial disagreements between Chekhov and Stanislavski after the original production of the play at Moscow Art Theatre in 1904. Chekhov disliked the production. He was disappointed by the way that Stanislavski had emphasized the sadness of the story at the expense of the comedy. For Chekhov the play is a comedy.

Katie is vehement in her notion that the play is a tragedy, with some laughter. She finds the notion of playing it as a comedy vile. I understand her position completely but find the comedy of the play unarguable.

Comedy comes in plays when characters fail to realize the awfulness of their own situation. The situation of the characters in *The Cherry Orchard* as they lose everything that they have lived for and fail to act on their capacity for love or truth is agonizing. Their inability to see it and the way in which they buffoon around, speaking too much, saying awful things, falling asleep then waking up suddenly, breaking furniture, bumping into doors is agonizing.

The comedy dramatizes their despair.

I wonder though if finally the two things are irreconcilable. If there will never be a perfect production that captures absolutely the synthesis of the two things, because at the same time that the despair and the comedy dramatize one another they also contradict one another. This contradiction is so fundamental that it may never be resolved happily.

This, though, rather than making the play weaker, is what makes it a masterpiece. It is why it is in constant production and why it is constantly being retranslated. It is defined by a fault-line, by an irreconcilable contradiction.

The piece I wrote on translation for the Guardian was published and there was a mild flurry of support.

I hope I haven't done either Michael Frayn or Gregory Motton a disservice. I think both of them are great writers. I was trying just to push the conversation about translation along a little.

19th October

It is always complicated negotiating the reviews that pour out after an opening. I made the resolution earlier this year to not read any reviews for any play written or produced and by and large I've stuck to my resolution.

I don't like the paranoia it engenders in me. I don't like how it destabilizes me. It allows me to take my eye away from my work and focus instead on my career and I think that doing that would be a mistake.

I have to trust my own sense of taste. I have to measure my own perception of what succeeds and what fails. The artist's capacity to honestly measure their own work is fundamental and the most difficult thing to hold on to. That capacity can be easily damaged by the boosts and bruises to their vanity that reviews necessarily entail.

The boosts can be as damaging as the bruises.

Sometimes I think it is a shame. Even a fleeting glance at many moments of great vitality in any art form will see a similar vitality in criticism. I look at the role of the great art critics at the explosion of modernism or the great music critics at the explosion of punk to see critical and artistic communities that fed off one another. I know that my work benefits from serious considered critical thought.

It may be that my inner confirmation bias immediately assumes that anybody who hates my plays is old fashioned or not serious. That is almost certainly the case.

I do think, though, that this is a complicated time for theatre criticism in the UK.

At one and the same time the form is both arid and alive. The state tends to depend on the medium.

Sadly, theatre criticism in newspapers is in a poor way. Word count is decimated to the point that critics are hidebound to offer nothing more than two paragraphs of description (normally of the story) and then a cursory comment of assessment. This grievously limits any depth of analysis.

In this culture two types of critics thrive. The best of them have a remarkable economy of phrase. At times Michael Billington, the Guardian theatre critic for the last forty years, has an astonishing capacity to capture the spirit of a performance in a single phrase. The problem is that many of these critics are now in their sixties and seventies and have been doing the work for decades and, despite their intelligence and skill and unarguable commitment to the art form, are sometimes blindsided by work that doesn't accord to the theatrical paradigms they defined themselves by in their twenties.

This is not exceptional. We all suffer from this. I do. Within a decade it will be what renders me arcane and old fashioned. But the extent to which it dominates serious broadsheet theatre criticism limits its relevance.

The second group type of critic who thrive in such contexts are the shitheads. Those like Tim Walker and Quentin Letts who have no interest in theatre as an art form whatsoever and merely enjoy the cock swagger of shitting on artists' work or rubbing their cock at the sight of a pretty young boy or actress in a frock. These are the lowest form of human life. They are miserable fuckholes who should get out of our fucking theatres.

I hasten to add that this is entirely my opinion.

In recent years arts editors have leaned towards this second type because they guarantee an increased internet traffic. Often outraged people like me will fail to resist the temptation to have a quick click on one of these shits just to exercise our incredulity and every time we do their traffic increases and their jobs are assured.

The state of theatre criticism on the internet as a whole, on the other hand, is quite extraordinary. Over the past five years, led by the determination of Lyn Gardner at the Guardian Blog and her acolytes Matt Trueman and Andrew Haydon there has been a remarkable explosion of theatre criticism on the web.

The lack of editorial policy of the internet might have led to a swamp of bloggers that is impossible to negotiate or one in which the voices of value are tricky to distinguish. But that hasn't happened.

Online theatre criticism, marshalled by the social media of Twitter and Facebook, is a genuine meritocracy. Led by one another, encouraged by one another and championed by one another, writers like Dan Rebellato, Dan Hutton, Meg Vaughan, Stewart Pringle, Catherine Love, and the aforementioned Trueman and Haydon (there are others, I've forgotten them) have led each other to the best of one another's work.

They remind me of the fanzines of the punk era. Many were shit but the best survived because readers recognized their quality.

These writers are unencumbered by word count. Nor are they encumbered by having to hit unrealistic and increasingly irrelevant and arbitrary deadlines. They have the capacity to think about the work they've seen and reflect on it before committing opinion to print or posting.

They can and openly do contradict themselves. They can change their mind. They can and are influenced by one another in a way which is more indicative of how people normally engage with art that it renders the false objectivity that the broadsheet critic poses behind increasingly absurd.

They have inspired me to be better. They have provoked me to think harder. And not only their complimentary reviews – also their frustrations or problems are as galvanizing as their kindness.

It is through their work that serious criticism becomes an oxygen for the artist.

I've missed the best of their work in trying to avoid most critics.

But the resolution this weekend seems kind of absurd. The gesture of avoiding criticism is as active as hungrily reading all of it and in that sense probably as distracting. Especially as somebody who uses Twitter often and enjoys it.

The fact that many of the people I follow on Twitter will have seen *The Cherry Orchard* and have thought about it and tweeted or posted their thoughts is disorientating to say the least. Like walking into a room and being certain that everybody has just been talking about you before you walk in. Even though they may not have been.

I should just read them. I have glanced at some of the headings so know them to be decidedly mixed. I know, for example, from the extremely scientific research of glancing at the headlines in the Guardian, that Michael Billington has damned my version with the beautifully poised adjective 'competent' and mourned its lack of humour. I suspect, without any evidence whatsoever, assuming that the lack of humour is entirely my drive and that Katie's work on the production was just to get the actors to learn their lines.

The best of the bloggers have a richer and more accurate understanding of the collaborative nature of the work and are likely to pay as much attention to the sound or lighting design as they are to the acting or the writing. Which is entirely as it should be.

This flurry of paranoia will pass. In a few days everybody will have stopped talking about the production and moved on to the next one.

But for now I'm mainly feeling a strange sense of anxiety. Assuming that everybody – not just people who work in theatre, but the people I pass on the school run and sit next to on the train – everybody has read the most mediocre of the reviews and is far too embarrassed to say.

20th October

It would be ironic if my headline glances at reviews are accurate and I am lambasted for removing all the comedy out of *The Cherry Orchard*. It would be ironic if Katie is given no credit for this decision and I am perceived as being entirely to blame.

Given the nature of our discussions for the last few years.

Terribly ironic.

In a kind of Chekhovian way.

Back working with Karl Hyde and Scott Graham on our *Fatherland* project. This time they interviewed me. It was draining. It was emotionally exhausting. Talking about my dad and his final words to me.

The funny truth is that I don't really know what his final words to me really were. They were either 'Thank you for my grandson' or 'Look after my grandson'. I didn't really hear him properly and didn't feel it appropriate to tell him.

They were, though, the last words he ever said to me.

They have sat, in some way, under everything that I've written in the past fifteen years.

22nd October

Back to Manchester to run a writing workshop with the writing group there. I did a workshop I'd not done before. I took the opening two pages of *Blindsided* and asked the group to identify the decisions that the writer has made in making the play.

It took some work to get them to think in terms of concrete decisions. But eventually they identified simple but urgent decisions. How many people are in the scene? Where is the scene? Who are the characters? How do they know each other? What do they say to each other? What do they do to each other? How old are they? Where are they? When is the scene set? What jobs do they do?

It is important to have moments, as a writer, when you identify the decisions that you might make intuitively. Identifying them allows the writer to take responsibility for them and to control the decisions with force and specificity.

Then we looked at a two-page extract from *Carmen Disruption*. I asked them the same questions. This was illuminating. They were forced to ask more complicated questions, or rather more fundamental questions. Are there characters? Do they speak? Who do they speak to? Is there a setting? Is there a location? Is there a time? Is there a story?

My point being that these fundamental questions DO sit under even the most naturalistic plays we write. It's just that tradition and culture and conventions mean that often we are not aware of them. Conventions lead to assumptions and so we stop thinking about fundamentals. Working in other contexts illustrates the assumptions and forces us to consider them and interrogate them. My hope wasn't that the writers go away and not write stories any more or not write characters. Rather that if they do write stories based on characters, they do that with an understanding that in even doing those things they have made active and deliberate decisions. Rather than just followed conventions because that is what they are meant to do.

Watched Sarah Frankcom's production of *Hamlet* with Maxine Peake as Hamlet. She was remarkable. Utterly charismatic and compelling. It was impossible to take my eyes off her.

Katie West played Ophelia and her madness scene was heart wrenching. She stood toe to toe with Maxine at that point. But it was Max's evening.

Her energy and physicality made her look like a boy prince. It was bracing to have an actor of her experience and range use the physicality of her gender to access the youthfulness of a boy. More women should play Hamlet. More women should play men in general.

1st November

A week off for half term with the kids. It was blissful spending time with them after a frenetic summer of travel. The more work I've done over the past year the more I hanker after just hanging out with the kids. Cooking their tea. Watching telly with them. Taking them to the park.

And then back to New York for the first previews of *Punk Rock*.

I saw two previews while I was there.

The cast is engaged and alert and keen to develop and sharpen. Their youth is inspiring. And ages me.

The first preview was slightly loose but had an energy and a shape to it. Mark Wendland's set is stunning. Carved out of photographs of disused Detroit high schools it carries the bruises of a culture on the cusp of catastrophe in every detail. It is lit exquisitely by Japhy Weideman. In the cavernous battered red velvet of the West Village's Lucille Lortel Theatre, a theatre graced with a history of staging the US's most significant playwrights, its broad wide space evokes the Lyttleton. I loved the juxtaposition of the decrepit beauty of the auditorium and the battered beauty of the set.

I met Trip Cullman, the morning after to share my thoughts with him. We agreed, I think completely, on everything, which was edifying. The actors need to be aware of the power of asking questions as though they very much want to know the answers to them.

Every time I have given this note it releases a performance. Too often in the first preview the cast were using questions to articulate feeling. As soon as they do that they kill the energy of the scene. The work is to stage interrogation and desire and that comes from asking questions.

The actors need to listen to each other. They rattled through the scenes with a compelling frenetic energy but the play works best when they have moments of stillness.

Douglas Smith as William was also playing his dislocation too early. The way to play William is to play him as normal and as human as possible. He needs to play every action with simplicity and ask every question with inquiry. His psychosis then becomes cumulative and interpreted by the audience and in the process of interpretation they come to recognize themselves. This play works when the audience recognize themselves in William. They recognize their own capacity for psychosis. This is much more frightening than watching a mad person kill people.

There were other smaller notes but these were the three main thoughts. Trip agreed. He took them on board and fed them into the actors.

The extent to which they took the notes was genuinely startling. It was a consequence of their youth. They took the notes and attacked them with real precision. So the second preview was much more alert and its cumulative force was shattering.

There is still some work to do. I think the kids can use the offstage presence of the school a bit more. I seem to be giving notes inspired by Katie Mitchell. They need to visualize with as much clarity as possible the off-stage characters so that Mr Lloyd can become a bigger presence and his death a bigger event and so that Chadwick's poverty, for example, can become a bigger presence. They need to use the ticking clock of the school day as a means of stopping them emoting. They can't sit in emotional states for too long because they have to get to class.

I am confident they will grapple with those things.

But the effect in the second preview surprised me. It felt extraordinary watching the school shooting in New York City. Last week in Washington DC a boy had tried to kill a girl who broke his heart and his friends who let him down. The cast tells me that in US schools 'shooting drills' happen regularly, the equivalent of 'fire drills' in the UK or 'earthquake drills' in New Zealand or California. They practise, from the age of four, what they would do in the event of what is called a 'lockdown'. To see this moment staged in front of an audience raised on this was electric. People screamed. People stood up in their seats. It was direct and startling.

Chris Shinn came. He told me that nobody in the US has properly wrested with the phenomenon of the school shooting. He was moved by the play and wrote a generous email to me.

5th November

Back from New York and back to the Lyric.

This week myself and Sean are hosting a week-long meeting with seven emerging writers whose work interests us. Brad Birch, Caroline Bird, Monsay Whitney, Ali McDowall, Luke Barnes, Charlotte Josephine and Andrew Sheridan.

The structure of the week is very simple.

We ask each writer to choose a play that they have seen in a theatre larger than 400 people and that they have loved. The idea is to get them thinking about how plays work in large spaces. To open up their lungs a little. To dare to sing a bit.

We then spend the mornings talking about these plays and highlighting what allows the plays to work. I ask them two quite particular questions. The first is to ask them what they would steal from the play. The second is to ask them how the playwright might fuck the play up.

I think the specificity of these questions is useful. It allows us to think specifically about the way in which writers have achieved the effects that they have achieved. In so doing we can emulate them.

I am also keen to have the writers think about the action of plays rather than their statements or their ideas. I am not interested in what writers are trying to *say* with their plays so much as what they are trying to *do*.

In the afternoons they have visiting speakers.

On Monday we talked about Shelagh Delaney's *A Taste of Honey* and Euripedes' *Medea*.

We talked about the tension between the honesty and detail of the world observed as though lived through and the flashes of remarkable linguistic poetry in *A Taste of Honey*. The juxtaposition of those two things is striking. Amidst an apparently drab conversation about tea and fags Delaney can floor us with a metaphor of wit and insight. The play also sits in a gap between the received conventions of what plays are meant to look at and what shape they are meant to be – five acts in living rooms – with the energy of looking at a world never staged before – the lives of the Mancunian poor of the fifties. She breaks the conventions because they restrict her. She does it perhaps unconsciously. Perhaps those things that limit and frustrate her in her world are the conventional norm accepted by most people.

Like many of the plays we are looking at this week, it examines that most fundamental of strictures, the family, and looks at power and death within that familiar convention. Maybe all great plays are about how we die and how we live under the shadow of death.

The presence of the body is strong in the play in its depiction of the agony of birth or the intimacy of sex. What renders it more than a documentary or a Sunday supplement is Delaney's capacity to write about the human body and her understanding of the political and social context of her time. In the midst of a play that seems socio-realistic Delaney examines the primal experiences of the body.

I love the idea that plays are dominated by characters who have a psychotic need to talk and to live their lives with an edge of performance. Through these extraordinary characters, characters who dominate all of the plays we've read, we see a glimpse of who we might be and so, through that, who we are. With language that is both mimetic and poetic, that uses unapologetic metaphor and simile, Delaney builds her play around a character who needs to speak.

Characters in plays speak because if they don't speak they will go insane. This is perhaps how we should judge our dialogue. Maybe we should only allow our characters to talk at moments at which, if they don't talk, they will die.

Jo in *A Taste of Honey* is driven by this need as much as is Medea.

And Delaney avoids the sentimental. She avoids the happy ending. She avoids the major third-act speech. So the audience is never sated and is always interrogating. Always asking of the characters – what are they doing and what are they going to do now?

Euripides in *Medea* takes a political context, in the same way as does Delaney in *A Taste of Honey* and opens it still further. This is a piece that plays out under the size of the universe. It is a play that looks ferociously at what it is to die and what it is to kill. It is contracted into an extraordinary time scale, the whole play playing out in four hours of real time. Even in this one space over one time the characters have a remarkable capacity to shift and change as the relationships in the room change. Euripides like Delaney dramatizes characters who are trapped and need to talk in order to release their containment. He is fearless in staging the awful. It inspires the sense of awe that Aristotle hankered after in *Poetics*.

A technique that emerging playwrights rarely use or try to use is that of dramatic irony. I think this is often because playwrights in the beginning of their career write plays that are led by the writer's instincts. They imagine the play as they write it. If you write like that it is difficult to lie. Dramatic irony – that sense when the audience know more than the characters do, but not necessarily more than the author – is a product of daring and involves having characters lie. In order to do that a writer needs to know more than their characters do.

There is a force of entrances and exits in scenes in the plays that sometimes I wish I used more. There can be a tremendous power in having a character leave a room. In order to do this the world off stage needs to be imagined completely. The great playwrights imagine not just the room next door but the whole world.

Both of these plays also are written with an understanding of sharing a room with the audience in the auditorium.

In the afternoon the writers met Tim Etchells, the founding Artistic Director of Forced Entertainment. He encouraged them to be empowered by the redundancy of playwrights, which felt like a bracing intervention.

On Tuesday we looked at Rebecca Lenkiewicz's *Her Naked Skin*. I'd never read this play before. It is in many ways the most conventional of the plays we've read this week. It looks, on the page, how contemporary plays are meant to look like. Stage directions top each scene and describe actions in between economically arranged dialogue. The first play by a woman writer ever to be staged on the Olivier stage at the National Theatre, it is a period piece. It recreates the lives of women involved in the early suffragette movement.

As I read it I was initially disengaged by the conventionality but as it progressed I was moved by it. It strikes me that Lenkiewicz was using the conventions of a period drama to investigate the agonies of impossible love. These agonies run through all the plays we've read this week. They all concern characters who can't love the way they yearn to and who can't stop themselves from dying.

She is driven by a refusal to mythologize the historical figure and a desire to find life and humanity in them. The play uses the mantle of the suffragettes to examine love in extremis and the despair of all terrorism.

I came to love the beautifully observed economy of the language. Characters speak in ways that are well behaved. They are defined by politeness as they carry out terrorist actions against the stage and fall in love with each other. These polite conventions are ripped through with images of vandalism and then prison brutality and forced feeding.

One of the play's great skills is the way Lenkiewicz places characters in different rooms in different situations and has them behave in different ways. A simple and exciting technique.

I read it with a sense that her main compassion is as much for William, the lead's husband, as it is for Celia, the lead. She writes him with real tenderness.

We looked at Rainer Werner Fassbinder's *Pre Paradise Sorry Now*. An atomized, fractured study of the fascism latent in all cultures crystallized through the story of Ian Brady and Myra Hindley. It was carved out of Fassbinder's fascination with the horror of the death camps and the cruelty of his parents' generation. That it distils a crime that continues to define Manchester's relationship to its children is coruscating.

It is a play that offers no stage directions and invites the director to play it in any order and use any number of actors. Some in the group were alienated by how difficult it was to read. I found it energizing and thrilling and the level of imagination it demanded of the artistic team arresting. As well as an aesthetic need it invites an enquiry into the moral world of the play. Artistic teams and actors have to ask themselves not only what the play is doing but why it is doing it.

The compulsive need to find the inhuman in the human and the human in the apparently inhuman defines the play's enquiry and resonates with everything I try to do with my plays.

In the afternoon the group met Edward Bond who talked to them for three and a half hours. I saw them again on Wednesday morning and the impact of Edward's session was legible. They looked changed. Three hours in the presence of one of the greatest figures of post-war theatre had rendered them in some way different to how they were before.

He teaches us many things, does Edward.

He teaches us to celebrate drama over theatre, to celebrate a consideration of the things people try to do rather than the staging of the spectacular. He teaches us to write in three dimensions. He teaches us most, though, the moral importance of drama and the dramatist.

It is our job to test whether laws are good or bad. It is our job to insist on moral interrogation. If we do this properly, then, in his words, the young dramatist has the potential to give our culture life rather than leave our culture as piles of corpses.

We talked today about Lucy Prebble's *Enron* and Arthur Miller's *The Crucible*.

We talked about the immaculate build quality of *The Crucible*. Every moment leading to an image: the execution of John Proctor. That image carrying the ideas that sit in Miller's investigation of the fragility of culture. Culture being a collaborative attempt to save humanity from nature and thus from death is rendered, in the play, fragile and uncertain. Writing as post-war America turned in on itself he finds a moment that crystallizes that fragility and builds everything in his play around it.

While I may prefer the messy poetry of Williams there is no denying the robustness of Miller's craft. I hate the sexual politics of the play. Every woman is hysterical. They all yearn for Proctor with his moral dignity. But as an excavation of panic and the horror of hysteria it is unarguable.

I enjoyed, in re-reading *Enron*, Lucy Prebble's capacity to startle with her line writing. That she can move effortlessly from scene to scene and always have characters take us by surprise by what they say and do is striking.

She shares a spirit of displacement with Miller. Like him she writes about her culture by dramatizing another. She writes about the 2008 economic collapse by finding its roots in the behaviour at Enron on the bridge of the twenty-first century. Neither writer is driven by the impulse that Delaney had to reimagine a world she had lived through or, as the shittier workshops have it, to write what they know.

Both plays are celebrations of the writer's imagination as a means of dramatizing the lives that they live through.

On Tuesday afternoon we had a reading of *Carmen Disruption* at the Almeida. It was invaluable. I need to link the stories together more. I need to make the Singer present tense. I need to place the motorbike crash more. I need to have the characters refer to their own names. I need to cut a couple of pages.

It was invaluable having Edward Bond at the Lyric workshop this week. His presence lingers. I sat through the reading of *Carmen Disruption* and imagined him sitting with me. It made me realize that I need to take the play more seriously. It has the potential to be an excavation of the psychosis of a life lived on screens.

We live all our lives on screens nowadays. The theatre needs to be a world that reclaims the humanity. Edward talked about this. I need to take responsibility of having ownership over this reclamation. I didn't in Hamburg and can now and it is imperative that I do. If there is any importance in this play it is in claiming that gesture is at its heart and owning it fully.

6th November

A morning workshop at the English National Opera with sixth form students organized by Mousetrap Theatre Projections to encourage students to write theatre criticism. They'd all been to see *The Curious Incident of the Dog in the Night-Time* and had to write reviews of it. They spent the day working with Lyn Gardner and Matt Trueman. I started their day for them being interviewed by Mat talking about the process of adaptation.

I talked to them about the absence of stage directions. Increasingly I'm interested in stage directions that are slight and suggestive rather than descriptive. I think that the job of the stage direction is as much to provoke creativity and charge imagination amongst the actors and artistic team as it is to describe the play that I see in my mind's eye. My job is to create a rehearsal room that is alert, not one that is slavish.

Then to the Tricycle. The writers from the Lyric had written short scenes that Sean Holmes directed with the brilliant actors Danny Webb and Lesley Sharp. It was a total joy to watch actors of that calibre playing with Sean. Free from the pressure of rehearsing a production or refining a play, the three of them were able to explore and take risks. Emptying the stage of anything artificial or the impulse to mimetically re-create a world they became more playful and more free as they found the essence of the scenes.

7th November

The last day of the week with the Lyric writers. We spent the morning talking about our writing practice. I urged them to think of their work as a job that they need to take seriously. They need to take responsibility for their financial welfare and their health. They need to anticipate the amount of time they require to write a play and the space they can best work in. They need to take responsibility for filling their imagination. Some of the most important days are those spent not working on something direct but watching a movie or reading a book or going for a walk or seeing an exhibition that might not directly relate to a commission or a play but might finally release four or five more plays. They need to figure out how much money they need to earn each week and spend the appropriate amount of time on each job that the fees for their commissions earn. They need to treat dramaturgs or script editors as peers not employers and make sure that note meetings have a clarity to them. This, in different ways, is as serious and as important as committing to the moral or aesthetic ideas that underpin their work. They need to treat writing like a job in which they are the staff and the employers alike and attack such work with the same seriousness and preparation as they would if they were running a cleaning company or a bar or a law firm.

In the afternoon we talked about the future of the Lyric. The challenge, it strikes me, is not to live off the laurels of *Three Kingdoms* and *Secret Theatre* but anticipate what will be next. To create an environment that allows artists to flourish. To stay ahead of the game.

It meant a lot to have writers in our unfinished theatre. Sharing fag breaks with the builders. It reminds us what all the work we've done there is actually for.

11th November

Two days at the University of York with Sean Holmes.

Both Sean and I were students at York at the end of the eighties. We never met. But I'd heard about him. He was in the year above mine. He was known for making great theatre and because several of my friends fancied him.

We did two workshops. One with undergraduate students and one with postgraduates.

We always do the same workshop. I led them through the writing of a scene. I led them to finding characters through music. I played the *Quartet for the End of Time* and bits of *Metal Box*, source material for *Wastwater* and *Morning,* and gave them simple automatic writing exercises in response to this. From this I built them up to write a brief fourteen-line scene.

Then Sean directed the scenes, without revealing the playwright, in front of the group.

Increasingly he's used this exercise to test the limits of naturalism. To find ways of staging the essence of scenes not the literal material. To find the metaphors at the heart of stage direction and stage the subtext implicit within it.

The students were good. They were smart. It was nice to go back.

We were hosted by one of the staff of the Theatre, Film and Television Department, Tom Cornford. He hosted us with grace and we went out with him in the evening.

He has a particular fascination with *Three Kingdoms*. He asked us about that in a Q&A and then over dinner.

What strikes me now about the whole phenomenon of that play is that the tenacity of the producers, from the Lyric and NO99 and Munich, was as remarkable as any of the imagination or creativity of the central practitioners.

They never gave up. Not when the Schauspielhaus in Hamburg pulled out or when Paul Ritter pulled out or when Paul Brennan left half way through rehearsals or when Muriel Gerstner the designer left. Not when the actors hated Sebastian. Not when the British critics battered us. They kept calm. They kept going.

Any of the success of the play is as down to them as to anybody else. It was a genuine masterclass in production.

It was good to spend forty-eight hours with Sean. Kicking around ideas for the future of the Lyric. He is fairly committed to reviving *Herons* in 2016. I am very fucking happy about that indeed.

We sat through the two-minute silence remembering Armistice Day as the train pulled slowly down through the country.

It was good to do a train journey without working.

Just watching the country pass.

Back to the office. Work on *Carmen Disruption*. Work on *Threepenny Opera*.

12th November

A morning reimagining my version of Brecht and Weill's 1928 musical *The Threepenny Opera* with the National Theatre's Associate, the avuncular and energizing Ben Power. Ben is a rare figure in British theatre. He is a writer and a good one but more prominently he is a dramaturg. He has been brilliant to work with on *Threepenny Opera*. I've been working with him on the piece for two years now.

He is smart and his passion is infectious. I bumped into Tessa Ross who I knew when she was head of Film 4 and has now become the Chief Executive at the National.

She was bursting with her faith in the work I can do there.

She laid me the gauntlet of stepping up as a senior writer.

13th November

More work with Ben Power on *Threepenny Opera*. He has an enthusiasm which is puppyish and charming, and which combined with a real understanding of how plays work and a proper intelligence means he is a quite invaluable figure.

He put it to me that it might be possible to revive *Sea Wall* on the Lyttleton. This is an insane idea that is completely inspiring. A little monologue that started off in a dark Bush theatre and was made into a film for the internet might finish its life on the stage for the 900-seat auditorium at the National. How unlikely and how exciting.

14th November

Ben couldn't join me this afternoon so I implemented the notes we talked about. I became excited by the idea of carving the play out of a timeless East London. The East London of which Iain Sinclair describes the psycho-geography. The East London of Alan Moore. Where Jack the Ripper and Mack the Knife and the Kray Twins and the London Riots alike all play out under the nightmare of the possibility of the gallows.

This might address the problem of the execution. If it is clear that is from the world of a nightmare.

In the evening I went with Marianne to see Ian Rickson's exquisite production of *Electra*. I found Kristin Scott Thomas's performance just riveting. Every decision she made felt surprising and honest.

Ian modulates his direction beautifully. Years ago I was trying to remember the word to describe the quality in his work I most admire. It is 'modulation'. There is something deeply musical about his work.

15th November

Saw *The Cherry Orchard* with my uncle Andrew and Kathy, his wife.

It was the first time I'd seen it since opening. The force of the production stands up but some of the performances seemed tired, so its cumulative effect was less powerful than when I last saw it. The show hasn't been a smash hit in the way that *A Doll's House* was and audiences do compare the two. It's unfair in a way. They are different plays and very different productions. What Katie lacks in a sense of a democratic relationship with her audience she makes up for with the startling precision and clarity of the acting she directs and the pictorial beauty of her stage.

16th November

In New York for the opening of *Punk Rock*. I landed at lunchtime and after getting washed and dressed at the hotel walked through the West Village to watch from Scene Three up in the balcony.

It was odd and rather lovely feeling so detached from the bulk of the audience. There were fifty students in from the Manhattan Class Company young company. They responded with startling energy. Shrieking and laughing and listening with intention.

I think the production is in fine shape. Some moments are better than I've seen them. The moment between Bennett and Nicholas when he is touching his leg is astonishingly tender. The moment when Bennett tells Cissy she's ridiculous is weirdly humane. There is an action to forgive that sits under it. William at the end yearning to be an architect.

The cast is extraordinary. It resonates in New York better than I ever dreamed it might.

Went for a beer with the Atlantic Theater's new Literary Manager, my friend Annie MacRae, and the playwright Nick Payne after. He's in town rehearsing *Constellations*. He was funny and kind.

17th November

It poured down all day in New York today. I had a decadent day. I had breakfast in my room and dinner in my room and I had a massage in the spa, and apart from coffee with Mark Brokaw to talk about *Heisenberg* next year, and a five-minute walk out to get cards for the cast, I didn't leave my room.

Casting for *Heisenberg* is tricky. The play has two actors. A forty-year-old American woman that we hope Mary-Louise Parker will play and a British man in his seventies. The impulse from Manhattan Theatre Club seems to be to send it more to star actors than actually actors who will do new plays. Fascinating actors like Anthony Hopkins, Jim Broadbent, Brian Cox and Jonathan Pryce have been offered the role. These actors don't do new plays. They will not say yes. They are simply wasting time.

But I gather that this is the culture of New York now. The off-Broadway theatres, even theatres which have an audience of a hundred seats, will be driven by a need to cast stars. I find it slightly ridiculous.

For the rest of the day I stayed in and watched the rain fall on the West Village.

I wrote my cards. I think it's important. It feels sometimes like a tedious ritual but there is something important in rituals and it felt important to me to try to tell the cast how grateful I am for how hard they had worked.

There's something in the simple physicality of writing cards that seems appropriate. As the world is fractured and atomized. It seems more important somehow to write something down.

To scratch it into a permanent shape.

Opening night of *Punk Rock* tonight.

18th November

Punk Rock opened beautifully. This time I enjoyed the absence of critics on the opening night. It was a much more relaxed affair than with *The Curious Incident of the Dog in the Night-Time*, indicative, certainly, of considerably less money involved in backing the thing.

The audience was warm and the actors played with clarity. It was a strong clean show. The audience lapped up the comedy of the first scene. They were taken by the shifts and changes as the play progressed.

I've found it fascinating returning to *Punk Rock*. In many ways I've not followed up on some of the play's dramaturgical decisions. In a way I really should have done. I should write more plays with lots of characters in a scene. I definitely should do that. I should use entrances and exits more skilfully. The opening scene of *Punk Rock* sees all of the characters come in with great opening lines.

Maybe the Faust play will see me make something bigger like this. Maybe it will see me have the confidence to put more characters on stage, to have them attack entrances and exits more. I hope so.

I've noticed this week as well that from the beginning the play leads inexorably to the massacre at the end. Early on in the play there are lines about incarceration. Throughout there are little clues that something awful is about to happen.

I should be more aware of that on the Faust play.

I enjoyed the context of the play. That too is something I need to be aware of as I go forward and write more. This is a piece that sets itself up to play out in the context of the history of the universe. So a story that is quite local and quite specific is rendered bigger by, mostly, Chadwick's observations on the size of the universe.

I need to hold on to that as well.

I panic that *Punk Rock* might be the best play that I've written. I look back over this year and much of the new work may disappear. I think *Birdland* stands up well next to *Punk Rock*. I think *Blindsided* and *Carmen Disruption* do too. And yet the most paralysing and difficult thing for any artist to do is measure the calibre of their own work. So maybe I'm wrong.

I lived most of my writing career keening for success. I had some success. Having had success I seem to spend most of my writing career terrified that I've written my best plays and enjoyed the biggest successes that I'll ever enjoy.

I know this is irrational. I know that actually art can't be compared qualitatively like that. I know that. But much of the work of being human involves being irrational. And probably it drives me on to try harder next time.

About half past eleven people kept on approaching me to tell me 'It's a rave'. Ben Brantley's review is, I gather, very warm. The energy of this news infused the party. I didn't read it. I don't think he wrote it for me to read. He's described my year in some ways. His *A Doll's House* and *The Curious Incident of the Dog in the Night-Time* reviews and now this.

I'm glad for the remarkable kids and the cast that they received such approval and glad for Trip and for the MCC. They've been very good to me on this production.

I sent them *Port*. Marin Ireland wants to do it. Trip wants to direct *Birdland*. I think my dad, a salesman to the last, would have been proud of me using the visit to place other ideas for future projects.

I left the party at midnight and went back to my hotel.

Woke up at five and showered and dressed and got a car at 5.30 to take me to JFK to bring me home.

It was a beautiful thing to drive through New York at that time of the morning. Some folk were getting up for work. Some were stumbling back to bed. The city sleeps deeply, of course it does. But there are pockets of it that wake throughout the night.

I've made perhaps seven visits to New York this year. There will be fewer next year but some. While I sometimes mourn its gentrification, its beauty and the force of its brief but remarkable history remains legible. Especially at 5.30 in the morning in a car on the way to JFK.

I'll miss the place.

I leave it with that sense of nostalgia that I've written about often in this diary. That interruption. That impulse to pick away at an open wound.

Got to the airport in good time.

The day flights start brutally but in the end I'll be happy to arrive home at bedtime.

Go to bed.

Start again tomorrow.

21st November

More work on *Threepenny Opera* with Ben Power. Ben is taking an increasingly central role in the artistic direction of the National. Rufus Norris, the new Artistic Director, is creating a collegiate environment there, in contrast to Nicholas Hytner's more controlling hand. Ben has become more integral.

Part of his mission is to bring the spirit of the Shed, the temporary space he led the building of on the river side of the theatre, into the larger auditorium.

With this in mind we met before we started work with George Perrin and Andrew Scott. We were looking at the possibility that Ben had teased me with last week, of staging *Sea Wall* in the Lyttleton.

It seemed a fucking crazy idea. Until the moment I saw Andrew alone on the stage there. Then I knew it could be sublime.

We'll see. Much depends on Andrew's availability but it was a thrilling thing to see and to watch Andrew's remarkable enthusiasm and intelligence in play within that space.

He gave a few readings from the piece. Moments of it still smash me up a bit.

22ⁿᵈ November

More work on *Threepenny Opera*.

I finally looked at the Evening Standard Awards shortlist. These awards cripple me. On the one hand I understand that they are nonsensical, specious and silly events and stand for everything I despise in the British theatre world. How can this year's theatre be celebrated without Chris Thorpe? Or *Show 5* of Secret Theatre? Or *Mr Burns*?

On the other hand the notion that my work this year hasn't been deemed worthy of consideration of some kind of celebration haunts my fucking stupid ego. I think *Birdland*, for example, is a play that I can stand by. Not perfect. Bits of it probably a bit shit. But much of it as good as anything I've written.

These award lists destabilize my sense of my ability to read my own work. Maybe I'm deluding myself. Maybe the only people who really liked *Birdland* were the Andrew Scott devotees.

I don't know. I never can tell. We just can't.

Although it is fucking insane that Andrew wasn't nominated. His performance was simply devastating.

I shouldn't give a shit, of course. The Evening Standard Awards are certainly the most conservative of them all. Why should I care what they think? They do throw a nice lunch though. I do sometimes get a bit too pissed.

I had a fine coffee with Brad Birch. He was talking to me about his interest in adaptation or writing versions. He wanted to know whether I perceived it as legitimate to be interested in these things.

The extent to which theatrical conventions established in the wake of the Second World War have become paradigms can lead to anxieties like this.

There is the notion that adapting or reimagining other texts in some sense betrays the innate authenticity of the artist.

This sense is, of course, bollocks.

For most periods in most of the history of theatre the work of the dramatist has been to adapt rather than to originate. There is a value in it. There is authorial characteristic in the gestures of adaptation that are as defined and particular as in originated plays.

I told him that the work of the artist is to work within conventions in order to test their edges. It is in the tension between conventions and authorial signature that the most important breakthroughs in artistic forms are made.

I tried to convince him to think of himself like Rembrandt. He would take commissions for private portraits and fulfil those commissions but within the conventions of those commissions redefine pictorial art forever.

He is a good writer, Brad. He has the potential to challenge and to test those conventions and I hope he does.

23rd November

My last day at the NT Studio, finishing off a redraft of *Threepenny Opera*. I'm as happy with it as I have ever been. It's been a hard play to write a version of. So much of the actual text is crocked. Its narrative is incoherent. It is predicated on ludicrous and ill-thought through devices – a series of repeats that are repetitious; an absolute absence of any judicial process or compelling penal system; a frankly absurd deus ex machina. It feels like it was knocked off while Brecht was drunk and shagging. So there is an impulse to repair its crooked dramaturgy and find a dramatic world that is cogent and resonant and which rises to the extraordinary music. Weill's score redefined musical theatre for a century and remains haunting.

I'm not sure that my idea for justifying the deus ex machina works completely. I leave the play with an unresolved sense of outrage at the injustice of Mack's survival and I'm not sure if that is right.

The bigger problem will be negotiating the puzzle of the demands of the Brecht and Weill estates with the demands from Rufus Norris to make it resonate in a contemporary way. The tangle of the two estates is particularly problematic.

I learnt at the NT that Richard Bean is trying to make a version for film. David Eldridge has made a version. So many contemporary playwrights have tried to make versions.

Fundamentally this is because the flaws in the play are compounded by intractable estates.

Based in New York, the Brecht and Weill estates are famously resistant to any intervention in either the musicology or the text. They also distrust one another – a distrust that concentrates their resistance to intervention

I think that it is this resistance that renders contemporary playwrights unable to change anything and leads us all to give up in the end. Two ageing, cumbersome estates wringing the life out of a text infused with beauty. In a spirit that absolutely contradicts the creative daring with which the two originating artists worked, they turn the thing into a museum piece.

Went to see Tim Stark's beautiful production of Robert Holman's *Jonah and Otto* at the Park Theatre. It is an even more extraordinary play than I remember it being. Robert remains a hero to me. He carves his plays slowly out of years of thought and feeling. He has the capacity to astonish me with every line. Watching last night I was struck by how his plays also lift off the page. They read like poetry but spoken they have a life.

Nobody excavates the sadness of kindness more beautifully or the strange joy and poetry of loneliness with more honesty.

The play's odd setting, the way an undertow of inertia is counterpointed with dialogue of vitality and surprise, the devastating exploration of grief and love and parenting and death left me euphoric and heartbroken.

It is one of my favourite plays of the century.

Forced Entertainment's remarkable durational piece *Quizoola!* was live streamed from midnight. It will last for twenty-four hours. From a theatre in Sheffield the company will play out a series of interrogations. They make their faces up as clowns and take it in turns to interview one another through a series of more than 2,000 questions. The questions range from the banal 'what's the weather like?' to the personal 'would you like to go to Afghanistan?' to the strange 'what is a leaf?'. The sheer volume and relentless speed of the questions and the wit and honesty of the answers and the remarkable length of the piece creates a human space that sits in tension with the simplicity of the convention. The performers also have their faces made up as deranged clowns. It is addictive. It is both very funny and very moving. It is kind of amazing watching it on an iPhone. So much humanity contained in such a dehumanizing device.

24th November

Stretched thin by a working weekend. I went to Madrid to watch a production of *Punk Rock* by the new company La Joven Compañía. The Young Company.

They are a company committed to making theatre for young audiences. By young they mean, I think, audiences in their teens and twenties. At a time when their country is economically decimated and where the young people in the country are affected with particular extremity, their work seems little short of heroic.

The production was bold and ferocious. An extreme, expressive sensibility running through every moment. It felt particularly Spanish.

I talked for an hour and a half before the play to an audience of about a hundred people. And then immediately after the play there was a question and answer session with the cast.

I got to bed at about four o'clock at the end of a very boozy night. Woke up the next morning. Straight to the airport.

Then up at six the next day to go to Manchester to start work on *The Funfair* with Walter Meierjohann and his wife, Petra Tauscher. We read the play with a group of Mancunian actors in the morning. Katie West read Caroline. It was a strong reading. The play lifted off the page in their hardcore Manc mouths. It felt as though we'd set it in Platt Fields or Wythenshawe Park. It felt contemporary and alive.

Walter was nervous at times that the actors settled too easily into Manc naturalism. With this play, to find the oddness of the rhythm and the silence you need to get your mouths round every word. Oddly when they read it in American accents it seemed to somehow lift the thing.

The potential for Home Theatre to shift the nature of Manchester's theatre, in a decade in which London is rendering itself increasingly impossible to live in for artists who want to take risks, is immense.

It will recalibrate the city. It will reposition theatre at its centre.

And the fact that Walter isn't English, so can't hear the nuances of accents, frees him from pursuing the type of naturalism so well served in that city's televisual culture.

25th November

More work with Walter and Petra and young director George Want. We worked through the whole play. Clarifying the silences. Finding spaces in which the language might be stranger. We need to find the poetry and the heightened gesture of speaking.

Horváth described language as a disease and his play is soaked in silence.

I was exhausted. But I felt charged by Walter's energy and the fact that the play is about to be announced and that it will open a new theatre. It felt like a great two days.

It was great to work in a part of Manchester that I'd rarely worked in before. Evoking childhood memories of the bruised architecture of Whitworth Street. Finally getting my head around the weird shape of the city. It curves east and then south from the Irwell like a weird urban knee joint.

26th November

A day at home working on Ignatius's *The Director* in anticipation of my meeting with Paul Greengrass tomorrow.

27th November

Paul Greengrass postponed the meeting. This is fine. It frees me up to re-read *The Director* completely. I implemented the changes on *The Funfair* that we worked on all week and sent them to Walter.

28th November

Moving slowly after going to Gary Lineker's birthday party last night. Becoming friends with Gary Lineker, former England football hero and currently one of television's most important figures, is utterly surprising to me. But more than it is surprising and flattering, it's just downright ace. He is a straight up solid gold human being. And his wife, Danielle, is a fucking star. She and Polly get on brilliantly.

We went out for dinner and then to the bewildering Annabel's nightclub. It was like one of the old nightclubs in Stockport. Like something out of the seventies. But with drinks at £16 a pop.

I managed hardly anything today apart from watching the Dardenne brothers' *Two Days, One Night*. A stark, beautiful study of a woman trying to get her job back after a period of illness. Carved from the same tradition as *The Bicycle Thief* or *Cathy Come Home* it is quietly devastating.

We watch the protagonist very, very closely. The camera hardly leaves her as she goes from house to house of all her colleagues trying to persuade them to vote for her in an upcoming referendum on her job.

The proximity of the camera to her face for so long becomes intensely moving. The simplicity of the structure as we watch her very simply trying to persuade her colleagues to vote against a considerable pay rise and in favour of her keeping her job is powerful. It's a rare thing to watch the extent to which drama is a playing out of simple choices played out with such clarity.

Her colleagues are never portrayed as inhuman or avaricious. The agony of their decision is clear and legible. It is a case study in drama being about the agony of choice-making. Every decision the characters make is sympathetic. The poisonous nature of poverty is dramatized with force and clarity.

29th November

On Friday night I saw David Kromer's production of *Our Town* at the Almeida. I'd never seen nor read the play before.

It was shattering.

On a simple open reconfigured thrust, the play unfolded with real clarity and simplicity.

And what a fucking great play. Edward Albee described it as maybe the greatest play ever written by an American.

It is simply structured. A first act dramatizing the daily lives of the characters in a small town at the turn of the twentieth century. A second act dramatizing with astonishing tenderness the love that develops between two of the protagonists, and the final act showing the dead awaiting the young wife at the heart of the second act who dies early in childbirth.

It is written without swear words. It is written against the backdrop of the universe and the history of the planet as a physical entity. It is written with generosity to every last character and built on a sense of their grace. The notion, from the final act that the dead remain waiting for us and alert but release themselves from the burden of the memories of their lives, is both unutterably sad and oddly uplifting.

Saturday was the last night of *The Cherry Orchard*. It coincided with the last night of *Far Away* in the Maria. David Lan asked me to speak. Somebody earlier had asked about whether the play would have a future life. It won't. But I like that. I think the dignity of theatre is that it ends. It has grace in its ephemerality. It carries a notion of death in its very form. As Churchill puts it in *Far Away*, 'You make beauty and it disappears'. I love that.

The actors had a beautiful last night. They played their notes with clarity and precision and this great play of farewell sang under them.

I'm proud of it. Sad it's over.

1st December

Went to the University of Reading to talk to students about *The Curious Incident of the Dog in the Night-Time* and *The Cherry Orchard*. I was hosted by the stalwart theatre academics Graham Saunders and John Bull. They interviewed me. It was robust and searching. I like Graham and John. Although they drink like bastards. They are committed to the form and talk and write with intelligence.

The arts need the academy because it operates and thinks in different ways to the ways most artists think in. Academics force us to reflect and consider that which we often just intuit. I love the intuition. I value it. But sometimes we need the space to articulate the ideas that underpin our instincts.

Lunch with Jon and NoraLee. We talked about the history of the devil. Jon presented me with the idea that the devil first came into thinking in the first century of Christianity as a response to the repressive nature of the Roman Empire. Jewish thinkers were unable to articulate their horror and revulsion because such articulation would lead to their death. The two thieves of Christian folklore on the cross were not thieves at all but revolutionaries. Christ a devout Jew was preceded two years earlier by another Christ figure and followed four years later by still another. In the throws of a repressive state and on the cusp of revolution, the Jewish thinkers would resort to the phantasmagorical.

I like the idea that Satan was given control over the world until God claimed it back. There was something of the Faustian pact in this. He can have everything but only if he accepts that he will surrender everything too.

The Evening Standard Awards on Sunday night. I wasn't invited.

2nd December

First day in nine months when I felt on top of my work. Finished compiling notes on the narrative of *The Director*.

In the evening I went to the Orange Tree Theatre and saw Ali McDowall's astonishing *Pomona*. A glorious, ribald, dark, nightmare of a play. An investigation of the devil under the ground in a Mancunian sex trade. It was funny and surprising and alert at every turn.

Watching it in the Orange Tree with an audience that was a real mix of the Richmond wealthy, many of who left very early, and a younger, more excited group whom seem to have travelled was vibrant and alert.

I've not had a more exciting time with a new play for a long time.

I think Ali is the real deal. I think his plays might last.

3rd December

Met the designer of the Melbourne production of *Birdland* this morning.
It made me happy to think that play will have another life.
It seems to have disappeared from people's consciousness as a thing
that happened this year.

That makes me sad. Not least for Andrew's performance as Paul,
which was startling, startling, startling.

I also met a German academic who is researching the impact of the
War on Terror on British theatre and wanted to talk to me.

I think my generation of playwrights was defined by political events
that made old ideas unstable. We lived with a new sense of
uncertainty. Our predecessors, galvanized by the new horrors of
neo-liberalism, were driven to protest against definable enemies. All
the definitions grew blurred for my generation. And those people we
thought were friends were revealed as enemies.

And just when it felt this uncertainty may pass, at a time when
Fukuyama was declaring the end of history, at a time of growing
affluence in the West and a rise in social democratic governments,
two jumbo jets were flown into the World Trade Center and everything
was dismantled again.

Enemies were hidden but omnipresent.

The sense of dread that Edward Bond infers when he talks about our
defining political catastrophe being ahead of us was made palpable
and made palpable everywhere.

Passenger jets become weapons. Tube trains. Discos. Commuter trains.

People are decapitated in London streets in broad daylight.

Social democratic governments became apologists for torture and war
criminals.

And the enemy is amorphous and destabilized and absent.

And, like Darth fucking Vader, grow stronger the more they are killed or arrested.

So our generation wasn't changed or altered. But rather our sense of uncertainty was affirmed and amplified.

The recession may change more than the War on Terror. Because the recession of 2008 presents real enemies and real bad guys and our generation of moral relativists finds that unsettling.

One of the great unifying themes of Ali McDowall's plays is this search for the possibility of goodness in a world so cleaved between the horrific gluttony of neo-liberalism and its consequent extraordinary poverty.

4th December

I took a train to the New Forest and talked to school kids about my work.

It felt important. It felt like they listened. Which is the best we can hope for.

And to get out of London and past Southampton and it's looming docks, into the marshlands and wild horses of the south coast felt like a real journey.

Meeting at British Film Institute on my return. They're nudging *Waterfall* ever closer.

5th December

Things winding down for the year now.

It seems lazy to be starting to slow up but it's been a fucking mental year, so feel slightly sanguine about a December dominated by nice lunches with people.

Had coffee with Nils Tabert, my German agent. When people talk about the reason my plays have succeeded in Germany they too rarely talk about him and his tenacious energy for work and his faith. That he also represents every other successful playwright in German theatre should be the main point.

My success like Mark Ravenhill's, Martin Crimp's, Dennis Kelly's is as down to him as to anybody else.

He is trying to place solid and exciting productions of both *Birdland* and *Blindsided* for 2016.

8th December

I went with Karl Hyde to watch *London Road* at the Archive of the National Theatre.

Odd and rather lovely to huddle around a computer with him.
It is a beautiful show and I regret not seeing it.

I love that Alecky Blythe, the playwright who made the show out of interviews with the residents of London Road in Ipswich living on the street at the time that Steven Wright murdered five prostitutes, built her piece around the community there, not the crime. It becomes a play about England and about England on the cusp of fear. The possibility of growing a garden in the face of murder.

The music was gorgeous. Adam Cork's score delicately captured the melodies of the speech of those people Alecky interviewed.

It was invaluable to watch for our *Fatherland* project.
We lack the unity of narrative, event, place and time that Alecky found and we need to find them.

I think that next year we will do our road trip around the country and build the show in the face of what we find.

But central to it will be finding those unities in the face of their atomization.

9th December

A lengthy lunch with Robert Holman and David Eldridge. Every Christmas since we wrote *A Thousand Stars Explode in the Sky* together we've met for lunch. It was good to see them and have a few drinks with them.

Their company is as galvanizing and inspiring as ever.

Then I walked from Blacks on Dean Street to Kennington and the White Bear to watch the fringe production of *Christmas*. I wrote *Christmas* in 1999, in my last year as a schoolteacher in Dagenham and it was my first commission for the Royal Court. It was eventually produced at the Bush in 2004 and I've not seen it since.

I lost my phone so, rather brilliantly, was walking without having to check tweets or emails and make phone calls.
A bracing harsh walk through cold London wind. Crossing Vauxhall Bridge was just beautiful. That big old cold smudge of the river.

And *Christmas* was just gorgeous to watch. It was an odd rush of nostalgia to see this play I've not even re-read for a decade.
Lines were like old friends. Bits of the dramaturgy are flawed and I could see myself working hard to keep a dramatic engine under something tangential.

But there was a beautiful wash of swearing in it. The swearing, deeply inspired by James Kelman's poetic, savage novels carved out of the Glasgow working class as I was at the time, felt organic and truthful.

And there were moments that were genuinely touching.
Moments of silence and tension.
And some good jokes.

The characters felt truthful and alive.

And the direction by the pub theatre's Artistic Director Michael Kingsbury was clear and strong.

The performances were far better than the writing.

It was a beautiful and nostalgic thing to see and made me wonder if perhaps the plays aren't necessarily all a bit shit.

The idea that a story I wrote fifteen years ago can still resonate and find a life means the world.

Starting to get my head around next year. Around the *Fatherland* project with Scott and Karl. Around the film for Paul Greengrass. Perhaps the *The Shining* adaptation for Ivo van Hove and the North project for 2016. And slowly starting to get ideas for the Faust play.

The idea of returning to the devil. Of researching that. Of reading Revelations. And getting my head around the contract involved in selling a soul to eternal hell.

I think it should be set deep in the City of London and Shoreditch. The old parts of the city. The dirt of it.

Jack the Ripper. The Krays. The contemporary City. The devil has been and will be everywhere always.

11th December

I met Jarvis Cocker this morning. I have an idea for a play with songs that I would like to write for the Royal Exchange. There would be nothing that would make me happier than if Jarvis wrote the songs.

It is a dislocating experience meeting artists who have informed your sense of self. I have loved Jarvis's writing for twenty years. I find his wit and savagery compelling. He writes with the natural span of a dramatic song writer. I wonder if the inspiration he took from Scott Walker, a man so deeply steeped in the songs of Kurt Weill, has afforded him that sweep. He writes with a natural narrative instinct. His songs have the detail and movement of great fiction. His understanding of the dirt and vitality of the North seems rich and appropriate for the piece.

He was charming company. He was self-effacing and watchful and listened with care. We talked about David Byrne's *True Stories* and Dylan Thomas's *Under Milk Wood* and Thornton Wilder's *Our Town*. I am fascinated by the idea of investigating whether or not there is such a thing as a northern spirit. I want to write without sentimentality. I want to write something rangy and maybe something long.

He wants to stay in touch and find out how our research progresses over the next year or so.

I saw Molly Davies's *God Bless the Child* at the Royal Court. It's a study of the political and ethical manipulation that sits in education policy. Set in a primary school classroom, recreated with stunning verisimilitude by Chloe Lamford and directed with a sense of truth and intelligence by Vicky Featherstone. Four brilliant performances by Julie Hesmondhalgh, Nikki Amuka Bird, Ony Uhiara and Amanda Abbington. A real pleasure to see intelligent women acting with nuance and truth, characters who were not in any sense defined by their relationship to men. There was a classroom cast of primary school aged children, actors aged from eight to eleven, that gave the play a sense of threat and hope and humour.

I had a cup of tea with Vicky. She confirmed that I will be at the Royal Court next year, as her Associate. I'll join the planning meetings and work with writers. I'll use the studio to explore ideas and write the theatre a play. It will be an extraordinary thing to be back there.

I'm looking forward to returning to a consideration of what a play is. It seems like the time is ripe for a reinterpretation of the form and the process of making theatre.

In the evening I went with her to meet Lucy Prebble, a brilliant and important writer who I first came across at the Young Writers Programme, and together we went to something called The Dramatists Club Dinner. It is a meeting of dramatists from the ages of twenty-five to ninety-one. In an opulent portrait-strewed room at the Garrick Club in Covent Garden. Stephen Jeffreys, a writer who taught and inspired me when I was resident at the Court, invited me to join and I took Lucy as my guest.

Saw Christopher Hampton and April De Angelis briefly and Roy Williams and met David Hare. He was avuncular and charming. The extent to which he has been thought of as something as a folk demon in British theatre by some of my peers is palpable. Sometimes his comments about younger writers can lack a spirit of generosity. But he has written consistently for stage for forty years and written significant plays. His writing about theatre always inspires me.

The Culture Secretary Ed Vaizey was the speaker. I'd never met a minister of state before. He was a curious man. He had a childhood surrounded by the arts and has consistently asked to keep his post. He spoke a little about his work and fielded some questions.

His speech was thin. He never articulated why he felt the arts were important. This lack of background is almost more dispiriting than the cuts. The questions he was asked were largely ludicrous. Everybody was pissed and nobody was listening. David Hare was passionate and Vicky and Lucy too. But people weren't interested in asking him anything. They just wanted to articulate what they thought. However pissed their thoughts were.

Julian Fellowes, the creator of the unwatchable television drama *Downton Abbey*, made odious right-wing fatuous insults and the whole thing had the feel of Prime Minister's Questions at its worst.

I've rarely seen the dislocation between the political discourse and the lives of most people in this country so baldly exposed.

I went to the smoking balcony with Ed Vaizey and Lucy after. I tried to get him to tell me why the arts were important to him. He largely failed. It was disorientating.

12th December

A day in Cardiff at the Royal Welsh College of Music and Drama. I ran a workshop with the Head of Acting there, Dave Bond. He is an inspiring figure who galvanizes his students and has created an environment, away from the rush and vanity of London, that encourages his students to think and to listen with nuance and rigour.

We looked at the work of the playwright and the nature of the human animal and the students wrote scenes that we looked at.

There were moments of real beauty.

When the actors imbued their dialogue, even dialogue that seemed slight and conversational, with a sense of risk, then it was almost startling. I explored with them the idea that in plays characters should only speak when it saves their lives. The need that sits under their language should be legible. It should be that they speak because if they don't, they will go insane. Every line, even lines like 'hi!', should have that bravery, however disguised it may be.

I am taking a post at Royal Welsh. I will be the International Chair of Drama. It's a ludicrous job title. The association with the college though and the students and Dave is thrilling.

Things are lined up for next year. The position at Royal Welsh and the Royal Court will sit alongside the Paul Greengrass film and the play for the Olivier and the possibility of *The Shining* adaptation and the work with Karl Hyde and Scott Graham. The collaborations I will have will inspire me. I am excited about working with Karl and Scott, Nick Cave on the Olivier show, Ivo, Marianne, Walter at home. On top of that there are productions I'm excited by. *Carmen Disruption* and *Song from Far Away* and *Heisenberg* and *The Funfair. The Curious Incident of the Dog in the Night-Time* will continue in the West End and Broadway and tour. There may be productions of *Blindsided* and *Birdland* in Germany.

15th December

Up early to head to Amsterdam for a day's rehearsal on *Song from Far Away*.

My flight was delayed by an hour.

But it was a pleasure to be back in Amsterdam and working with Toneelgroep Amsterdam at their exquisite rehearsal rooms in the Stadsschouwburg, the city's theatre house in the middle of the canal district.

And a privilege to be working with Ivo.

There is something remarkable about the rehearsal rooms at Toneelgroep Amsterdam. Huge open windows look out onto the street. Jan Versweyveld's design has been recreated with meticulous detail for a rehearsal stage. It must be at considerable expense.

And it is an exquisite design. A blank empty room, built according to the physical characteristics of Eelco Smits who will play Willem, it offers a haunted ante-room to the stage right and two large mirrors reflecting back on Willem.

Ivo has made the quite brilliant decision to have Willem talking to the ghost of his younger brother, rather than to the audience. Its like we're peering into the insanity of a grieving man, talking to a ghost whose absence we are startled by. There is something rich in this image for our age atrophied by technology away from actual interaction.

The more he plays the presence of his absent brother – teasing him, enticing him, inspiring him, moving him – the more his grief is revealed without it being made explicit.

I think the text holds up.

I think the counterpoint between the text and Mark Eitzel's haunting, aching song is sublime.

There are some things I notice that may be of use. When a character asks a question in my plays it is always a question. When a character describes something as fascinating it is because they are fascinated. When a character is doing something awful they normally should play it with a spirit of adventure and joy.

But watching Ivo work is remarkable. He has the same synthesis of reverence and playfulness that I saw in Patrice Chéreau, the great French director, who directed *I Am the Wind*.

He elevates Eelco's performance.

If Eelco can find a way to avoid a repetition of tone in his paragraphs, then I think this production might work.

Went out with Mark and his boyfriend Jeremy and had dinner. Was joined by Rik van den Bos, a young Dutch playwright enjoying some success now.

Wandering through Amsterdam, it feels like the city is oddly haunted to me by the imaginary ghosts of *Song from Far Away*. Real place names resonate from the play. I've imagined this city more than I've lived through it because ordinarily I just go from hotel to theatre rehearsal room. Wandering round it briefly tonight I recognized more places from the play I'd imagined with Mark than I did from memories of being here before.

16th December

A fine second day.

There is part of me that is again enjoying rehearsing a play in a second language. Dutch is curious in that its energy feels similar to the energy of English but the words are simply NOT English, so sometimes it feels like I'm having a stroke.

I like interpreting what the people in the room are saying to one another just by interrogating their energies. It dislocates me from the conversations but sometimes feeling more like an observer is useful.

Ivo isn't used to working with a living writer and finds me making notes in my notebook unnerving. The demands on his time, as Artistic Director of the theatre company meant that I wasn't able to have a conversation with him about yesterday's rehearsal, so I sent him an email instead. I like the process of writing the emails as collations of my thoughts but I worry that it makes me seem in some way authorial.

There is nothing useful about a writer having an authorial presence in the rehearsal room. I just laugh too much at my own jokes and get the coffees in.

There is something moving about watching Ivo rehearse. There is no sense of self-deprecation that defines an English rehearsal room. There is no doubt that there is something important about this. There is an unapologetic sense of grace about him working.

Sometimes Ivo can seem a little awkward socially. In the rehearsal room this awkwardness disappears. He is playful and light alongside his sense of commitment.

He talked about how he loves the mock-up rehearsal set. He had the same while working on *A View from the Bridge*. It crystallizes his imagination into something more real.

To an extent this may be a consequence of the wealth of his company but it is more than that. It is an aesthetic decision. Other directors (he told me that Chéreau was an example of this) prefer the open space that frees their imagination and won't have a set until late. But Ivo likes the convergence of his imagination that having a set allows him.

Ivo is having Eelco play much of the play naked. There is always something vulnerable about nakedness on stage. There is an unarguable honesty to it. Eelco's body in the context of Jan's blank, empty hotel room speaks of the themes in the play. A search for the possibility of human compassion in a man who has wilfully tried to abandon that humanity.

It might make English audiences a bit embarrassed but it shouldn't. I find it moving.

I learned something about the play today. It feels weirdly like the most optimistic play I've written for some time. In the form of Anka, Willem's nine-year-old niece with her insistence on engaging him, there is a sense that in the face of any ecological catastrophe or economic despair there might be hope that humans might survive or thrive. It's an optimism that sits under the end of the play.

It seems to be what the play is about.

The complicated possibility and contradictory mess of being human might be enough to save the whole fucking species.

17th December

Went with Camilla Bray and Marianne Elliott to meet Christine Langan, the Head of Development at BBC Films. She had some smart notes for making *Waterfall* leaner, less cluttered and more built around Emily's point of view. Marianne is driven to make the film a real consideration of the gender politics that sit under what happens to women over forty. Is there a notion that their function after childbirth is just to wait till death? I'm not certain but it is a provocative thought and her energy galvanizes me. Certainly the exploration of sexual desire of a teenager for a woman of fifty provokes conversation.

Feel my energy winding down at the end of the year.

I was mortified this morning to realize that I missed a board meeting at Paines Plough last night. I've been on the board there for five years now. I was on the interview committee that appointed George Perrin and James Grieve as joint Artistic Directors. Watching them grow into their post and building a team around them and establishing themselves as leaders in the theatre world has been inspiring. So long as playwriting remains at the heart of British theatre Paines Plough will remain a company of significance. Its track record of producing and touring plays by emerging and established writers is exemplary.

To have missed my farewell board meeting is mortifying.

I hope playwriting does retain its significance.

It is rightly under interrogation from many exciting areas. A generation of designers has emerged that is concerned with creating energy and aesthetic on our stages, more likely to be inspired by the imaginative force of contemporary art or dance than an interest in staging the imaginary world that a playwright prescribes through stage directions. This is precisely as it should be.

A generation of directors has emerged with a commitment to claiming their authorial validity. They are inspired by many of the directors coming out of the German state-subsidized theatre worlds. They are provoked by the punk imagination coming out of the best of the fringe theatres in recent years – the immersive provocations and devised interventions that the Battersea Arts Centre has championed with precision and determination. They are keen to not just stage the worlds that playwrights describe and teach their actors how to read them, but rather to create fully realized theatrical experiences.

I am inspired by them and keen to encourage them.

Ten years ago this energy provoked the then incumbent Artistic Director of the Lyric Hammersmith, David Farr to claim that the playwright had died. For a brief period it led to a flurry of largely forgettable bickering on chat rooms between the entrenched camps of the playwrights and the devised theatre makers. It was silly.

The challenge facing the playwright and the producer of new plays is how to engage with and be inspired by these energies. To reject them and to hold onto entrenched positions and ideological certainties from another time would render the playwright's work arcane.

It should be the reverse.

When I think of those playwrights I love – when I think of Robert Holman or Caryl Churchill or Ali McDowall – I am reminded of the exceptional event that is the creation of a new play. When those writers write, they imagine something previously unimaginable. They carve nights in the theatre out of their perception of the world and they control the energy and the language, the narrative and the imagery of those nights with singularity. In doing so they create metaphor.

Metaphor is the element most absent from devised work. It is the element most damaged by a theatre aesthetic that is fascinated only by visual style. It is the element most compromised by collective devising.

It is through metaphor that as audiences we come to understand ourselves. It is through metaphor that we examine our empathy. This examination is, finally for me, the key function of theatre. It is an empathy machine. Its machinations make us better at being human. They play out in rooms defined by a collection of strangers sharing an experience. The impulse to share these experiences, to engage in these stories and to confront a collective sense of self, whether in the euphoric celebration of the pantomime or the musical or the intimate forensic auditoria of our small theatres, is fundamental to human culture.

If our culture is going to survive. If, in fact, it is going to thrive, then it is dependent on this self-examination.

Sitting on a train on my way back to Manchester for the opening of *The Curious Incident of the Dog in the Night-Time* on the first night of its national tour I am watching England pass by. 2015 will see a

General Election. As I write the possibility of the pernicious, cynical force of UKIP playing an instrumental part in that election seems palpable. Our country is moving to the right. Nationalism is rising as it does in times of uncertainty. As we become more afraid we become less generous and more cynical. UKIP preys on this uncertainty.

Our economies are becoming uncertain.

Our political structures leave electorates disaffected.

Our national infrastructure feels strained by the response to economic difficulties coming from largely neo-liberal, monetarist economic thinkers, defined by the assumption that the theories of Milton Friedman enshrined by Margaret Thatcher in the eighties are not theoretical possibilities but the normal thing to do.

Terrorism is a real threat. Two days ago in Pakistan the Taliban attacked a school and killed 136 school children. This morning it seems clear that the North Korean government commissioned a cyber attack on the Sony Corporation in response to a satirical attack on their country at the heart of the Sony film *The Interview*. Sony have subsequently removed the film from all forms of distribution and have deleted all references to it on their website.

Our ecology remains in a state of perilous fragility.

How can theatre mean anything at a time of such a shit storm of crises? I think only by clinging to what is at its heart – that impulse to test and exercise our capacity to empathize. The simplicity of this idea leaves me optimistic. I think the playwright creates and imagines a theatre built on the communication of metaphor with a directness and force that is to be cherished.

If we cling onto old models of working, especially because these models appeal to our vanity, then we will render ourselves anachronistic. What the playwright has to do is engage in the intelligent fearlessness that interrogates their position within the theatre-making process. If we do that, then we will write better plays. If we write better plays, we will make more remarkable theatrical experiences. I think there is a value in that.

18th December

The Lyric Theatre at the Lowry in Salford holds 1,700 people and on the first preview of *The Curious Incident of the Dog in the Night-Time* it was near capacity.

It felt cavernous and there was part of me that worried that the play was exposed in a theatre so big. I was sat near the front of the stalls but the play still felt distant to me. The first preview suffered a little from the usual problems of a first preview. The cues were slow and there was a tentativeness in the face of such an extraordinarily large audience. The play was slow. For much of it I worried that the production lacked visceral force and was more impressive than it was shattering.

As it went on though the actors picked up confidence and so picked up pace. And by the end of the play it felt more like we were in the same room as the actors. The production works when it feels as though we, as an audience, are inside Christopher's mind. Towards the end of the production we were nearly there.

The cast was variously buoyed by the achievement of getting through the night, pleased by its reception, which was undeniable, and frustrated by a sense of how far they have to move.

With Katy Rudd and Marianne Elliott in charge they will get there and this production will continue its remarkable journey around the country.

I went with twelve members of my family. My mum and Steve her husband. Her three brothers and their wives, including Uncle Andrew, the same Andrew who produced the film of *Sea Wall* and throughout my life has been something of a hero. He brought his kids and his brother Art brought his son Ben and his girlfriend. It meant the world to take my family to see the night. Without their support, quiet and constant, I wouldn't have been able to write the things I've written or achieve any of the things that I've achieved in this strange, marginal art form.

19th December

An interview for Granada Reports at the theatre that was later bumped for coverage of a local murder.

Lunch with Sarah Frankcom. It was brilliant to see her. We talked about why *Birdland* hasn't been part of the year's discussion of new plays and why in fact the Royal Court hasn't. The theatre missed the year's key new plays. I wonder what can be done, structurally, to ensure that doesn't happen next year.

Few people talk as openly to me about my work as she does. To have somebody of her rigour and intelligence talk as honestly as she does sustains me.

31st December

At the end of a two-week Christmas break I took Polly and the kids and ten of our friends to see *Dick Whittington and His Cat*, this year's Pantomime at the Lyric Hammersmith.

The panto is such a peculiar and British phenomenon. It exists in the residue of the working-class music hall and many of its theatrical tropes – women playing boys, men playing women, songs being sung, the audience singing along and joining in onstage – are bewildering to non-English audiences.

It is a theatrical form built absolutely on the acknowledgement that the audience is in the same room as the actors. Much more Sebastian Nübling than Katie Mitchell in that sense.

It was a great afternoon. The kids all clapping along and clambering for sweets and the adults laughing at the dirty jokes that the kids missed entirely.

For so many people in theatre the panto is their first experience of the theatre. One of our friends brought their eighteen-month-old baby. He bobbed about and gazed at the lights and was captivated.

It was brilliant to go back to the Lyric, to see that auditorium open again.

It felt like the perfect way to end the year.

Over the past two weeks I've thought a lot about the writing ahead of me. I think I will try to slow down. Maybe write only four more plays in my forties. One for the Exchange, one for Sebastian, one for the Court and one for the National Theatre. To take eighteen months over a play rather than four. To step up. To try to write bigger plays. To try to be better. To fail, no doubt, but to try.